Reading Du Bois

SUNY series in African American Studies

Robert C. Smith and John R. Howard, editors

Reading Du Bois

An Afrocentric Critique of the Color Line

Aaron X. Smith (Jabali Ade) and Molefi Kete Asante

Published by State University of New York Press, Albany
© 2025 State University of New York
All rights reserved
Printed in the United States of America

No part of this book may be used or reproduced in any manner whatsoever without written permission. No part of this book may be stored in a retrieval system or transmitted in any form or by any means including electronic, electrostatic, magnetic tape, mechanical, photocopying, recording, or otherwise without the prior permission in writing of the publisher.

Links to third-party websites are provided as a convenience and for informational purposes only. They do not constitute an endorsement or an approval of any of the products, services, or opinions of the organization, companies, or individuals. SUNY Press bears no responsibility for the accuracy, legality, or content of a URL, the external website, or for that of subsequent websites.

EU GPSR Authorised Representative:
Logos Europe, 9 rue Nicolas Poussin, 17000, La Rochelle, France
contact@logoseurope.eu

For information, contact State University of New York Press, Albany, NY
www.sunypress.edu

Library of Congress Cataloging-in-Publication Data

Names: Smith, Aaron X., author. | Asante, Molefi Kete, 1942– author.
Title: Reading Du Bois : an Afrocentric critique of the color line / Aaron X. Smith and Molefi Kete Asante.
Description: Albany : State University of New York Press, 2025. | Series: SUNY series in African American studies | Includes bibliographical references and index.
Identifiers: LCCN 2024044586 | ISBN 9798855802443 (hardcover) | ISBN 9798855802450 (ebook) | 9798855802436 (paperback)
Subjects: LCSH: Du Bois, W. E. B. (William Edward Burghardt), 1868–1963—Criticism and interpretation. | Afrocentrism—Philosophy. | African Americans—Race identity. | African diaspora in literature. | LCGFT: Literary criticism.
Classification: LCC PS3507.U147 Z86 2025 | DDC 818/.5209—dc23/eng/20250131
LC record available at https://lccn.loc.gov/2024044586

To Jeniece and Bakari, to Aion, Nova, Akila, and Akira, whose paths will crisscross Du Bois's for generations

Now is the accepted time, not tomorrow, not some more convenient season. It is today that our best work can be done and not some future day or future year. It is today that we fit ourselves for the greater usefulness of tomorrow. Today is the seed time, now are the hours of work, and tomorrow comes the harvest and the playtime.

— William Edward Burghardt Du Bois

Contents

Preface	xi
Acknowledgments	xiii
Chapter 1: A Performative Biography: Who Was Du Bois?	1
Chapter 2: Du Bois's Central Contributions to the Race Discourse	15
Chapter 3: The Entrapment of Ambition: Talented Tenth	29
Chapter 4: The Narrative of Socialism Considering Democracy	43
Chapter 5: Restorative Imagination in Du Bois's "The Comet"	57
Chapter 6: Du Bois and the Color Line: Battling the Toxic Social Construction of Race	75
Chapter 7: The Evolution of Du Bois into a Pan African Race Organizer	89
Chapter 8: The Afrocentric Corrective at the Crest of Victory	103
Notes	115
Bibliography	133
Index	143

Preface

The background to *Reading Du Bois: An Afrocentric Critique of the Color Line* lies in the work of a State University of New York Press author, Ana Monteiro-Ferreira, whose book *The Demise of The Inhuman: Afrocentricity, Modernism, and Postmodernism*, which was published in 2014, was one of the first full-length attempts at applying the principles of Afrocentricity to theoretical projects outside of intradiscipline areas. Ferreira's discourse gave birth to numerous uses of Afrocentricity as a mature theoretical approach to phenomena, events, activities, and personalities. Hence it was only a matter of time before Afrocentrists would examine the work of the greatest African American scholar of the twentieth century, William Edward Burghardt Du Bois.

Consequently, we wanted to critically engage Du Bois at the level of agency, culture, and orientation, something we had not read in other works on Du Bois. Although we recognize valuable work done by David Levering Lewis, Manning Marable, and Reiland Rabaka on Du Bois, we found a niche that had not been explored. Most contemporary readings of Du Bois clearly leaned to the Marxist positioning partly because of the substantive theoretical work that the Marxist tradition has developed. The other reason is because Du Bois was punished and persecuted by the American government in his later years, had his passport revoked, and then when it was returned, fled to Ghana where he was made a citizen. Our objective was to rescue Du Bois not from Marxian rhetoric but from the inadequacy of a purely Marxist analysis of his body of work. Our use of Afrocentricity is directly informed by African history and culture, language, and politics, and we have arrived at our conclusions based on Du Bois's own words. A careful reading of Du Bois is demanded not so much by the times that we live in but by the advancement of theory since the end of the last century.

Afrocentricity has rapidly risen in Africa, South America, and North America, affecting the social sciences and arts in Europe and Asia. Reliance on other scholars is made to buttress our own understanding of the location or dislocation of certain terminology or statements in Du Bois's writing. An Afrocentric reading of Du Bois challenges the racialized history in some ways encouraged by Du Bois and brings the cultural question to the forefront because we are seeking to understand the centeredness, the cultural core, from which Du Bois speaks. The epitome of Du Bois's work was racial analysis and racial inequality, but we believe that culture is a more powerful predictor of action than the false concept of race. This is the reason we have announced and insisted upon readers' understanding the close reading of Du Bois Afrocentrically. Who and what is marginalized, that is, pushed to the periphery, in Du Bois's work?

This is a provocative question that gets at the heart of his challenge to keep himself and his people above the raging ocean of physical and psychological dangers that threatened, and often did, trouble him. Our study pursues Du Bois for orientation, always knowing that his rich life was so complex and active that whatever is captured in this book is just a small portion of who he was and what he said. We can only vouch for what we have said in this book about the man. Much of his life was spent as an agitator for equality. While the cast and context of that agitation during his lifetime was behind the veil of inequality and racial domination, his ambition and objective lay in trying to resolve satisfactorily the question of white racial domination, that is, the idea that whites were superior to blacks.

This was something he objected to from the depths of his soul, and he sought to prove that it could never be a part of the reality of a decent democratic America. Our work, therefore, is a celebration of his courage and stellar contribution while it remains an Afrocentric critique of his practice to assist students in locating him in historical context.

Acknowledgments

There are many people to acknowledge in an adventure such as this. Du Bois, of course. There are many books written about this intellectual giant, but no one has done an Afrocentric reading of Du Bois. Our former students Taharka Ade, at San Diego State University, and Reiland Rabaka, at the University of Colorado, have written provocative works on Du Bois. A pivot toward reading Du Bois Afrocentrically challenged us to have numerous discussions with our colleagues in and outside of our department. We are grateful to the Department of Africology where the Temple Circle of Afrocentric Scholars is engaged in research grounded in an African perspective. Thanks especially to Professors Kimani Nehusi, Sonja Peterson-Lewis, Reynaldo Anderson, and Nah Dove for consistent support and wise counsel and to our brilliant graduate students Hope Dove, Christina Hudson, and Michelle Taylor who convinced us that this would be a proper work for assisting students and others in reading Du Bois Afrocentrically.

This book is an expression of collegiality, cordiality, and dedication to excellence in Africology. Thank you to the Charles Blockson Afro American Collection at Temple University, Diane Turner, the curator, and the great legacy of the famed Charles Blockson himself whom we knew and will cherish always. Our special thanks go to Michael Rinella, editor at the State University of New York Press, for responding positively to our plan for the book. We have benefited from a progressively minded editorial team that understands the need for this work. Thanks to our students, undergraduates and graduates, who have allowed us to test these ideas on them, and who, in some cases, have taught us through their comments and critiques. Our families have shared the pain and pleasure of our long hours at work, and we gladly acknowledge them.

Aaron Smith (Jabali Ade), Montclair, New Jersey
Molefi Kete Asante, Valdosta, Georgia

Chapter 1
A Performative Biography

Who Was Du Bois?

The study of William Edward Burghardt Du Bois is clouded with myth, sometimes of the subject's own making, and consequently secreted behind great walls of mystery.[1] Our intention is to unmask as much as we can of the biographical rendition of Du Bois's life to examine critically how he constructed patterns of behavior that lifted him, as well as his people, in the national imagination. Our reading, an Afrocentric one, is by its nature critical of dislocation, patriarchy, and illusion, and although we comment on aspects of the life of the eminent scholar we tread lightly on ethical judgments.

There is enough evidence in Du Bois's autobiography to suggest that he was a master at arranging the pieces of his life and career to assert a rhetorically provocative image of the person he wanted to be, and of who he became. In other words, he performed his biography in a dramatic historical fashion, deciding missions, strategies, and operations for uplifting his people as much as he could through personal initiative. He would be the exemplary African man, brilliant, well dressed, cultured, competitive, and invincible. No wonder he had vowed as a young person that he would devote his entire life to the mission of raising the race. Confident, resourceful, well mannered, but relentless in his fight against ignorance, Du Bois managed his life as a performance of the possible.

John Hope Franklin, an eminent historian in his own right, told a personal story about his interaction with Du Bois to the historian Manning Marable that characterizes the performativity of Du Bois's life.[2] One must know that Du Bois had been for years an icon in Franklin's family in Oklahoma.[3] His parents had named him John Hope after the name of Du Bois's best friend.

They had sent him to Fisk for education much like Du Bois had done, and there he had heard the great one give several speeches to the students. In fact, Franklin recalled that Du Bois had given a speech in 1924 at Fisk that created a revolution and drove the white president, Fayette McKenzie, away from the campus. Furthermore, Franklin had left Fisk for Harvard to study history in the tradition that Du Bois had started. He was, in the academy, a Du Boisian man. Franklin says that he saw Du Bois "close up for the first time" at a Raleigh, North Carolina hotel dining room in 1939; the Arcade Hotel was the only place between Atlanta and Washington where black people could eat or go to the toilet. In his matter-of-fact style, Franklin says:

> I sat there eating my dinner one evening and I saw across the room: the man. So, I said, "This is my chance. I got him all to myself and I am going to make the most of it." So, pulling myself up and taking all the courage I had (I was all of twenty-three at the time or something like that), I went over to him. He was eating or reading, and I said, "Dr. Du Bois, my name is John Hope Franklin." I wanted him to hear "John Hope-John Hope" — I was named for his best friend. He did not even act like I was in the room. He was reading and eating.[4]

Disappointed, Franklin thought that he had a couple more points to stress, so he said, "I am a graduate of Fisk University, Class of 1935,"[5] playing on the close-knit tendencies of Fisk graduates.

Everyone knew who was in which class, and Franklin knew Du Bois was in the Class of 1888. But Du Bois said not a word. Franklin then tried one more gambit. "I am a graduate student at Harvard University in the field of history and I am now working on my doctoral dissertation." He says, "without even looking up to see what I was or who I was or how I was, he said, 'How do you do?'"[6] Later, after Franklin had received his doctorate and became a professor, he met Du Bois at a meeting and asked him what that earlier exchange was about. Du Bois told him, "Well, you know I am very shy; you know I am also always very preoccupied." This encounter between two of the greatest historians of the twentieth century is our entry into the performativity of Du Bois's life.

Performing as an Intellectual Act

All the world may be a stage, but Du Bois's life was an ever-evolving performance of the mastery of the creative ethos, without evidence of pathos, in the intellectual arena where he made himself, an African American man, the model for his race. One might see him as a director, choreographer, or circus ringmaster, but Du Bois was not necessarily concerned about configuring or making images for art's sake. Du Bois projected himself as the pure man, the "A plus African"[7] who could not only speak for the race but also demonstrate in his person that he was equal to any other human on the earth. This was his permanent mission; all other attributes of Du Bois must be seen in the light of this performative biography. Du Bois was the most perfect example of an original African American intellectual of the twentieth century.

In *Black Marxism: The Making of the Black Radical Tradition*, Cedric Robinson acknowledges that "William Edward Burghardt Du Bois was one of the finest historians ever developed in the United States."[8] Of course, he did not appear in our history fully developed or in full bloom; this would take years of observation, experiences, and training. However, as an African person born in Massachusetts from a complex social and biological background, Du Bois was thrown into the discourse about race from the time he was in high school in Great Barrington. Traveling to the South to attend Fisk University would be one avenue for liberation, but it would also bring him close to his mission in an American nation that saw black people as inferior to whites. Who was he as a person during this American paranoia and confusion about the issue of race?

The First Act: A Creative Origin

Du Bois's search for origin started while he was a very young man. Indeed, he was the one in his family who discovered and spread the word that his ancestor Thomas Burghardt had been stolen from the west coast of Africa and brought to America in 1730 by Dutch captors. Thomas Burghardt grew up as a servant in the household of these Dutch slaveowners. However, because Thomas enlisted in the Revolutionary War in 1775, Du Bois discovered the records of his ancestor, the fourth grandfather, a private for the Berkshire County Regiment. Service in the Revolutionary War freed Thomas, and his family lived as free people. By 1780 the state Bill of Rights had declared all enslaved Africans in Massachusetts free. The Burghardts, primarily because of Thomas's enlistment in the Revolutionary Army, had settled in Massachusetts on large acres of land as a reward for this military service.

They became a leading family that soon headed a large clan of African Americans in Massachusetts. Thomas Burghardt died in 1787 and the leadership of the clan passed to Jack Burghardt, who married Betty, and they were blessed with several children among whom was a young man named Othello Burghardt, who was Du Bois's grandfather. In fact, Du Bois claims that he knew his grandfather. The family was enlarged because Jack was a polygamist and had several other children. Other African people moved to the area of Egremont and helped create a substantial number of African people in the community. Intermarriages among these black families enlarged the Burghardt's clan, and Du Bois came to appreciate the intense relationship with his mother's Burghardt relatives. However, a search for his father proved much more complex, but Du Bois cracked the code to his satisfaction. His paternal ancestry was Du Bois, as that was the name his father carried.

Du Bois claimed to have some Dutch ancestry as well, saying that his blood comprised "a flood of Negro blood, a strain of French, and a bit of Dutch."[9] According to him he inherited the Dutch from the paternal side of his family. In the early seventeenth century, a Frenchman named Jacques Du Bois had left the city of Lille, France, to travel to America. His wife was Dutch. They settled in New York state and one of Jacques's children, James Du Bois, became a physician in America. He happened to be Du Bois's great-grandfather and hence the so-called Dutch blood. James the physician then settled in the Bahamas and became a landholder. He married an African woman and had two children by her, Alexander and John. When their mother died, the father sent them to the

United States for education in 1810. Alexander chose to associate with blacks and John crossed over to associate with whites.

Alexander, who was Du Bois's grandfather, also migrated to Haiti and married a black woman. When he lost his wife, he was compelled to send his children to the United States, and they settled in New Haven. In fact, Du Bois's grandfather Alexander was a cofounder of the New Haven Episcopal Parish Church for Colored People. Du Bois's father, Alfred the son of Alexander, was born in 1825 in Haiti. From the description given by Du Bois, Alfred was a whimsical figure, adventurous, with somewhat of a wanderlust, and worked variously as a barber and a merchant. It was in Berkshire Valley, Massachusetts, where he met and married Mary Burghardt who gave birth to the great intellectual. Alfred was forty-two years old at the time and his wife, Mary, was thirty-six, so that is the gist of the record of Du Bois's genealogy.

Modeling Academic Success

Du Bois was a studious and obedient child. His mother, even with a little income she made from domestic services, kept her son interested and active in school activities. She raised him as a devoted Christian and from the time he was six years old he regularly attended the Congregational church in his community. He attended public school in Great Barrington and in high school he was the only African out of thirteen students but always the one making the highest grades. Nothing in his academic record showed any cracks in his intellectual capacity. Indeed, his work's superiority caught the attention of his peers and the community leaders in Great Barrington. He said that he had extraordinarily little recognition of discrimination against him by his peers. It is hard to say whether this had something to do with the fact that Du Bois in his youth had a light complexion, even enough European ancestry to have crossed the color line. He admits, however, that by the time he was in high school, his brown complexion had matured.

His frizzy hair was noticeable, and this brought about a change of attitudes on the part of his schoolmates. Yet he did not experience the kind of racial rejection or discrimination the majority of African Americans found in the United States, particularly in the South in the nineteenth century. Du Bois writes in *Darkwater*, "I found myself assuming quite placidly that I was different from other children. At first, I connected the difference with a manifest ability to get lessons better than most of them."[10] He also understood something else, and he was able to write about that in *Darkwater*: "Then slowly I realized that some folk a few even several actually considered my brown skin a misfortune; once or twice I became painfully aware that some human beings even thought it was a crime."[11]

Daniel Agbeyebiawo writes in *The Life and Works of W.E.B. Du Bois* that even though Du Bois suffered discrimination, this never discouraged him, he worked tirelessly to control academic leadership in his class. As a boy he was totally confined to his hometown and seldom travelled. His first major trip from town was when he visited his paternal grandfather, Alexander Du Bois, in New Bedford, Massachusetts. He was by then a final year high school student at 16.

The journey, for the first time, made it possible for him to see a multitude of African people in festive moods. That was in Providence, Rhode Island where the blacks were celebrating the West Indian emancipation. He said he "became filled with pride of his African heritage."[12]

In 1884 Du Bois completed high school and worked as a timekeeper for construction companies and as a correspondent for the newspaper *Springfield Republican*. Three prominent whites assisted him in establishing himself on the road to higher education. Recognizing his intelligence and seriousness of purpose, Frank Hosmer, his high school principal; Edward van Lennep, the principal of the local private school; and Reverend C. C. Painter, a Congregational preacher, sought opportunities to keep him engaged with moving forward.[13] Du Bois, also recognizing his talents, allowed the concerned citizens to give him advice. Although he had wanted to enroll at Harvard University after high school, this seemed like an impossible objective given that "Harvard was a mighty conjure-word in that hill town, and even the mill owners' sons had aimed lower."[14] In the end, he was advised to apply to Fisk University in Nashville, Tennessee, in the fall of 1885. While he was unable to attend Harvard immediately and was disappointed because of the impossibility of entering that university, he accepted enrollment into Fisk. His supporters in Great Barrington provided a scholarship of $25 per year for his matriculation at Fisk University. Four churches came together and, for the time it took for him to complete his degree, gave him $25 each year.

Learning the Acts of Liberation

Du Bois did not consider going to Fisk University a setback. In fact, it was a world where the student body was 100 percent African and just the environment he needed to add to his cultural and social toolbox. Although the teachers were white, they were mostly progressive and liberal with the idea that a great wrong had been perpetrated on the black people. Furthermore, the gathering of black students from all over the nation, but especially from the South, grounded him in the remnants of African culture. Hearing the great spiritual songs called the Negro spirituals, and later called by Du Bois "The Master Songs" because of their majesty, set his soul on fire. Fisk had released in him something that his Burghardtian ancestry could not — the visual, visceral, and powerful act of freedom. There was something special about the South that he had not seen in Great Barrington. During the summer holidays he went into the rural areas of Tennessee and taught the poverty stricken African American farm workers basic reading and writing. Du Bois graduated from Fisk University in June 1888 after obtaining a bachelor's degree in philosophy and social sciences.

Ready for the Big Stage

Du Bois wrote of his admission to Harvard with boundless joy. "I willed and lo! I was walking beneath the elms of Harvard — the name of allurement, the college of my youngest, wildest visions!"[15] In some incredibly important ways one must see his presence at Harvard as a moment for him to bring his passionate African sensibilities into convergence with his desire to be at the place of his youthful wish. But was Harvard, in some strange way, what Michael Tillotson calls an agency reduction formation for black people? In his book *Invisible Jim Crow: Contemporary Ideological Threats to the Internal Security of African Americans* (2011), Tillotson developed and introduced the theoretical construct *agency reduction formation*, operationalized as "any system of thought that distracts, neutralizes, or reduces the need and desire for assertive collective agency by African Americans."[16]

Du Bois's love for Harvard can be seen in some odd way as a seduction that was to distort his perceptions and trouble his conceptions of Africa. He had no positive ideas about Africa while a student at Harvard, Fisk, and the University of Berlin, because he had not yet understood fully the underdevelopment of Africa in every sector of human possibility. Of course, the Africa he knew was a colonized, degraded, and marginalized Africa, almost reminiscent of a Hegelian Africa "without history." This was a false Africa, a truncated narrative of the longest civilized history in the world, but Du Bois, a lover of the highest citadel of white intellectual dominance in America, to which he was beholden, could not know Africa in the fullness of its history. On the other hand, when he had arrived at Fisk in Nashville, Tennessee, he was immediately struck by the physical presence of black students. This would help him with the Harvard sojourn, but it would not erase his feeling of conquest. Fisk, with its powerful Jubilee Singers and its language of poetry and song of Africa, combined with its intellectual posture, had prepared him well for socialization into the southern African American culture.[17] Although Du Bois gained admission to Harvard, and loved the college, it did not accept his bachelor's degree from Fisk, and he was admitted to Harvard as a third-year student and had to gain another BA from Harvard. However, in 1890 he received his BA in philosophy, economics, and history from Harvard, having achieved a goal for which he had dreamed. There had always been in Du Bois a competitive spirit that allowed him to put forward the best face of the African person in any situation. At his undergraduate commencement he was one of six chosen student speakers. Compelled to perform at the top of his capabilities, Du Bois spent several days mulling over his address. In his mind, he had to establish himself as a serious scholar. As a young person, he was thinking of making his case for history; indeed, his attitude of competition rescued him from the neutralization offered by Eurocentric education. But reading Du Bois one must be careful to compensate for the lure of Harvard, which for him was the epitome of his dreams.

The chosen subject of his speech at the graduation for the bachelor's degree was Jefferson Davis, the former president of the Confederacy, who had led the armies of the South against the Union government. This was a bold proposal and an important statement to be made by a young, brilliant African American. What he planned to do was to discuss not the man himself but the type of civilization that such a life represented. We still speak in terms of the times making the person. Some people rise above the influences of their times; others succumb to the depths. Jefferson Davis, as Du Bois saw him, had certain traits and characteristics that might have led him down another path. However, he succumbed to the strong man individualism with an emphasis on ruling by might. Du Bois started his speech by saying "it made a naturally brave and generous man, Jefferson Davis: now advancing civilization by murdering Indians, now hero of a national disgrace, called by courtesy, the Mexican war: and finally, as a crowning absurdity, the peculiar champion of a people fighting to be free in order that another people should not be free."[18]

This speech was itself a rhetorical performance of the highest order because Du Bois took the symbolic nature of Jefferson Davis and argued that whether he appeared "as a man, as race, or as nation his type only met that part of the world that should advance at the expense of the whole."[19] At twenty-two years of age Du Bois had made a mark on the history of education, the African American people, and the United States. He had demonstrated genius in drawing the contradictions between the realities and the symbols, between the ideas of civilization and the demands of racial domination. Criticism of the speech came as one can imagine, but praise was more than enough to overcome the short-sighted vision of the few who held sympathies for the Confederacy.

For Du Bois, as it would become ever more evident, it would be necessary to speak out against the bigotry that made American life miserable for the descendants of Africa. Sociology was a new field, and Du Bois was attracted to it for its potential in social and racial research and analysis. Upon discovering that this new discipline was being developed and taught at the University of Berlin, now called Humboldt University, he applied to join the department. Feeling that it was the best in the world for sociology he decided that Berlin was his next destination. Soon after receiving a master's degree from Harvard in 1892, he successfully pursued a Slater Fund scholarship for study in Berlin.

The Slater Fund scholarship from the estate of a Connecticut millionaire provided him $750, half of it a loan to be paid back at 6 percent interest. Du Bois repaid the loan once he started working as an academic. He lived in Berlin from 1892 to 1894, working toward his doctorate, but because his loan was not enough to cover the completion of the degree he had to return to Harvard, and in the fall of 1895 Harvard University gave him a doctorate in history and government. His dissertation was "The Suppression of the African Slave Trade to the United States of America, 1638–1870," which became the first volume of the Harvard historical studies series in 1896.

Into the Cauldron

Where could a brilliant African American scholar with degrees from Fisk, Harvard, and years of study at the University of Berlin find employment? In any generation, a person so qualified and credentialed should have found a position at a good college or university. Du Bois, therefore, with an attitude of competence and confidence, applied to many colleges and universities. Among the historically black universities and colleges to which he applied were Tuskegee Institute, Wilberforce College, Howard University, Fisk, and Hampton University. Du Bois was confident that he could make substantial contributions to any of those colleges. He would undertake his role in uplifting the race and benefit from his training and expertise. Yet he underestimated the opposition and criticism to his commencement speech at Harvard on Jefferson Davis, and he consequently met resistance from some university faculties, particularly in the elite African American colleges and universities where most of the professors at the time were white.

There was some trepidation about a black man with a Harvard education and a European experience entering the world that had been created by liberal whites. Du Bois, they were sure, would make their lives difficult. Nevertheless, he pressed forward. Wilberforce asked him to come and teach Greek and Latin at an income of $800 per year. Du Bois wanted to teach sociology, but this was the only job that appeared immediately for him. Wilberforce was an African Methodist Episcopal Church school set up by the church to educate African Americans in Xenia, Ohio. The young professor arrived at Wilberforce with his high silk hat, white gloves, and a walking cane, an influence from his two years as a student in Germany. He taught Greek, Latin, and English. While those subjects were outside of his interests, he was prepared to teach until the college responded to his request to create a program in sociology.

At length he felt that Wilberforce would never introduce sociology into the curriculum. Since the school authorities did not allow him to teach sociology as the subject he had mastered, and it also resisted innovations he proposed, he resigned his professorship after two years. As fortune would have it, the University of Pennsylvania offered him a one-year contract as an assistant instructor in sociology, paying him $900 a year, which he accepted in 1896. He was a lecturer on contract without an office; without recognition for his training and skill, he saw himself used for a project Penn wanted, a study of the Philadelphia Negro, but did not want to highlight Professor Du Bois's position.

A Harvard PhD, without an office, and without official recognition as a professional, took the position and the contract that was offered and created a product that would affect the rest of his career.

Du Bois undertook the study of the social and economic conditions of African people in Philadelphia. The aim was to determine statistically whatever problems existed. Du Bois started the study of the Philadelphia Negro in 1897. Instead of hiring research assistants he personally interviewed about five thousand black people in the Seventh Ward of Philadelphia. At the forty-second meeting of the American Academy of Political and Social Science in the fall of 1897 in Philadelphia, Du Bois gave a report entitled "The Study of the Negro Problem." It was his philosophy of researching, revealing, and explaining the social condition of African Americans that he believed would help to resolve many of the issues confronted by populations that had been discriminated against for decades. His extensive urban sociology was the first of its kind in the United States and when he left the University of Pennsylvania for Atlanta University, he went to an institution willing to take the risk of allowing him to do sociology.

Because of his excellent work at the University of Pennsylvania he was given a position at Atlanta University as a professor of history and economics at an initial salary of $1,200 a year. Du Bois held that position from 1897 to 1910. The burning desire in the heart of Du Bois was to explain to the rest of the nation the circumstances out of which African American people created families, homes, churches, and visions of the possible. To do this he believed it was essential that the history and the culture of African people had to be at the center of all interpretations and all explanations of the social condition of black people in the United States. He had not yet developed a theory, but he had a plan based on his learning about the social elements that created conditions of poverty, segregation, and prejudice.

Therefore, the Atlanta series of sociological studies became his main scholarly work. He contended that he wanted to have a program of research and study that would cover most aspects of the lives of African people. Research studies at Atlanta began in 1896 and ended in 1914. The papers included "Mortality among Negroes in Cities," "Social and Physical Condition of Negroes in Cities," "The Negro Business," "The Negro Church," "The College-Bred Negro," "The Negro Artisan," and "The Negro American Family." Highly praised for its comprehensive nature, the Atlanta University series had resonance with much research done at the top of the twentieth century. Indeed, Du Bois himself said, "It may be said without undue boasting that between 1896 and 1920 there was no study of the race problem in America that did not depend to some degree upon the investigations made at Atlanta University."[20]

Du Bois had entered Atlanta University at a time when the Bureau of Labor Statistics had begun to collaborate with the university on projects that would be modeled after *The Philadelphia Negro*. A trustee of the university, George G. Bradford, who was also a pioneer in labor studies, and Carroll D. Wright, the leader of the Bureau of Labor and a friend of the university, felt strongly that Atlanta was the place to forge urban studies of African Americans. Jonathan Grossman is correct to say regarding Atlanta University's studies, "W. E. B. Du Bois' later and greater fame came as a militant leader of black aspirations. But his training at German universities and his Ph.D. at Harvard in the 1890s inculcated in him a devotion to objectivity which won for him in his early career distinction as a careful and creative scholar."[21] While Du Bois was engaged in teaching and research at Atlanta University he was also deeply entrenched in the struggle for civil rights.

He did not relinquish his role in the national battle for equality and justice. This disturbed some of his peers who felt he threatened their position with his increasingly militant stances against the treatment of blacks in the country. Alongside the suspicion of his colleagues, he also had to contend with the Tuskegee Machine, as Booker T. Washington's assemblage of supporters and followers was called. It was a formidable formation that could be called upon by Washington to discredit or credit any black politician or professor. Yet out of the cauldron set for him, Du Bois was able to make excellent opportunities for himself as well as for the research conducted about African Americans. In Paris in 1900, he displayed the research he started at Atlanta at the World's Fair and received a Gold Medal for the graphs and charts he showed at the exhibition. Already by now becoming a household name among African American intellectuals, Du Bois was preparing for more stellar events and activities in his career. Although Du Bois departed his first stint at Atlanta University in 1910 his publications went on until 1914.

Of Booker T. Washington

It might be said that the controversy between Washington and Du Bois sent shock waves through the academic community.[22] Booker T. Washington was the charismatic leader of Tuskegee Institute and a major supporter of industrial education. Du Bois at Atlanta University had sought to make research the focus of black education. The ensuing controversy between Washington and Du Bois created financial pressures for Atlanta University as philanthropists refused to donate to the school. Du Bois, conscious of the situation, felt that it was best for him to leave the post that he had used to define his research agenda.

Yet twenty years later, in 1934, Atlanta University asked Du Bois to return to the university as professor and head of the department of sociology. Booker T. Washington had passed away in 1915 and now there was no controversy between Atlanta University and the Tuskegee Machine. Du Bois was comfortable in his role of researcher and as initiator of the Encyclopedia of the Negro. By 1945 he had published the preparatory volume to the encyclopedia and had also completed three additional books including *Black Reconstruction* (1935), *Black Folk, Then and Now* (1939), and *Dusk of Dawn* (1940). Subsequently, in

1940 he founded the social sciences journal *Phylon*.[23] It was devoted to publishing the kind of research that could transform understanding of the African American community.

Nonetheless, by 1944 Atlanta University's new president compulsorily retired the great scholar at the age of seventy-six. According to President Rufus Early Clement, the age for retirement was sixty-five and Du Bois, who had been appointed when he was sixty-six, was now seventy-six and therefore was forced into retirement. A person of Du Bois's physical and mental health, despite his age, could continue to contribute to society. Believing strongly that his work was not completed, Du Bois was by far the most significant African American intellectual of his time. His forced retirement from his post brought many letters of protest and offers for jobs. But it was not a job that Du Bois sought. Rather, he needed a platform that would allow him to continue his dedication and devotion to the cause of civil rights for the masses of black people. Fortunately, for Du Bois, he had always maintained a relationship with the movement for African American rights. In some ways he was the most identifiable black spokesperson of his time because of his militant stand as one of the fifty-nine black people who created the Niagara Movement.

He had been thirty-seven years old when he helped to stand that organization up in 1905 to speak for the black community, even though it had been stillborn in the sense that it did not last long past its first anniversary, which was held at Harpers Ferry, West Virginia, in honor of John Brown. When the National Association for the Advancement of Colored People was organized a couple of years later, Du Bois was not just in the mix, he had the only black leadership role. From Niagara Falls and Buffalo, the locus of activism seemed to move to New York City where the involvement of numerous white philanthropists gave the NAACP a more credible path to longevity. Du Bois had worked alongside several progressive blacks who held views like his about the equality of African Americans. One of these was the journalist and publisher William Monroe Trotter, whose battle against the Tuskegee Machine had inspired many northern militants. Although Trotter had died from an accidental fall from the roof of his Boston house in 1934, ten years before Du Bois's forced retirement from Atlanta University, the memory of warrior giants like Trotter and C. Bentley and A. M. Hershaw must have sustained his vision of a society imbued with equality and justice. Du Bois insisted that all tasks could be accomplished with organization. This truism to him was just as meaningful to African American organizations as to others. Consequently, he was dedicated to writing out in concrete and rational ways what strategies should be followed to bring into existence the required objective.

In July 1905, Du Bois, after being urged by his friends to establish a "national strategy board" of radicals, invited a few select persons to the secret sessions of the Niagara Movement, which were held at Fort Erie, Ontario.[24] Never one to misunderstand the abiding racism in American society, Du Bois received criticism from many whites and some blacks who felt that he was exercising great audacity to lay down these principles for the Niagara Movement. Some people even thought that Du Bois was acting out of envy of Booker T. Washington. One must remember that only ten years earlier in 1895 Washington had given his great defining speech, "Cast Down Your Buckets Where You Are,"[25] to an enthusiastic white southern audience at the Atlanta Exposition. Our contention is that Du Bois was performing civil rights; indeed, he was performing individualism to the degree that he felt it was necessary for a conscious black person to lead a movement of civil protests in response to oppression.

Furthermore, this incipient struggle with the Tuskegee Machine created problems for the Niagara Movement, which was unable to find wide support among African Americans or financial support from white liberals. Those two problems, combined with the loss of news coverage, handicapped the Niagara Movement. Within three years of the Buffalo meeting the organization had disappeared. A small magazine named the *Horizon* served as a source of information about the movement's activities. Four years later, Du Bois helped create the National Association for the Advancement of Colored People. One year later, in 1910, he founded *The Crisis*, which became the main instrument for advancing the goals of the NAACP, and Du Bois's great propaganda instrument. The NAACP was founded by an interracial conference held in New York City and created with an initial membership of forty people. Du Bois and the core members of the Niagara Movement must be credited with being cofounders of the National Negro Committee. The group changed its name to the National Association for the Advancement of Colored People and held its first meeting on February 12, 1909, the anniversary of Abraham Lincoln's birthday.

Home Again

Du Bois knew when he left Atlanta University that he would be active in the civil rights movement for the rest of his life. From Atlanta University to the founding of the NAACP and later Ghana, his legacy of service remained consistent and consequential. He was given the post of director of publicity and research, which included being the editor of *The Crisis*.

As the editor of *The Crisis*, he supported the goal of creating a truly democratic society and integrating Africans into the main body of American society. The way to do this of course for them was to eliminate all intolerance or prejudice and all racism. The organization found itself without the support of many of the usual philanthropists for black organizations. Many believe that the organization's political actions would give them a tarnished image and name. Nevertheless, the organization and its lawyers continued to perform in the black community's interest regardless of philanthropists. These actions were especially important for those who lived in southern states. By 1919 *The Crisis* was selling over 100,000 copies per issue, and it became the voice of the highest ideals of American democracy and for reasonable but earnest and persistent attempts to realize these ideas.

Du Bois was always on one road. And that road was the achievement of equality for African Americans in the United States. That meant that his first twenty-five years at the NAACP were steps on the journey, and when he left that organization in 1934, it was a shock to African Americans. His desire to go to Atlanta University and establish a research program and an encyclopedia was based on his intellectual battle for African American equality. Once he left Atlanta University in 1944, he slipped into his previous role at the NAACP. It seemed to have needed him as much as he needed it. By September 1, 1944, Du Bois had returned to New York and focused on the study of the colonized people in Africa and the oppressed people worldwide. He had also worked to revive the Pan African Congress movement and it was during this time that plans were laid for the Fifth Pan African Congress at Manchester, England, in 1945.

It was not possible for Du Bois to remain on the fringes of the Pan African movement. He had run the First Pan African Congress in 1919 in London, years after Sylvester Williams had coordinated the Pan African Conference in London in 1900. But by the middle 1940s Du Bois was very much interested in having a relationship with the NAACP and the Council on African Affairs, an organization dependent on Max Yergan and Paul Robeson as intellectual leaders. Their aim was to liberate the continent of Africa and alongside these two major actors was Alphaeus Hunton of Howard University. The Council was able to raise funds for poor people throughout the continent of Africa and this was particularly the case in South Africa where Yergan had lived for a while. Du Bois was given a position at the NAACP as director of special research, but it did not last long. There were those in the NAACP who felt that he had an uncompromising personality regarding racial injustice and abuse of power. They felt that it was difficult for him to understand the position of people who may have been a little more conservative than he was at times.

The organization was in a furor over his strongly held beliefs and fired him in the fall of 1948 at age eighty. Like a "cat with nine lives" Du Bois was immediately offered a job at the Council on African Affairs as vice chairperson. Although this group was accused of being filled with Communists and sympathizers, it did outstanding work informing the black community about activities in Africa. The United States confiscated Du Bois's passport in 1951, and by 1955 the American government, in a particularly conversative mood, had forced the Council on African Affairs to close its doors.

Although Du Bois's desire was to travel to Africa, he was prohibited by the American government when it would not renew his passport. When Ghana became independent in 1957 it encouraged Du Bois to come to the celebration of independence, but he was unable to do so until 1961 when President Kwame Nkrumah asked him to come to Ghana. At the age of ninety-three, he landed in Ghana to take up the editorship of the Encyclopedia Africana. Even then, the

United States would not renew his passport, and in 1963 he became a naturalized citizen of Ghana. Du Bois lived to be ninety-five years of age. He was married to Nina Gomer for fifty-four years. After the death of Nina, Du Bois would later get married to Shirley Graham, for the final thirteen years of his life. One catches a glimpse of him in his office, at the lectern, sitting at his desk at *The Crisis*, but in the end, he was a husband and father who adored his children.

His son, Burghardt Gomer Du Bois, died of dysentery after a year and a half of life. It is said that the death of the son brought a gloom over Nina that would not disappear for the rest of her life, so devastated was she over the loss of the child. In 1900 the couple gave birth to Yolande Du Bois who was sent to school in England and upon her return to the United States attended Fisk University. Yolande married the outstanding poet Countee Cullen at his father's Salem Episcopal Methodist Church in Harlem in September 1928, at a wedding that attracted three thousand people, many of whom had been inspired by W. E. B. Du Bois.

The marriage did not last, and by the spring of 1930 it ended in Paris with Du Bois as mediator. Both Cullen and Yolande soon remarried. Yolande married Arnette Franklin Williams, a football player, in 1931. A daughter, Du Bois Williams, was born to this union. However, by 1936 Yolande was divorced from Williams. She and her daughter, Du Bois Williams, lived in Baltimore. Du Bois Williams, W. E. B. Du Bois's granddaughter, married Arthur McFarlane and had a son named Arthur, to whom Du Bois dedicated a portion of *The Souls of Black Folk*.

When Nina Gomer Du Bois passed away on June 26, 1950, Du Bois had her buried in Great Barrington besides the son Burghardt whom she had forever mourned. Nina had been his wife for over a half a century and he regretted her loss. However, Du Bois would marry Shirley Graham the next year. Graham became a constant companion to the elderly Du Bois and went with him to Ghana in 1961. They are both interred in Ghana at the Du Bois Shrine near the house that they had been given by the Ghana government. W. E. B. Du Bois left the stage of human life in 1963 at the age of ninety-five having performed his biography as a model of what needed to be, what could be, and what had to be for African Americans to rise from the unfair and unscripted adventures of an American society bent on subjugating them forever. We have shown in this chapter that Du Bois, more than any one of his peers, took charge of his personal life and merged his soul with that of the souls of Black Folk.

Chapter 2
Du Bois's Central Contributions to the Race Discourse

Race is a term that was introduced by a radical cadre of European thinkers and religious leaders to classify humans biologically, physically, and genetically for hierarchical purposes. In their minds humans could be divided into separate groups and ranked according to the quality of their physical characteristics. Of course, the ideal group was European, and the most important traits were those exhibited by the "white" race. During the height of the late nineteenth and twentieth century racial doctrine movement in which white supremacy was the primary ideology of European dominance, colonialism, and imperialism, Du Bois endeavored to slow the train of race so that it could be properly understood. In fact, he wanted to discern its origin and its course in human history.[1] Du Bois was intrigued with the political and social motivations behind the race discourse. His thinking about race was based on examinations and investigations of social issues to see how the practices of race and the persistence of the idea reinforced inequalities.[2]

One could, by speaking so much about race, inadvertently make race the subject of social discourse. The twentieth century, so famously highlighted by Du Bois's civil rights, political, and scholarly work, stands out as the century of the battleground of race. Du Bois was aware of it and made much ado about how to deal with its energizing capacity among the less educated whites in American society. However, he was aware of the overwhelming nature of race in the white elites' imagination. Patricia Reid-Merritt has shown in her books on race that it permeated all classes and every region of the United States.[3] In one of the more remarkable feats of scholarship Reid-Merritt produced *A State-by-State History of Race and Racism in the United States,* a work of more than one thousand pages documenting race and racism in every state of the union. Du Bois said that "the problem of the twentieth century is the problem of the color line."[4] He was correct, but he was also a principal in making the twentieth century about race in terms of his social and political practice. To combat racism, he had to create intellectual avenues for relief that gathered collateral damage for decades, generating responses, setting agendas for resistance, and establishing the political and social opposition to racial domination.

The Term *Race*

In the English language the word *race* was first used in a poem in 1508 by William Dunbar with the meaning of a certain class of objects; however, by the nineteenth century it had morphed into applications of physical characteristics that were transmitted by descent.[5] One can appreciate that when Du Bois went to Germany in the late 1800s, he was already swimming in the racial waters that had become by the 1600s the preferred way that whites described humanity. Francois Bernier had arrived at several categories of humans based on complexion and facial characteristics in the late seventeenth century and other European thinkers had followed in kind, always with the white group at the top, and all other "races" below.

Du Bois made several important contributions to the discourse on race and was prepared for the hellish times ahead by virtue of his experiences and education. African Americans would have had to create or construct a Du Bois avatar had he not been born in Great Barrington because the gifts he brought to the table were abundant and consequently used and digested by a people and a nation intensely engaged in explaining its historical contradictions. Du Bois's education at Fisk, Harvard, and Berlin gave him a wide view of the African world by virtue of his paternity and maternity, and a passionate desire to understand the racial disease that he saw in America. For him, race was the immovable object in the road to American democracy. His German experience had taught him that *der Geist* was key to unlocking the conundrums of the American social order. *The Souls of Black Folk* was for him an ever-powerful work of race construction.

The Orientation to Race

One comes to the question: How should we understand Du Bois who sought to transform society but could not reform it? A serious reading of Du Bois requires both a political and a historical eye. He was convinced over his long life that the United States could have produced a more progressive politics had its people known more. One of the reasons he edited *The Crisis* and made the NAACP his instrument for bringing about change was that he had seen the limits of research. It was a time for activists, those who would work incessantly to make change happen. Seeing America as a democracy that promised a politics free of domination, Du Bois felt that the Civil War was a manifestation of the corrupted idea of American politics. From the founding of the nation, American politics had produced the elements that led to the Civil War.

Thus, the corruption had been in the founding documents that did not see Africans and Native Americans as parts of the society being constructed on racial domination. We understand that for Du Bois, born so close to the Civil War, it was such a major aspect of his socialization in a country that was trying to find its way from the woods of division. Clearly the disease of white supremacy had shaped Du Bois's willingness to fight with vigor the dangers he saw in the American nation.

In this chapter, we intend to show that reading Du Bois in the twentieth century is putting on stage his immense contributions to the theory of race backhandedly. It is not so much that Du Bois spread the theory, but rather that in his intense and energetic drive to defeat it, to cripple it, to exhaust it, he gave language and space to the overwhelming sociological and political discourse on race during the twentieth century.

One can examine his corpus and see that his intentions were honorable but because he was trapped in the web of race, surrounded by the doctrine of white purity and white supremacy, he had to dispense with those issues to see freedom. He was a prodigious champion of antiracism.

The Impact of *The Philadelphia Negro*

Most scholars agree that *The Philadelphia Negro* established Du Bois's leadership in urban sociology and gave him a preeminent place in how Africologists, sociologists, and political scientists see the issue of race.[6] In the late nineteenth century the University of Pennsylvania was ensconced in the race paradigm and refused to give him a proper academic position as a Harvard PhD who had spent two years at Berlin and held two bachelor's degrees, one from Harvard and the other from Fisk, because he was of African descent. However, they did offer him a research position if he would make a survey of the condition of the black community in Philadelphia, largely residing in the Seventh Ward, and make a report on their health, political, religious, and economic conditions.

Du Bois understood that American racism dictated his opportunities, and he took the job and made the best of it. Indeed, when he completed his work, it was impossible for anyone to consider urban sociology without referring to Du Bois's massive work. The fact that race was seen by leading white intellectuals as biological and genetic at the time meant that Du Bois entered the discourse with some sense that whites saw black inferiority and white superiority as natural and permanent.

The specific physical markers that could be seen in black people by white people meant that there was something deeply entrenched in the natural realities of black people. The same was true for white people, but the exception was that their traits were considered superior and did not hold them back.

The Changing Nature of Race

Several scholars have shown that Du Bois was not alone in his attempt to deal with the race paradigm. In fact, Italians, Irish, and Jewish people were not considered white by the politically and economically dominant white Anglo-Saxon Protestant community. It would take the twentieth century for certain European groups to make it into the white race club. Du Bois, born in Massachusetts, understood the depths of race only after his experiences at Fisk University in Nashville, Tennessee, where he confronted himself in a way that he had not seen in the North. In the South, he was unquestionably black.

In 1751, "Benjamin Franklin classified the world's population by color: there were black, tawny, swarthy, and white complexioned peoples on the globe. Some will be surprised to discover that Franklin listed the French, Germans, Russians, and Swedes among the swarthy. The only whites to his mind were the English and the Saxons."[7]

Karen Brodkin's *How Jews Became White Folks and What That Says About Race in America* suggested that transforming Jews into whites had race, class, and gender aspects to race-making.[8] Racial assignments find energy in polarizations, segregations, and separations. What Brodkin understands is that options open to "alien" others and those not considered "white" start with them seeking to become "white."

The alternative to this whitening for Jews, Italians, Turks, Portuguese, and Irish was to be given an inferior place in the world of white racial domination. Consequently, many Jews made the transition from being "aliens" to being accepted as white. Brodkin's work questions the construction of racial and political identities and demonstrates that the governing myths of race create anxieties about identity in a world where superiority is based on race. In a probing work, *Are Italians White? How Race Is Made in America*, Jennifer Guglieimo and Salvatore Salerno concluded that Italians moved from a nineteenth-century position as pariahs in the imagination of white Protestants to white Americans in the late twentieth century.[9] Whiteness studies suggest that the study of the transformation of Europeans to white status was part of the bargain of accepting the hatred of blacks. Indeed, we agree with Matthew Wills's evaluation "that whiteness should be abolished, that whiteness should be reconfigured, that the whole notion of race in general should be abolished. Race may be a categorization we make, yet the need for these constructions have deep roots. Whiteness studies reveal how arbitrary those roots can be, suggesting as well that nothing is permanent."[10]

The Twoness Conundrum

One of the more significant contributions Du Bois made to the discourse on race had to do with his provocative and often quoted statement about "twoness." Writing in *The Souls of Black Folk*, he says:

> It is a peculiar sensation, this double consciousness, this sense of always looking at oneself through the eyes of others, of

> measuring one by the tape of a world that looks on in amused contempt and pity. One ever feels his two-ness, — an American, a Negro . . . two thoughts, two unreconciled strivings; two warring ideals in one dark body, whose dogged strength alone keeps it from being torn asunder. The history of the American Negro is the history of this strife, — this longing to attain self-conscious manhood, to merge his double self into a better and truer self.[11]

Unfortunately, as we see it, this passage has not been read Afrocentrically by many of the literary giants of African American studies. First, what Du Bois referred to in double consciousness is perhaps more akin to double-sightedness; one can only have one consciousness at a time. It might be possible to experience serial consciousness, but the idea that we have dual conscientious awareness simultaneously is strange and difficult to imagine unless you are truly in the race paradigm and have lost sense of all cultural anchors.

Du Bois, growing up in Massachusetts, in the overwhelmingly white town of Great Barrington, might have had a different reality than most African people in the United States whose consciousness, defined by environmental and cultural designs and contextual circumstances governed by historical facts, did not have this "two-ness." What were the "warring ideals" in Du Bois's mind? Does this concept refer to being white and being black, or is it simply the mental struggle of trying to determine the meaning of a reality of inferiority and one of superiority? Is it really whether one is black or not? Our interrogation of Du Bois's sense of this idea is to illuminate the extent of its weight in the discourse on race. While this Du Boisian "two-ness" idea in the African American is a major contribution to the race paradigm, even if we can say that it is inadvertent since Du Bois was trying to understand race conflict, it is only a part of his additions to the discourse.

One of our former students, Ibram Kendi, whose books *Stamped from the Beginning* and *How to Be an Antiracist*, became bestsellers, advanced the race discourse, much like Du Bois, by seeking to expose the inadequacy of it as rational for human society, community, and culture. Kendi announces his intentions when he says that "the good news is that racist and antiracist are not fixed identities. We can be a racist one minute and an antiracist the next. What we say about race, what we do about race, in each moment, determines what — not who — we are."[12]

Kendi is a champion of antiracism, believing and teaching that racist policies rather than racist individuals are at the base of America's social problems. Indeed, he explains: "Critiquing racism is not activism. Changing minds is not activism. An activist produces power and policy change, not mental change. If a person has no record of power or policy change, then that person is not an activist."[13]

Racial Identity

Du Bois's legacy included giving legitimacy to the idea of racial identity, thus inspiring numerous studies and reports measuring various aspects of identity formation, setting up interrogations into differences between groups defined as black and white. Race was the primary reason for the study of *The Philadelphia Negro* in 1896 when Du Bois went from house to house in the Seventh Ward of Philadelphia to interview nearly five thousand African Americans. What he discovered was that the black population was younger than the white population and the mortality rate among blacks was higher than among whites, thus cementing the idea that racial identity could suggest differences in life chances.

He also discovered that almost all of the negative indices of black life could be tied not to racial inferiority but to racial prejudice, opening another entry into the question of race. Du Bois demonstrated that any example of dysfunction in the black community could be traced back to lack of access, not to biology. Almost all the issues about race promoted and developed by Africologists and sociologists must be laid at the feet of Du Bois. Racial formation theory, urged by Michael Omi and Howard Winant, could also be seen as related to the opening given by Du Bois in the works of the twentieth century.[14] Social forces must be seen, according to racial formation theory, as influencing racial categories and racial prejudices.

Even before Omi and Winant, Du Bois had inferred that racial formation shaped the idea of race. He was aware of the role that D. W. Griffith's 1915 racist film, *The Birth of a Nation*, had on abetting the racist language and memes that formed the discourse of the twentieth century.[15] How does one combat this fierce attack on the humanity of Africans? Our reading of Du Bois must allow African agency to assert itself in any interpretation of his argumentative discourse where he seeks to explain social differences based on race. Du Bois's writings show that he became acutely conscious of the class distinctions that proved capitalism's companionship with racial attitudes. His work anticipated William Julius Wilson's *The Declining Significance of Race* when he embraced the socialist position on the conflict of classes.[16]

Race and Policies

As Kendi has shown, the presence of racism without racists is dependent upon the policy structures and systems that deliver racism regardless of individual beliefs or attitudes. Our position is that reading Du Bois means that we must introduce his political activism as a part of his fight against racial preference, prejudice, and discrimination. Du Bois was a cofounder of the National Association for the Advancement of Colored People at the same time he was confronting the Tuskegee Machine created by Booker T. Washington. In his judgment, Washington, a natural organizer, had developed a school that would assure whites in the South that they would have black workers. Indeed, Washington's famous 1895 Atlanta Exposition speech had this statement:

> A ship lost at sea for many days suddenly sighted a friendly vessel. From the mast of the unfortunate vessel was seen a signal, "Water, water; we die of thirst!" The answer from the friendly vessel at once came back, "Cast down your bucket where you are." A second time the signal said, "Water, water; send us water!" ran up from the distressed vessel, and was answered, "Cast down your bucket where you are." And a third and fourth signal for water was answered, "Cast down your bucket where you are." The captain of the distressed vessel, at last heeding the injunction, cast down his bucket, and it came up full of fresh, sparkling water from the mouth of the Amazon River. To those of my race who depend on bettering their condition in a foreign land or who underestimate the importance of cultivating friendly relations with the Southern white man, who is their next-door neighbor, I would say: "Cast down your bucket where you are" — cast it down in making friends in every manly way of the people of all races by whom we are surrounded.[17]

Furthermore, Washington's idea was to train African Americans in a way that would be fruitful for the white population:

> Cast it down among the eight million of Negroes whose habits you know, whose fidelity and love you have tested in days when to have proved treacherous meant the ruin of your firesides. Cast down your bucket among these people who have, without strikes and labour wars, tilled your fields, cleared your forests, built your railroads and cities, and brought forth treasures from the bowels of the earth, and helped make possible this magnificent representation of the progress of the South. Casting down your bucket among my people, helping and encouraging them as you are doing on these grounds, and to education of head, hand, and heart, you will find that they will buy your surplus land, make blossom the waste places in your fields, and run your factories.
>
> While doing this, you can be sure in the future, as in the past, that you and your family will be surrounded by the most patient, faithful, law-abiding, and unresentful people that the world has seen. As we have proved our loyalty to you in the past, in nursing your children, watching by the sickbed of your mothers and fathers, and often following them with tear-dimmed eyes to their graves, so in the future, in our humble way, we shall stand by you with a devotion that no foreigner can approach, ready to lay down our lives, if need be, in defense of yours, interlacing our industrial, commercial, civil, and religious life with yours in a way that shall make the interest of both races one. In all

things that are purely social we can be as separate as the fingers, yet one as the hand in all things essential to mutual progress.[18]

Du Bois and the NAACP carried out an alternative path toward justice in society. For Du Bois it was essential that the African American population fight for voting rights, civic responsibilities, and education to secure economic power and social justice.

Resistance to Racism

Du Bois must be read as a bulwark against the doctrine of white racial supremacy, the abiding disease of white exclusivity in the American polity. The Buffalo, New York, mass shooter, Payton Gendrone, wrote in 2022 that he wanted to kill black people for "the future of the white race"[19] more than a hundred years after Du Bois declared the color line to be the problem of the twentieth century. Thus, the issue is the changing of the structure of racial power, that is, the resistance to the doctrine that says some humans are superior to others. Du Bois believed that African Americans had to enter the house of ordinary citizenship as an act of resistance to all forms of racism; being trained to work for people who believed that blacks were inferior would not transform the condition of the masses of black people. Du Bois knew, as he had written in *Mansart*, how whites felt about their superiority because he has Manuel Mansart going to work in a small Georgia town that he calls Jerusalem where "there was always a certain tenseness in the air which at times, especially on drunken Saturdays, brought one or two quick police to rush some black man to jail."[20]

He knew from history in the South that "mobs could suddenly be gathered, and lynching arranged by whites. Riots and murders were carried out by rule. One or two police officers watched the Negroes. These towns by the thousands in the South kept the interracial pattern intact, held political control of the state, and were the center of stern religious dogma. It was no empty joke to assert in this land, 'Man made the city, God made the country, but the Devil made the small town.'"[21] No matter how much eloquence we hear in Du Bois's language it is clear to the reader that he understands the collaboration of the segregationist South with the malignancy of white racial domination. One does not have to listen to or read the rhetorical incontinent sentences of racists, bigots, and segregationists of the twentieth century to know that Du Bois's challenge was mammoth.

Religion

Most of Du Bois's career was spent as a free thinker although he had grown up in a New England Protestant community. His academic experiences, political and social environments, personal convictions, and sensibilities accompanied him through various responses to the spirituality that he found in African people in the United States. His reaction to religion was skeptical: "Du Bois seemed to be one of those persons who, when asked about their religion, reply that they have 'none to speak of.'"[22]

He wrote in a posthumously published piece, "On Christianity," that "the theology of the average-colored church is basing itself far too much upon 'Hell and Damnation' — upon an attempt to scare people into being decent and threatening them with the terrors of death and punishment. We are still trained to believe a good deal that is simply childish in theology. The outward and visible punishment of every wrong deed that men do, the repeated declaration that anything can be gotten by anyone at any time by prayer."[23]

Anthony B. Pinn has problematized the entire discourse on Du Bois and religion by examining three of the most important works on this subject in his review article "Reading Du Bois Through Religion and Religious Commitment." After discussing in some detail the works of Edward J. Blum, *W. E. B. Du Bois: American Prophet*, Jonathan S. Kahn, *Divine Discontent: The Religious Imagination of W. E. B. Du Bois*, and Terrence L. Johnson, *Tragic Soul-Life: W. E. B. Du Bois and the Moral Crisis Facing American Democracy*, Pinn states: "With no unquestionable argument on the topic in place, perhaps we must be comfortable with the idea that Du Bois's thinking on and use of religion is complex, layered, thick, as well as full of tensions and paradox. Ultimately, Du Bois's continuing importance rests not on his personal religious beliefs — whatever form they did or did not take — but on the sharpness of his insights and his profound ability to unpack and interrogate the inner workings of racialized life in the United States."[24] Consequently, we believe that the reading of Du Bois, to be fair, must include all of the complexities that he confronted in his search for truth. While it is true that Du Bois was steeped in the rich tradition of black religion, especially by his association with, and experiencing the life of, the historically black colleges and universities, he was still skeptical of its transformative power.

Thus, his language was imbued with the metaphors and figures of the robust African American spiritual and poetic sensibilities, although he was clearly agnostic in his personal responses to the sorrow songs' capabilities when it came to restorative justice.

Historical Alienation

A critical reading of Du Bois must consider his eventual state of alienation from a society that was not fully accepting of black people. There is no wonder why Reiland Rabaka, one of the dominant contemporary writers on Du Bois, found that he was involved in discourses of race, race-based antiracism, race relations, racial colonialism, racial idealism, racial identity, racial materialism, racial polity, racial reasoning, the racial state, racist politics, and racist culture.[25] A first stage of his life was spent seeking to become a whole part of the society, learning as much as he could of the culture, even mastering the Yankee aspect of the Civil War, and immersing himself in the German culture that had modeled graduate education for the American academy.

He was not pleased to be a spectator to the doctrine of white supremacy; he wanted to demonstrate that it was a false idea, an artificial construct that could not stand the test of humanity. When we read Du Bois we have to cross many roads that have been traveled by numerous European philosophers as we encounter themes deeply embedded in his training at Harvard and Berlin. Fisk is truly there, but at the time he attended Fisk it was saturated with the same intellectual wines that had made German and American academics, and it was his college readings that first suggested an alienation between European culture and African American culture. Resolving the contradictions, leveling the playing fields, and creating new spaces for progressive social meetings overtook his mind, and he followed his passion into activism.

A social activist challenges the conditions, interrogates the status quo, describes political and social reality in detail, and responds with the necessary remedies to the issues. Du Bois knew from reading the fundamental texts of the American nation that his work would be no easy walk to victory. His challenge was to himself and his community because he knew that the social and economic conditions of African Americans were not self-generated. The so-called Negro Problem was really a white problem in theory and practice, and when one reads Du Bois one must constantly be reminded that he is rethinking the race problem in every article and book like a man trapped in a cage looking for an escape hatch. Sometimes he sings a song of beauty based on the coolness of soul, *itutu* in Yoruba, calmness gained from living among black people in the American South.

For him, this is the essence of the soul of black folk, elegant and luxurious laughter, ritual soprano greetings of friends, and rhetorical flourishes that rival the charismatic oratory from the ordinary church down the street from one's house. This is the reason Du Bois inhabits our social constructions because of his historical genius. What appears to be true in a critical Afrocentric reading of Du Bois is his reliance on history to solve some of the social problems. His tool of choice is a historical scalpel used to carve away at falsehoods and misrepresentations of African history as he becomes more attuned to his own and his people's authenticity. Du Bois embraced his human beingness as a resistance methodology used against those who sought to erase him. In grasping humanity as a shield, he runs away from deformation, showing no interest in being anyone's freak, or Negro exhibit, and toward the equality of humans. He is above all nothing but a man.

One is not able to read Du Bois through the lens of classical Africa, as we could Cheikh Anta Diop or Maulana Karenga, for instance, because during his time the consciousness of Africa in the classical period had not become a concentration of many African American intellectuals. Neither Harvard nor Fisk, and certainly not Berlin, would have considered the Nile Valley civilizations critical areas of discourse. Nevertheless, and with some interest in Egyptology, Du Bois discussed race with William Matthew Flinders Petrie, a British archaeologist and Egyptologist. Petrie had read Du Bois's *The Souls of Black Folk and* wrote to him in this fashion:

> Dear Sir, I write to thank you for having said all you have in *The Souls of Black Folk*. I have long wanted to grasp the Negro problem, and your prudent, balanced statement is extremely helpful. As I am a stranger, I must say what my point of view is. It is as an anthropologist and historian; my work for over thirty years has been digging up the civilization of Egypt.
>
> Many years ago, when president of the Anthropological Section, North British Association, I made native races the subject of that meeting, insisting on the iniquity of crushing lower civilizations by Europeanizing natives. Later I did the Huxley lectures on migrations, mapping all the movements from 0-1,000 A. D. in Europe. The subject of race mixture is of special interest to me, and only this autumn I was addressing London journalists on the subject by request. Excuse my saying so much, just to show you my standpoint: It is that of native culture and rights, without European uniformity.[26]

Du Bois's reply to the rather lengthy letter was terse and direct:

> My Dear Sir: I thank you very much for your letter of January 3 and for your kind words concerning my book. You will also permit me, I know, to comment on some of the matters upon which you have touched on in your letter. The Englishman's objection to the native sounds very familiar to me.
>
> I can see nothing in the objection except the very human dislike for cheating and ignorance and lack of self-respect. This objection is worldwide and age old. The great point is, however, how to meet it, and I am sorry to see that apparently you sympathize with methods of meeting it which have been, to my mind, only too much in vogue during the world's history — the stern driving of men, the denial of education, and the general assumption that men must remain as they are for an indefinite time. To all these I take profoundly serious exception.[27]

In this exchange Petrie does not reveal his ideas on the blackness of the ancient Egyptians, paying more attention to the Christian "Copts" than to the black Africa foundation of Egypt. Du Bois, while stern in his response to some of the racial nonsense promoted by Petrie, did not have the classical knowledge of ancient Egypt that could have truly closed the mouth of Petrie.

Du Bois did not engage classical Africa at Harvard, Fisk, or Berlin; he was a black man with a culture almost indistinguishable from that of white and black intellectuals with whom he corresponded in addition to Flinders Petrie, such as Jane Addams, Ralph Bunche, Andrew Carnegie, Charles Chesnutt, Countee Cullen, Paul Laurence Dunbar, Albert Einstein, Mahatma Gandhi, W. C. Handy, Langston Hughes, William James, James Weldon Johnson, Jomo Kenyatta, Martin Luther King Jr., Claude McKay, Margaret Mead, Kwame Nkrumah, Eugene O'Neill, Sylvia Pankhurst, A. Phillip Randolph, Paul Robeson, Eleanor, Franklin, and Theodore Roosevelt, Bertrand Russell, George Bernard Shaw, Arthur and Joel Spingarn, Mary Church Terrell, Carl Van Vechten, Booker T. Washington, H. G. Wells, Walter White, and Roy Wilkins.

Equal Opportunity

To read Du Bois properly one must see that the race question for him is false. It is not that the African is black that the social and economic ills to which he or she must respond exist, but because the society does not give Africans equal opportunity in any segment of the society. Thus, Du Bois understood that there was no problem for black people except the lack of equality of opportunity. Blackness was neither a crime nor a curse; the cruel injustice of racial discrimination and inequality promoted by whites was the real problem. To bring into existence a more just society it was necessary to identify the streams of inequality that turn into the rivers of domination. Shutting off the water to such malicious streams is the only way to annihilate race and racism.

Our reading of Du Bois must be done in conjunction with his political ideology. Every text dealing with race confirms his attitude toward its irrelevance when it comes to black success. Although he spent time laying out the need, at one time, for the Talented Tenth, he would later reject this notion for a more generalized understanding of mass elevation based on the socialist idea. It was clear in his response to Williams Flinders Petrie and to the Tuskegee Machine led by Booker T. Washington that he saw the political kingdom before the economic kingdom because he felt that black people had to be prepared to protect and defend their rights.

A fiercely independent, quick to debate, and brilliant personality, Du Bois took equal opportunity as one of his shields in discourse with other leaders. He believed that black people were the equal to other people and that there did not have to be any specialized treatment except to provide a society where white racists would not put their hands on the scale. Du Bois maintained that there was absolutely nothing wrong with black people except white hostility and inequality: "The history of the American Negro is the history of this strife, — this longing to attain self-conscious manhood, to merge his double self into a better and truer self. In this merging he wishes neither of the older selves to be lost. . . . He simply wishes to make it possible for a man to be both a Negro and an American."[28]

In the pioneering article "Toward An Afrocentric Research Methodology," Ruth Reviere of the University of the West Indies posits Afrocentric criteria that can be used to determine the quality of a text.[29] For her, the Kiswahili terms *ukweli, uhaki, kujitoa, ujamaa,* and *utulivu* are fundamental to examining the works of African scholars seeking to demonstrate a relationship to African agency. Although Du Bois is writing long before Reviere, she insists, looking backwards, that "any inquiry must satisfy these five canons to be truly legitimate."[30] According to Michelle Taylor, "Reviere defines these terms as follows: *Ukweli* is the groundedness of research in the experiences of the community being researched; *Kujitoa* requires that the researcher emphasize considerations of how knowledge is structured and used over the need for dispassion and objectivity; *Utulivu* requires that the researcher actively avoid creating, exaggerating, or sustaining divisions between or within communities but rather strive to create harmonious relationships between and within these groups; *Ujamaa* requires that the researcher reject the researcher/participant separation."[31]

One could easily fit Du Bois's entire argument in Reviere's methodological structure because in the end it helps to defeat the inequality, bias, racism, and discrimination that appear endemic in American society. Du Bois himself responds with a powerful and provocative declaration of his humanity:

> I sit with Shakespeare, and he winces not. Across the color line I move arm and arm with Balzac and Dumas, where smiling men and welcoming women glide in gilded halls. From out of the caves of evening that swing between the strong-limbed Earth and the tracery of stars, I summon condescension. So, wed with Truth, I dwell above the veil. Is this the life you grudge us, O Aristotle and Aurelius and what soul I will, and they come all graciously with no scorn nor knightly America? Is this the life you long to change into the dull red hideousness of Georgia? Are you so afraid lest peering from this high Pisgah, between Philistine and Amalekite, we sight the Promised Land?[32]

Furthermore, he sums up his belief in the unity of humanity by saying what he saw in the English toward the Irish: "The racial angle was more clearly defined against the Irish than against me. It was a matter of income and ancestry more than color."[33]

In fact, he was quite vehement that

> the equality in political, industrial, and social life which modern men must have to live, is not to be confounded with sameness. On the contrary, in our case, it is rather insistence upon the right of diversity; — upon the right of a human being to be a man even if he does not wear the same cut of vest, the same curl of

hair or the same color of skin. Human equality does not even entail, as it is sometimes said, absolute equality of opportunity; for certainly the natural inequalities of inherent genius and varying gifts make this a dubious phrase. But there is increasingly clearly recognized minimum of opportunity and maximum of freedom to be, to move and to think, which the modern world denies to no being which it recognizes as a real man.[34]

Hence, to read Du Bois properly one must see that he utilized race in his rhetoric to destroy its essence.

Chapter 3
The Entrapment of Ambition

Talented Tenth

Our objective in this chapter is to provide a guided inquiry into one of the abiding ideas in Du Bois's work. We will center on provocative and evocative arguments to help us decipher Du Bois's strategies for African uplift. This will take close readings, critique of sources, text-based interpretations, and social contexts to show historical and political literacy.

The depressing statistics related to the condition of African people who had been forced to work for 246 years in the most oppressive situations imaginable created in Du Bois an adversary role against the political and economic powers in America. Du Bois combined his skill in data collection with his historical interest as he was the first urban sociologist to document not just the conditions of suffering, but to offer what he considered to be options for emerging out of the poor economic situations.[1] All African Americans who had developed social consciousness were thinking about solutions to the conditions thrust upon the African people. Help was needed in a critical sense with insight into the problem and willingness to explore possibilities for resolving the situations of dire poverty. The Civil War ended in 1865 and Reconstruction ended in 1877, a mere twelve years, and after that time the blanket of death was dragged over the destitute four million Africans seeking, by Du Bois's time, to rise and assert their humanity.

In other places he would enlarge upon this idea both in lectures and in print, and then finally he would speak of the Guiding 100, which might be seen as a corrective to the Talented Tenth.[2] In recent years it has become fair game to question whether Du Bois was the first to propose this idea of the Talented Tenth.[3] We concede that there were several suggestions made in speech and print about the role of free blacks in the South and the Northeast to support the uplift of the general African population. However, it was Du Bois's relentless and direct call for the professional class of African Americans to be engaged in the battle to gain rights, education, and economic success for others. This is why we say that to read Du Bois Afrocentrically demands a historical insight that allows for a view of Du Bois's consciousness of his role in the ongoing fight to end discrimination. Let us put it another way: Du Bois, as we have said, was confident in his abilities and aware that he had not met a white person who could make him bow to a greater intellect. Some called it arrogant but for the role he saw for himself it was necessary that he felt a sense of responsibility for the uplift of the millions of Africans whose chances for success had never been secured by the society. He was not alone in seeking to develop a moral responsibility in the Talented Tenth to build a leadership cadre that would guarantee the route of successful citizenship. Of course, he was challenged by, and he would critique, the philosophy espoused by Booker T. Washington. In some respects, both individuals achieved powerful aims in their careers. Washington set Tuskegee Institute on a sound financial and academic footing and Du Bois succeeded in establishing a tradition at the National Association for the Advancement of Colored People that has endured into the twenty-first century. One could say, as we believe, that the idea of the Talented Tenth was not simply tied to the intellectual class but also to those who studied industrial education for the sake of economic progress as propounded by Washington. Nevertheless, when one reads Du Bois, especially the early Du Bois, one must turn the pages slowly and see that he is convinced that Washington's "Atlanta Exposition Address" in 1895, dubbed by Du Bois and others "the Atlanta Compromise," was a threat to the notion of black equality in political, social, and economic terms.[4]

How could African people defend whatever industrial achievements occurred through hard work and study if civil rights were not secured?

Read Du Bois's Talented Tenth with attention to attorneys, teachers, ministers, and professors who, as Du Bois said, could leaven the lump and inspire the masses. Now this type of reading is not simply following words on a page, but seeking the inferences, nuances, and implications of his overall project of African uplift. Du Bois was to trouble his virgin rendering of this idea in the "Talented Tenth Memorial Address" when he spoke of a new realization that he had about the proposal: "I realized that it was quite possible that my plan of training a talented tenth might put in control and power, a group of selfish, self-indulgent, well-to-do-men, whose basic interest in solving the Negro problem was personal."[5]

Du Bois's early idea was not a narrow one; he saw the Talented Tenth as a catalyst for moral change as well as uplift economically and educationally. In effect, his intention was to have the Talented Tenth guide the majority of blacks and others as well away from "the contamination and death of the worst."[6] What an admirable ambition for Du Bois as a young observer of culture and society in 1903! Reading Du Bois on the Talented Tenth cannot be adequately done without some appreciation of the original mention of the term by Henry Lyman Morehouse, for whom Morehouse College is named. In his essay "The Talented Tenth," Morehouse wrote, "In the discussion concerning Negro education we should not forget the talented tenth man. An ordinary education may answer for the nine men of mediocrity; but if this is all we offer the talented tenth man, we make a prodigious mistake."[7] Morehouse, then, writing as a missionary with an eye toward the general uplift of those a few decades out of enslavement, continued:

> The tenth man, with superior natural endowments, symmetrically trained and highly developed, may become a mightier influence, a greater inspiration to others than all the other nine, or nine times nine like them. Without disparagement of faithful men of moderate abilities, it may be said that in all ages the mighty impulses that have propelled a people onward in their progressive career, have proceeded from a few gifted souls. Sometimes these have been "self-made" men, so-called, whose best powers were evoked by rare opportunities. Oftener, they have been men of thoroughly disciplined minds, of sharpened perceptive faculties, trained to analyze and to generalize, men of well-balanced judgments and power of clear and forceful statement.[8]

There is no question that Du Bois engaged with this reflection on the part of Henry Lyman Morehouse. It is a profound prologue to Du Bois's acceptance of the idea as befitting the campaign for raising the level of the masses of African people. At the dawn of the twentieth century Morehouse's words rang as true to the educated African Americans as they did to the Christian believers who saw redemption in the figure of the great person. Thus, Morehouse continued in a matter-of-fact way:

> It is this talented tenth man of our colleges that in after years reflects more honor on his alma mater than the other nine; it is this tenth man that is the recognized leader in his profession and the leader of public opinion. To him, rather than to the other nine, the many looks for suggestion and advice in important matters. He is an uncrowned king in his sphere. This being true, I repeat that not to make proper provision for the high education of the talented tenth man of the colored people is a prodigious mistake. It is to dwarf the tree that has the potent of a grand oak. Industrial education is good for the nine; the common English branches are good for the nine; but that tenth man ought to have the best opportunities for making the most of himself for humanity and God.[9]

Du Bois Channeling Morehouse

Here is what Du Bois wrote about the Talented Tenth:

> Strange to relate! for this is certain, no secure civilization can be built in the South with the Negro as an ignorant, turbulent proletariat. Suppose we seek to remedy this by making them laborers and nothing more: they are not fools, they have tasted of the Tree of Life, and they will not cease to think, will not cease attempting to read the riddle of the world. By taking

away their best equipped teachers and leaders, by slamming the door of opportunity in the faces of their bolder and brighter minds, will you make them satisfied with their lot? or will you not rather transfer their leading from the hands of men taught to think to the hands of untrained demagogues? We ought not to forget that despite the pressure of poverty, and despite the active discouragement and even ridicule of friends, the demand for higher training steadily increases among Negro youth: there were, in the years from 1875 to 1880, 22 Negro graduates from Northern colleges; from 1885 to 1890 there were 43, and from 1895 to 1900, nearly 100 graduates. From Southern Negro colleges there were, in the same three periods, 143, 413, and over 500 graduates. Here, then, is the plain thirst for training; by refusing to give this Talented Tenth the key to knowledge, can any sane man imagine that they will lightly lay aside their yearning and contentedly become hewers of wood and drawers of water?[10]

Du Bois had successfully captured the attitude, perspective, and essence of Henry Morehouse's argument for the training of the Talented Tenth. Morehouse was making a statement about human populations and the distribution of talent and the applicability of the theory to the black population. However, Du Bois, with an eye toward the elevation of the African people, thought that this Talented Tenth could be used as an inspiration for the education of African Americans.

In 1906 the Atlanta Baptist Seminary hired its first African American president, John Hope, who was a brilliant visionary. Hope led the institution with a strong emphasis on financial security and enrollment. He saw the institution as an antithesis to Booker T. Washington's Tuskegee Institute. Where Washington relied upon agriculture and trade as his emphasis for Tuskegee, Hope challenged this view by asserting the need for Africans to have top liberal arts training. By 1913, the Atlanta Baptist Seminary had changed its name to Morehouse College to honor the memory of the person who had first proposed the Talented Tenth idea. Morehouse had been the corresponding secretary of the American Baptist Home Mission Society and his involvement with the seminary led to the Rockefeller family's gifts to the school. Du Bois had been in Atlanta, having begun his work at Atlanta University in 1897, soon after his Philadelphia experience, during the transformation of the American Baptist Seminary, although he was not there in 1913. His tenure ending in 1910, Du Bois nevertheless had heard enough and read enough about the Morehouse doctrine to become an expert on the issue of uplift of the African people. In reading Du Bois we must keep coming back to *The Philadelphia Negro* because in this study he put as much as he could of what he saw in the character and potential of the black population. Du Bois provides vivid accounts of some of the data, such as information about saloons and drinking habits, which he heard about from the work of Wharton School students assisting S. M. Lindsay in his research. As low as his salary was during the study of Philadelphia in 1897, Du Bois was still considered, and he saw himself, as a part of the bourgeoisie.

This class of black people, mostly teachers and ministers, was "curiously hampered" because although they were in the leadership class many of them were unprepared for their roles and the masses had not yet become accustomed to looking to them for direction. Unsaid in Du Bois's account was the fact that dependence, driven home by two centuries and more of habit, had compelled the black masses to see solutions only in what whites could produce. Yet Du Bois knew in his heart that the solution was neither the white community nor the agricultural and industrial path of Booker T. Washington. "The Negro race, like all races, is going to be saved by its exceptional men," said Du Bois, himself a graduate of Fisk University and Harvard University. "The problem of education, then, among Negroes must first of all deal with the Talented Tenth; it is the problem of developing the Best of this race that they may guide the Mass away from the contamination and death of the Worst, in their own and other races."[11] He had declared himself a part of the Atlanta fortress against the extraordinary Tuskegee Machine. Of course, Washington's response was always the following: "No race can prosper till it learns that there is as much dignity in tilling a field as in writing a poem. It is at the bottom of life we must begin, and not at the top. Nor should we permit our grievances to overshadow our opportunities."[12] This argument would direct the attention of numerous civil rights leaders and educators for decades. Nonetheless, Du Bois must be read as supporting academic excellence to build "race" capacity where leaders could elevate the masses with their higher education experience.

Therefore, for Du Bois, the duty of the so-called Talented Tenth was to serve the lower classes. This was not a doctrine of whites; this was the radical doctrine of black progress through the eyes of the African American first citizen, defender of the race, hero of the war against the masses, and commander of the language necessary to quell any attacks on the black people of America. He carried on his work with a noblesse oblige for the vast ocean of poor black people he saw in the South. Nothing evil, brutal, or savage said or done to black people escaped his attention; he held the ramparts against bias and domination for decades in scholarly publications and in articles written for *The Crisis* magazine, the official organ of the National Association for the Advancement of Colored People.

Embellished by experiences, but deeply engraved in Du Bois's soul, were the ever-present demands of duty. Since his time at Harvard University, he had developed and promoted a personal ethics of duty. In the "Renaissance of Ethics: A Critical Comparison of Scholastic and Modern Ethics," a college paper for William James's class, Du Bois had written: "The fundamental question of the Universe, for ages past, present, and to come, is Duty. Given a universe with two horrible futures and the question becomes to each individual How much difference will it make if This be tomorrow's universe rather than

That's. In other words the great question the world asks is How much better is the best possible universe I can help make, than the worst possible?"[13]

The twentieth century was certainly an age of patriarchy and Du Bois, filled with duty, showed patriarchal tendencies, especially in relationship with those who were of the lower classes. Ethically, he saw his search for routes for the elevation of his people as an essential duty for one who had been granted so many opportunities of the mind. For him, as it was for many people of that day, it was his moral responsibility to carry out the Christian doctrine of helping the poor, caring for the sick, and elevating the suffering masses, most of whom were the darker races of the world. There was an entrapment in the Talented Tenth notion that hovered over all attempts to define duty and that was personal ambition. We do not contend that Du Bois held duty high in his moral character only because of ambition, but rather that Du Bois's central mission seemed to be outright determination to raise the level of Africans. This was not so much an entrapment, but a sacred duty placed on the altar of human elevation.

As one reads Du Bois it is good to remember that the argumentative setup between Du Bois and Booker T. Washington did not at first involve Du Bois. It was Washington who with his bold assertions and passionate beliefs convinced many whites to follow his logic to the separation of the races with blacks being educated to serve the interests of white people. This was the easy way out for whites who wanted nothing to do with bettering the lives of black people, but who felt that something had to be done. So these Washingtonian whites were pitted against whites like Henry Morehouse and the Rockefellers. The Atlanta Baptist Seminary with its aim to educate black students at the higher levels was in direct conflict with Tuskegee, and hence Du Bois enters the fray with an ideological and personal commitment to raising the lower classes through educating the Talented Tenth to the highest possible degree. He became the great nemesis to Tuskegee. Every time Washington raised his voice in support of the sons and daughters of formerly enslaved people working to please the sons and daughters of the enslavers through industrial, agricultural, or domestic work, Du Bois objected. There was no way that a self-loving, thoughtful, and diligent African person could ever acquiesce to a lower form of education.

While it would become increasingly clear to Du Bois through the years that historical and material conditions of life in the United States were changing and that he would have to revisit the Talented Tenth idea, he did not abandon the idea of educating African people in the best traditions. In fact, his engagement with socialism helped to direct many of his ideas after the Manchester Pan African Congress in 1945. It gave him a definitive framework for articulating his ideas about the struggle between the classes without completely wiping away what Du Bois saw as the natural road to "race" uplift.

Kelly Miller, one of the early intellectuals after Reconstruction, wrote a paper on "The Education of the Negro."[14] In this paper he made this statement, "Mr. Du Bois has done more to give scientific accuracy and method to the study of the race question than any other American who has essayed to deal with it."[15] Although Du Bois would have considered few men to be his equal, certainly Francis James Grimké, Kelly Miller, alongside Alexander Crummell and Martin Delany, older than he was, would have been in the emerging pantheon of talented African Americans. Of these, Crummell had the most impact on Du Bois, and by the time he had completed his education at Harvard and published *The Souls of Black Folk*, his mind had been filled with the life and wisdom of Crummell. In fact, when Crummell died at Red Bank, New Jersey, in 1898, Du Bois recognized it as the passing of an age. Delany, on the other hand, who died in 1885, had a more convoluted course to the apex of the black intellectual tradition; yet for Du Bois he was a sentinel of the light that was to come. Delany had studied medicine at Harvard long before Du Bois had studied history at that institution, but Delany's pre–Civil War glory was somewhat tarnished by his post–Civil War activities in the South. Nevertheless, like Francis Grimké, William Ferris, Crummell, and Archibald Grimké, he existed in Du Bois's frame of reference for the black elite.

Committee of Twelve

The Committee of Twelve was prompted by the Carnegie Hall Conference held between January 6 and 8, 1904, with the objective of mending the growing split among black intellectuals. Enough had been done and said by various units of "leading" voices of the community that it was clear to philanthropists and well-wishers that something had to be done to quell the rift between Du Bois and Washington. In some respects, it was a Goliath and David story in the sense that Washington had no peer when it came to raising money for the causes of black uplift in the South, and he felt and acted like the champion he had become through support from the Carnegies and other rich white patrons. Du Bois, on the other hand, had managed by virtue of *The Philadelphia Negro* to capture the imagination of prominent northern intellectuals, progressives, and humanitarians.

The "Wizard of Tuskegee" seemed to control everything, from education to politics to the press. He emphasized economic advancement and industrial education for the African American masses and eschewed political rights and social equality; his opponents, led by Du Bois, demanded immediate social equality and full civil rights as well as access to higher education. Some people felt that the "Wizard of Tuskegee" sat in the captain's chair and presided over the table of issues that confronted the black community.

Individuals from across the nation had been invited and some, like Du Bois, were reluctant to attend because they saw the conference as a Washingtonian production. Booker T. Washington and his compatriots had gathered fifty black and white men for the conference. Most of the participants were squarely in Washington's ideological camp. Without William Monroe Trotter, his potent and provocative friend and editor from the *Boston Guardian*, or William Ferris, a true activist intellectual and journalist, Du Bois was essentially walking into the lion's den without weapons or prominent supporters. He had asked the organizers to invite Kelly Miller, eventually securing an invitation for him since he was a prominent Washington minister and sociologist at Howard University.

The Carnegie conference made some progress initially with participants agreeing to the right of all people regardless of race to be educated, with higher education for the elite and industrial education for the black majority in the South. Washington accepted the idea of universal suffrage and publicly said that segregation should be challenged in the court system. A resolution was passed that condemned lynching, mob violence, and rape against the black community. They also agreed on cooperation with those whites who were open to progressive social action. As part of the follow-up action, the conferees created the Committee of Twelve, with Washington and Du Bois as leaders. The aim of this elite group was to keep everyone informed about conditions in the black community, from racial achievements to racial oppression. However, the ideological differences were real and the agreement between Du Bois and Washington made on January 8, 1904, at the end of the conference, was to prove impossible to carry out.

Du Bois could not agree with Washington, and although two of his friends, Kelly Miller and Archibald Grimké, Francis's older brother, served as secretary and treasurer, respectively, the fact that Washington was chairman and sought to dominate made the situation intolerable for Du Bois. On April 23, 1904, Kelly Miller wrote to Du Bois expressing astonishment at Booker T. Washington's sarcastic remarks about higher education for African Americans. Miller felt that Washington would turn the committee into an attack on liberal education, but Du Bois, feeling quite confident of his own and Miller's abilities to help steer the committee, told Miller that withdrawing from the Committee of Twelve would give Washington a free hand to do what he wanted to do. Three months later, Du Bois resigned from the committee. The elite Committee of Twelve lasted for four years and by 1908 was finished. In the meantime, Du Bois took his talents, and those of his closest friends, to a new organizational initiative that they called the Niagara Movement in 1905. Four years later in 1909 they organized the NAACP with the aim of confronting all forms of racism and segregation in southern courts.

The twentieth century opened with the overwhelming majority of African Americans, 90 percent, living in the southern states. Fifty percent of black men and 35 percent of black women worked as farmers or farm laborers. Others were left to unskilled and service positions. Few children were in school during this time because they, too, worked on the farms.[16] When President Franklin Roosevelt introduced the New Deal and created Social Security in 1935, the majority of black people were either working in agriculture as farmers or farm laborers, or as domestics, and they were not covered by the Social Security Act. Du Bois, who had campaigned forcefully for the rights of the masses of black people, became increasingly convinced that there had to be a radical democratic transformation of society.

Du Bois's activism as one of the *talented* took him to many venues. His lecture at the 1900 Pan African Conference organized by the Trinidadian H. Sylvester Williams, a practicing London attorney, put him on the Pan African map. This international conference of July 23 to 25 in London, attended by Anna Julia Cooper, A.M.E. Zion bishop Alexander Walters, and others, made Du Bois more famous at home in the United States. His lecture was called "To the Nations of the World" and came about because he was asked to chair a committee to Address the Nations of the World to which he responded with a document that he read at the conference on the closing day. Included in this speech were some of the terms we would later read in other books and articles. This is a part of Du Bois's speech:

> In the metropolis of the modern world, in this the closing year of the Nineteenth Century, there has been assembled a Congress of men and women of African blood, to deliberate solemnly upon the present situation and outlook of the darker races of mankind. The problem of the Twentieth Century is the problem of the color line, the question as to how far differences of race, which show themselves chiefly in the color of the skin and the texture of the hair, are going to be made, hereafter, the basis of denying to over half the world the right of sharing to their utmost ability the opportunities and privileges of modern civilization.[17]

While scholars are most inclined to quote Du Bois on the "problem of the color line" from *The Souls of Black Folk* (1903) or "The Freedmen's Bureau" in 1901, he had proffered this line in 1900 in London at Sylvester Williams's Pan African Conference. He was likely inspired by the impending century change and sought to insert into the conference, as a historical marker, this iconic phrase that has been sustained in the literature for decades.

Reading Du Bois in His Time

The Afrocentric reader is attuned to place and time, so it is not altogether strange for one to see how reading a text without consideration for situation and chronology could be quite confusing. In our opinion, Du Bois, clothed as he was in the best tradition of African people buttressing themselves against the vicissitudes of prejudices and biases, lived at a time when the voices of dominant European philosophers had thoroughly led their people down the ignominious road of bigotry. For example, the British philosopher David Hume, more than a century earlier, had already written and rewritten negative statements about African people:

> I am apt to suspect the Negroes to be naturally inferior to the Whites. There never was a civilized nation of any other complexion than white, nor even any individual eminent either in action or speculation. No ingenious manufacturer amongst them, no arts, no sciences. On the other hand, the most rude and barbarous of the Whites, such as the ancient German, the present Tartars, still have something eminent about them, in their valor, form of government, or some other particular. Such a uniform and constant difference could not happen in so many countries and ages, if nature had not made an original distinction betwixt these breeds of men. Not to mention our colonies, there are Negro slaves dispersed all over Europe, of whom none ever discovered any symptoms of ingenuity; though low people, without education, will start up amongst us, and distinguish themselves in every profession. In Jamaica, indeed, they talk of one Negro as a man of parts and learning; but it is likely he is admired for slender accomplishments, like a parrot who speaks a few words plainly.[18]

We know that Du Bois knew the traditions that had been advanced at the top American universities about the greatness of Europe's intellectual leaders, and yet we know that

> Locke was heavily involved in the slave trade, both through his investments and through his administrative supervision of England's burgeoning colonial activities. . . . The attempt to reconcile Locke's involvement in the slave trade with his reputation as a philosopher of liberal freedom has a long history, beginning shortly after the abolition of the slave trade. . . . Locke's readers are faced with the problem of how he could have been so intimately involved in promoting an activity that he apparently knew to be unjustified. . . . We are disturbed by the ease with which some commentators excuse Locke of racism or minimize its significance. . . . to advocate, administer, and profit from a specifically racialized form of slavery is clear evidence of [Locke's] racism, if the word is to have any meaning at all.[19]

Of course, Du Bois was aware of the various statements of the American philosopher Thomas Jefferson in *Notes on the State of Virginia* in 1784. For example, Jefferson says:

> Comparing them by their faculties of memory, reason, and imagination, it appears to me, that in memory they are equal to the whites; in reason much inferior, as I think one could scarcely be found capable of tracing and comprehending the investigations of Euclid; and that in imagination they are dull, tasteless, and anomalous. . . . Never yet could I find that a black had uttered a thought above the level of plain narration; never

> see even an elementary trait of painting or sculpture. In music they are more generally gifted than the whites with accurate ears for tune, and time. . . . I advance it therefore as a suspicion only, that the blacks, whether originally a distinct race, or made distinct by time and circumstances, are inferior to the whites in the endowments both of body and mind.[20]

Du Bois knew from his own humanity that the statements of white racial superiority were lies. Furthermore, he knew for a fact, a scientific one that he had proved with his urban sociology in Philadelphia, that the condition of African Americans had more to do with white prejudice, politics, and policies. Denied opportunities to compete and then condemned for not winning, black people had to create and organize for their own redemption. The leadership class, in Du Bois's mind, ought to be out in the front of this drive for equality. Increasingly confronted with the growing influence of the socialist revolution, Du Bois knew that he would have to revise the idea of the Talented Tenth. For four decades or more he preached the doctrine of educating the Talented Tenth so that they could elevate the masses. Many writers, including the influential Reiland Rabaka, see Du Bois's emphasis on the Talented Tenth as a form of elitism. We caution reading this too directly in the proposal that was asserted by Du Bois because he never stated, at least in earlier years, that this was an elitist position. To be talented did not mean that one was from the elite community or aspired to be set apart from the masses in interests. For Du Bois, the Talented Tenth referred more to those individuals who by skill and will made it to higher education while maintaining the drive to raise the impoverished masses. He was to regret later that some of the Talented Tenth turned to selfishness and became impervious to other African Americans. His objective, in our judgment, was pure; the actuality of it was fraught with corrupted views and practices.

Reading the Talented Tenth Through World Events

Near the middle of the twentieth century Du Bois had begun to see the impact of world events on the condition of Africans in the Americas. He felt that human beings were beginning to see that the clash between the rich and the poor, the workers and the bourgeoisie was almost as significant as the doctrine of white supremacy in the division of humanity. Evidence of the entrenched alienation of the working class from the capitalist production of goods was obvious to political and social observers.

The realities of life inside Russia where the poor people had been oppressed by the nineteenth-century Tsarist regime became for Du Bois a new site of comparative study in societal transformation. Alexander Plekhanov and Vladimir I. Lenin started to examine how the ideas of Karl Marx and Friedrich Engels could be used in the twentieth century to elevate the masses of Russian people. In 1847 Marx and Engels were asked to write the *Communist Manifesto* to demonstrate how the working poor could take power from the owners and managers. Both theorists were asked to help form the International Workingmen's Association. The organization, after creating spaces for working-class people to organize, split into pieces because of the very rigid views of anarchists such as Mikhail Bakunin. One of the parties that emerged from the breakup of the First International was the Russian Social Democratic Labor Party, Bolshevik. The party sought to use Marxism to construct a centralized working-class party that would guarantee the self-determination of nations. Consequently, at the 1903 Congress it adopted a program for self-determination, which meant the right of any nation to secede from an oppressive government. While Du Bois was still carefully analyzing the situation of his own people, he became increasingly aware of the situation in Tsarist Russia. Nations inside the Romanoff's iron grasp wanted more and more to have their own governments as federated states under a bourgeois democratic republic or under socialism. Du Bois, an avid student of European politics and views, watched with interest the unfolding of Russia's future.

Russia had two revolutions in 1917. The first is called the February Revolution; the second is the October Revolution. After the abdication of Czar Nicholas Romanoff II, Alexander Kerensky assumed the headship of the Russian state and the provisional government until its demise during the October Revolution, which overthrew the entire state structure. On October 24, 1917, the Russian Social Democratic Labor Party, Bolshevik, took over all soviets of the workers. The next day the Bolsheviks met and handed land and power to the serfs, workers, and ordinary citizens who did not have to pay compensation.[21] The October Revolution had many lessons and one of the most important for Du Bois was the reconsideration of the class question.

Rabaka quite pointedly sees Du Bois's pivot to the "Guiding Hundredth" as a nod to the class issue: "In revising and reformulating his Talented Tenth thesis into a theory of the Guiding Hundredth, Du Bois democratized and internationalized his black liberation and leadership thought, asserting that it must be based on 'group leadership, not simply educated and self-sacrificing, but with a clear vision of present world conditions and dangers and conducting American Negroes to alliance with cultural groups in Europe. America, Asia and Africa, looking toward a new world culture.'"[22] Rabaka is justified by the texts to see that "character became the greatest gauge of radical political potential."[23] Yet the circumstances Du Bois confronted, and other African American leaders encountered, were different from those of the Russian state. This means that character, whether one is a part of the Talented Tenth or the Guiding Hundredth, or a hypothetical 250,000, as was once suggested, is at the core of translating ability to action for the masses.[24] This chapter has demonstrated the complexity of the Talented Tenth notion, although it captured the imagination of scholars and activists alike without ever being articulated in any ideological framework.

Reading Du Bois Afrocentrically, we are persuaded to see his attempt at radical social transformation by asking those with talent to assist in raising the intellectual and economic profile as profoundly ethical.

Du Bois, for all his brilliance, never developed a full-fledged theoretical platform for his numerous struggles. In some respects, this was a failure; but, in others, it showed that he was much too engaged in practical actions to give more thought to the reflective task of making theory. In not developing a theory he also did not choose to apply the theories of others in any consistent and rigorous manner. This is where and how Plekhanov and Lenin were able to organize a massive response to the Russian Empire. They had at their disposal the works of Karl Marx and Friedrich Engels as guiding path lights to power and transformation of the Russian people, ultimately to revolution. Not even the Talented Tenth were given a platform, or guiding ideology, in any detailed manner, and hence it was impossible for them, even if they had formed a mighty organization, to follow through on bringing into existence a new African person.

Chapter 4
The Narrative of Socialism Considering Democracy

The American socialist Herbert Aptheker wasted no time in outlining the distinctions between Du Bois and Washington. Du Bois was without peer for more than four decades of the twentieth century as the iconic scholar of the African American struggle for democracy. Herbert Aptheker, born in 1915, who became a prominent Marxist historian, took to Du Bois's works as promoter, organizer, and interpreter. The publication of Aptheker's edited version of Du Bois's papers, *The Correspondence of W.E.B. Du Bois, Volume 1, Selections, 1877-1934*, by the University of Massachusetts Press, helped to reintroduce Du Bois's works as historically significant for the understanding of his differences with Washington. The anti-Communist campaign fever of the 1950s had tainted even the mention of Du Bois's name and work by academics. Du Bois had been indicted, tried, and acquitted of being an agent of a foreign principal in 1951 because of his membership in the Peace Information Center. As a persona non grata in his own country Du Bois had trouble getting his books and articles published in the United States. When Kwame Nkrumah invited him to come to Ghana and found the Encyclopedia Africana, he leaped at the opportunity to demonstrate that he could still contribute to the progress of the African world. And slowly his star rose on the horizon as a guide during the civil rights era.

It must be admitted that the narrative of socialism, so prominent in Du Bois's thinking in the mid-twentieth century, had really been elevated by the rhetoric of the 1940s and 1950s. At the age of ninety-three in 1961, he joined the Communist Party. Du Bois had followed the socialist revolutions around the world and had seen the Russian Revolution sentiments enter the ordinary vocabulary of the world's masses, changing the lexicon of curricula and the language of sociology. Impacted by the ideological position taken by the October Revolution of 1917, Du Bois had gravitated toward a realization of the special political power of organized ordinary people such as soldiers, truck drivers, railroad workers, and civil servants. Furthermore, in the rural areas, away from the huge metropolises, lived people who worked in agriculture, often as serfs, but were prepared to sacrifice everything to discover their own freedom, and to have their own land. Du Bois slowly recognized that the Russians and the Chinese were seeking a new way to raise the level of the masses. Lenin and his compatriots in Russia had managed to introduce the *soviet*, elected district or national council, system upon which the Soviet Union was based in 1922. In the meantime, the Chinese leader Mao Zedong (1893–1976), after a protracted struggle, including the Long March, founded the People's Republic of China in 1949. These events directed the attention of Du Bois to two phenomena: (1) the inability of democracy to deliver a mass revolution, and (2) the importance of raising the consciousness of the masses.

In this chapter we will examine the reading of Du Bois's relationship with democracy and individual freedom and we shall present his narrative of socialism regarding international and national politics. Obviously, Du Bois lived long enough to have contradictions, to manage them, and to accept those that did not destroy his mission. John Henrik Clarke, the late historian, contrasting Du Bois with Booker T. Washington, said, "W. E. B. Du Bois was a New England petty aristocrat. In New England, you could be an aristocrat with no money, if you had a good family, good status, good manners, if you went to church, and had not disgraced yourself."[1] As we have shown, Du Bois came from a regular family in Great Barrington, Massachusetts, and because it was a small town and he essentially was the child of a single mother and had shown great promise, the townspeople embraced him and thought of him as someone who would make a good student, but although he might have appeared, largely to himself, to be an aristocrat, few in the town would have thought of him that way. Du Bois was neither a member of a superior class nor a member of a privileged group. He was a talented youth whose ambition would bring him far in life. As he matured and found himself in the struggle for the oppressed masses, he wrestled with strategies for reform to a democratic system that gave feints to possibilities but never fully delivered the goods.

Democracy and Revolution

American historians are quick to begin a discussion of American democracy through the eyes of the Frenchman Alexis de Tocqueville, who wrote *De la démocratie en Amérique* in two volumes published in 1835 and 1840. Tocqueville studied the idea of democracy that had been developing in the Western world for a few centuries but had burst forth in America after the 1776 Revolution. A little over fifty years since the Revolution, the French government commissioned Tocqueville and Gustave de Beaumont to study how the American prison system worked, but once in the United States, they studied American society itself. When they returned to France, they submitted their report on the prisons, but Beaumont also published a book on slavery and Tocqueville on American democracy.

Tocqueville believed that society was getting more equal, and that the aristocracy was slowly disappearing in the United States and other democracies. In fact, this equality, as he saw it, was present when one looked at the number of men who were being permitted to enter the clergy, engage in economic competition because of increased commercial activity and the abolition of primogeniture where the firstborn inherits everything from the father's, or mother's, estate, depending on whether patrilineal or matrilineal customs apply. Of course, Tocqueville is lauded for his observations and praised for his understanding of America.

To read Du Bois's frustrations with the United States one must understand that what Tocqueville saw is not what the average African in the United States saw during the time of Tocqueville's nine-month visit in 1831 and 1832. Critics have rightly observed that Tocqueville ignored the writings of the American Founding Fathers, especially the writings of James Madison and Thomas Jefferson, as they sought to work out the type of government the new society should adopt. The idea in Tocqueville that industrialization leads to democracy might be used to suggest that it can equally lead to a greater gap in wealth. If democracy is about representative government, universal suffrage, and majority-based government, where is the analysis that explains the enslavement of millions of people?

We read Du Bois's writing, more than a hundred years after Tocqueville, and acting for transformation in the same society that was to eliminate inequality, as a prophet because neither equality nor justice had been achieved by the 1940s. Tocqueville's America was a hypothetical nation without a just reality for Native Americans and Africans. The Indian Removal Act of 1830 had been signed into law by President Andrew Jackson and of course, at the time, Africans were still in bondage. Obviously, the democracy that he observed was not anything that would have impressed Du Bois, and even after the Civil War ended in 1865 the American nation never had a revolution that produced the equality predicted by Tocqueville.

For us, reading Du Bois during his formative years after graduating from Fisk and Harvard we see a young man determined to make his mark on the world and to help in righting the wrongs against African people through an activist intellectual platform in the best traditions of democratic reforms. From the time of his Harvard speech on Jefferson Davis, the leader of the Confederacy, and his publication of *The Suppression of the African Slave-Trade to the United States of America*, to the 1940s he retained a belief in the transformability of United States' democracy. Every action that he took, all avenues explored, and each attempt to address the issues of racial domination, brutality against black people, and voter intimidation stretched democratic principles to their limits. It might be said that he had been trained in the United States and Germany to take up the white man's burden as if he was a surrogate for the white man. He was extremely well educated, worldly, sophisticated, well-traveled, and spoke several languages; in addition, he knew more about the political scaffolding of the American nation than most of his peers. Leaving no channel of petition unchallenged, he helped to create the NAACP, wrote research papers outlining the undemocratic practices of society, and appealed to the moral conscience of the nation until he realized that the problem was not lack of hearing but lack of moral interest in making democracy work for African people.

American democracy was born with tremendous handicaps in the enslavement of the Africans and the genocide of the Native Americans. Consequently, these two populations were defined by the white Americans as "problems" that needed to be resolved in the American nation. In 1890 Rutherford B. Hayes held a conference "On the Negro" just as earlier leading American industrialists had held conferences on the Native Americans, called at the time the "Indian Question." The black people, like the brown people, were "problems" that had to be solved. The solution to these "problems" had to leave the white people in their "proper" place as superior to the "problems." One can imagine in reading Du Bois that he must have thought of all of this when he was seeking to transform American democracy.

But what must be your mental state when you know that your fellow Americans see you as a problem? Thus, the idea of the "Negro Problem" permeates the democratic institutions in America during the middle to the late twentieth century, posing an issue for civil rights and human rights for organizations committed to change. Yet to achieve all that he achieved in education, contribution to scholarship, and leadership, and then be considered a part of a problem where his person, his body, was rendered second class and inferior, was the height of ignorance and arrogance. By virtue of the whites' declaration of him and his people as "the Negro Problem," he was immediately taken out of history and placed into a box that could be discarded or selected for special persecution. Du Bois began his journey toward a new reality by rejecting the idea of the "Negro" as the inferior other. He was a part of the citizenry that was like a limp demographic of quasi citizenry. But this was contradictory in the trajectory of democracy that was to lead to a more progressive body politic. The insinuation of the "Negro" into every social, political, and economic sinew of the American nation assured the whites that the overwhelming response to its appearance, because it was not human, would be rejection. African people knew that it was not real, and that we were the opposite of what whites thought, but without power we were unable to make change.

Amir Jaima contends that "the idea of the Negro is metaphysically and epistemologically problematic. Whereas the Negro 'Problem' is measurable and concrete, there is no consistent empirical correlate to the 'Negro' per se. In other words, though the problem is often framed in terms of racial *identity*, the sociological frame of *racism* is ontologically prior."[2] Overreading is not possible when we consider the multiple layers of the social context out of which Du Bois developed his response to the social sites of democratic contradictions. We are aware of his social and organizational activities among the highly educated class of staff workers for the NAACP and educators at the university within the context of the group thinking about racism in American society. And, certainly, we cannot misread his analysis of race to think of him as out of touch with the true problem of race. As Ta-Nehesi Coates says, in *Between the World and Me*, race is the child of racism, not the father.[3] The inferiority of "the Negro" and all the structures around the trope had to be created and then the thing named.

The collapse of the possibility of a democratic revolution that would ensure African American equality and that of other people in the society sat right at the front door of any discussion of justice, truth, equality, or a common humanity. It was not so much that democracy as a system was unable to perform as it ought, but rather that American democracy with its ingrained and reactionary racism based on what Molefi Kete Asante and Nah Dove called the "racial ladder" made a truly democratic revolution impossible.[4] Du Bois understood this reality and looked elsewhere for ways to confront the problem of race and racism. Therefore, it is difficult to read, almost useless to read, Du Bois without some interest in his idea of social revolution. What he observed in the American nation and saw in the example of mass revolutions were two systems supposed to be delivering better lives to people, and he could not resist the idea that one was doing it and the other had no proper mechanism for delivering mass transformation.

Socialism and the Masses

The appeal of socialism for Du Bois was the same as it had been for Plato in the *Republic*, Thomas More in *Utopia*, and Lenin. With a different education he would have also found deep within the African culture the communal nature of society. It is what Julius Nyerere instituted with the Umoja villages, what Stanlake Samkange and Desmond Tutu talked about with *Ubuntu* as a philosophy. What attracted Du Bois, however, was the idea of a system of political, economic, and social organization where the means of production, distribution, and exchange are owned and regulated by the community rather than by individuals. Du Bois saw the rapid changes that had been brought about by the Industrial Revolution where the steam engine had shuttled in an important advance in production. He had been a recipient of its contributions to travel and to manufacture, but just as Marx and Engels had seen in the nineteenth century, and Lenin and others had seen in the twentieth century, the gap between the owners of the machines of production and the workers who produced the goods grew at an astronomical rate. The owners dominated the workers, established private estates, measured out punishment, and even worked children as laborers. Two systems in one society meant that there was extreme wealth and extreme poverty. Du Bois did not have to look farther than his own African American community to see that the condition of the black masses, workers and producers of wealth, was one of increasing poverty and bleakness, while the condition of the owners of factories, as occurred on the plantations, enjoyed the fruits of other people's labor. Reading Du Bois on this side of the breakup of the Soviet Union could never be like reading him during his lifetime. Du Bois died in 1963 and the Soviet Union lasted for almost another three decades as a formidable political and military power. During his life the Soviet Union was a purveyor of the socialist doctrine that gave birth to many of the revolutionary independence movements for the freedom of Africa from colonial powers. Peoples' republics were established in many countries and socialist union movements happened as a matter of ideological course. To be progressive meant to be socialist; thus, siding with the masses against the wealthy exploiters was not only essential to sustaining mass consciousness but a moral act of conscience.

Du Bois's *Black Reconstruction* is considered one of his best analytical works because in it he applied much of what he had experienced and learned about the contemporary global situation to the post–Civil War era. He was an astute observer of realities and once said, "Today I see more clearly than yesterday that back of the problem of race and color lies a greater problem which both obscures and implements it: and that is the fact that so many civilized persons are willing to live in comfort even if the price of this is poverty, ignorance, and disease of the majority of their fellow men."[5]

Du Bois found that socialism was betrayed by the labor movement itself. If labor could have coalesced and brought black and whites together the nation would have created a much more equal society. Thus, he can write that "negroes moved from unionism toward political action, white labor in the North not only moved in the opposite direction from political action to union organization, but also evolved the American Blindspot for the Negro and his problems. It lost interest and vital touch with Southern labor and acted as though the millions of laborers in the South did not exist."[6] Clearly the issue of a collective phalanx against the imperialists and capitalists could not be resolved so long as whites embraced notions of white superiority. As a committed socialist, Du Bois arrived at the position where he hoped for a change of attitude among whites. History had recorded that

> labor went into the great war of 1877 against Northern capitalists unsupported by the black man, and the black man went his way in the South to strengthen and consolidate his power, unsupported by Northern labor. Suppose for a moment that Northern labor had stopped the bargain of 1876 and maintained the power of the labor vote in the South; and suppose that the Negro with new and dawning consciousness of the demands of labor as differentiated from the demands of capitalists, had used his vote more specifically for the benefit of white labor, South and North?[7]

Du Bois assessed the situation in the country and concluded that the barons of industry in the North had "coupled with privilege and monopoly" to create death and chaos after the war between the Union and the Confederacy. For him, the war had not succeeded in making equals of the whites and the blacks; in fact, it brought about much more inequality and anarchy.

The journey to socialism had many stops and interventions but curved in the direction of the working classes. This was his guiding star whether he had been influenced by the Social Democratic Party in Pankow while studying at Berlin, or reading essays by Eugene V. Debs, or becoming more interested in Africa as a source of inspiration. The 1900 conference in London led by H. Sylvester Williams had shown him the interconnectedness of the African people to many other dark people of the world. When the first international European war broke out on July 28, 1914, Du Bois saw it as an intracolonial war to decide who would control how much of the labor and land of the colonized people. He traced the war to the Berlin Conference of 1884–1885, seeing the African continent and people as the prized possession to be cut up, divided, distributed, and exploited by the great and not-so-great European nations. During the period of the war, the Russians had their revolution and the people had declared a government of the masses. When the war, called World War I, ended in November 1918, much of Europe had been destroyed and poison gas had been used in battle for the first time. Du Bois claimed and wrote vehemently that the war was "the result of jealousies engendered by the recent rise of armed national associations of labor and capital whose aim is the exploitation of the wealth of the world mainly outside the European circle of nations."[8]

Du Bois's generation, spanning the end of the nineteenth century and the first half or more of the twentieth century, was the time of giants who vied more with themselves than with each other to shape the future of African American history. As Europe gathered for war over the colonial enterprises in Africa and Asia, there was stirring among the most innovative leaders of the African American community. The ideas of Booker T. Washington, Carter G. Woodson, and Du Bois would not only help define the era but would usher in the time of the New Negro, in the midst of the disturbance in Europe. Each one of these leaders in their own lane brought a dynamic response to the nadir in human rights that appeared at the turn of the century. By 1915, Booker T. Washington was dead, just after the start of the world war, but he had left behind a powerful Tuskegee Institute machine whose imprint was on most major institutions in the black community. Woodson, who had received his PhD in history from Harvard University three years before Washington's death, pursued African American history with a passionate missionary zeal. By his transition in 1950, he had established the national celebration that morphed into Black History Month. Woodson devoted his entire life to making African American history a constant theme in all social and educational settings. Woodson was preoccupied with scholarship and publication at a different level than Du Bois, whose work was dedicated to intellectual and social activism. Woodson's aim was the ordinary reader; Du Bois's was the specialized reader. While both were compelled to work in the interest of social justice, Du Bois went the political and legal route while Woodson fought to influence education and American history. Neither Du Bois nor Woodson followed Booker T. Washington's industrial education path, but both were disturbed by the war and sought to rally African Americans to defend themselves. Woodson founded the Association for the Study of Negro Life and History in 1915; the next year he started the *Journal of Negro History*.

In fact, by the turn of the twentieth century Washington's views were well accepted by the leading white educational voices in the nation but had been questioned as early as 1906 by Du Bois in a speech at Hampton in which he criticized the Washingtonian model, calling for a more liberal arts orientation to the education of African Americans. But the war brought more urgent interest to Du Bois than Washington's Tuskegee Machine. He took to *The Crisis* to write about his feelings about the European powers gathering for war. In her article "W. E. B. Du Bois and the Wounded World: Seeking Meaning in the First World War for African Americans," Jennifer D. Keene wrote about Du Bois's ambivalence initially and then his acceptance of the fact that black Americans and white Americans had to come together to fight in World War I. He wanted the white race to take note of the bravery of the black soldiers.[9] Clearly, Du Bois was challenged to explain the fact that the war was caused by capitalist imperialists who wanted to increase their control over Africa, and his belief that black people were equal to any other "races" and could prove it by participating in a war that was in fact about robbing Africa of its resources and power. Historical records and observations are sharp on these points. By this time Du Bois was a known pacifist; nevertheless, he used his considerable influence and public platform as the editor of *The Crisis to* urge readers to see the war as beneficial to African Americans. In a July 1918 editorial, he wrote that "the colored race" ought to "forget our special grievances and close our ranks shoulder to shoulder with our own white fellow citizens and the allied nations that are fighting for democracy."[10] Moving from pacifism to war hawkishness proved to be a regretted position for Du Bois who found that the war did not serve the black community well. Resentment, anti-African attitudes, and bitterness over the fact that many African American soldiers had fought and conquered white German soldiers and fraternized with white women in Europe caused some veterans to wonder why their world was not free for democracy. Our critique is that race as a paradigm could never deliver what Du Bois wanted: a society free from the clutches of ranking of people phenotypically. This is precisely the problem Afrocentrists see with all analyses based on the illusion of race. Du Bois was not immune from this position.

Carter G. Woodson may have had a better appreciation for the power of culture in the exchange of human wills. Woodson seemed to have captured the sharp culture difference from the beginning of his career work. From an Afrocentric perspective Woodson was more theoretically inclined by his stark statement of the problem in *The Miseducation of the Negro* in 1933 where he criticized the fact that black colleges had taught black students to love European culture more than their own. One might say that he was at this point oriented toward understanding how Eurocentric culture had dominated the minds and brains of the educated class of African Americans. On the other hand, Du Bois, a gifted writer and observer, would at length join that stream of thinking in his 1936 speech at Hampton Institute, possibly influenced by Woodson, and chastened by succumbing to the "Leading Nations" meme of warring nations. But by then the world was on the verge of another international European war with Germany in the middle of the narrative once again.

The issue was race itself. Du Bois took a situation and massaged it into the racial framework that had been prepared by whites. Race defined the condition of black people and race defined Du Bois's initial and then final response. On the one hand, he knew that the war was not about saving black people but, as the war progressed, he recognized that for the black world in general, and black Americans particularly, the war might help to resolve some lingering issues about the capabilities of blacks. In the end, after the war the black community went through one of its worst periods of persecution. Black veterans were treated especially badly in the South and many could not wear their uniforms without being harassed.

Du Bois went to Russia in 1926. It proved to be a turning point for his consciousness and an experience that allowed him to put a stake in the ground of his own intellectual development. He saw a society that gave him hope that nations could concentrate on raising the masses out of dire poverty and dependency on capitalist exploitation. He wrote with a renewed vigor and both *Darkwater: Voices from Within the Veil* and *Black Reconstruction* reflected his new experiences.

As the astute reader can see, he folded his socialist views, developed in the early part of the twentieth century and sparked by the October Revolution, into his writing of *Darkwater: Voices from Within the Veil* and *Black Reconstruction*, both considered provocative in different ways. *Darkwater* was first published in 1920, and in it one finds the sense of what could happen in a world revolution. Rabaka is correct to make the powerful point that Du Bois was postcolonial before there was a concept of postcolonial because he engaged the discourse as one engulfed in the milieu created by colonial and imperial powers.[11]

Black Reconstruction showed how African people took their freedom, and working with the Freedman's Bureau and the Northerners who went to the South to assist the newly freed Africans, established churches, colleges, and free public schools. In a tribute to the brilliance of black plantation and factory workers in the South, Du Bois makes a novel discovery about the Civil War. The black workers won the war by participating in a general strike against the plantation system, effectively transferring their labor from the slave-holding Southern elites to the Northern invaders whose army lines began to use the new labor force to defeat the South.

Democracy crawled to the door of freedom and refused to open it. It would take decades more of petitions, marches, protests, and threats of violence to bring into existence a spirit of equality. Given his own life of activism his politics resonated with the Black Reconstruction and the civil rights movement of the 1950s and 1960s. He stated that "the Negro is coming more and more to look upon law and justice, not as protecting safeguards, but as sources of humiliation and oppression."[12] This reality made resistance virtually inevitable.

Drawing attention to the worldwide significance of the changes that had started in the United States, Du Bois depicted an America blind to the emancipation of African people as a part of the international revolution of workers against their abuse. An Afrocentric reading of Du Bois's attraction to socialism must consider the African legacy of communality that spurred many liberated African nations during Du Bois's last days to take on the mantle of socialism. Just a few years before, he had agreed to go to Ghana under the leadership of Kwame Nkrumah, a preeminent African socialist.

His disappointment with the failure of American democracy had begun years before his transfer to Ghana. Indeed, he had declared: "In 1956, I shall not go to the polls, I have not registered. I believe that democracy has so far disappeared in the United States that no 'two evils' exist. There is but one evil party with two names, and it will be elected despite all I can do or say."[13] A person so filled with the optimism that democracy should have brought to America by the 1940s or earlier could say, "What a world this will be when human abilities are freed, when we discover each other, when the stranger is no longer the potential criminal, the certain inferior!"[14]

Although most authors who write on Du Bois acknowledge that he was deeply committed to socialism, others cite his links to Africa and Pan-African liberation. For many he represents one of the most critical and contradictory race theorists of the twentieth century. Another group of scholars argues that he is the "father of Pan-Africanism" and played a pivotal role in the decolonization of Africa.[15] Bill Mullen's analysis of Du Bois's work is one of the most progressive because he excavates Du Bois's jewels about socialism that are buried in plain sight.

The reader of Du Bois's international essays and global opinions and arguments will do well to remember him as "the father of Pan Africanism" according to George Padmore whom he influenced and worked with at the 1945 Manchester Pan African Congress.

Although Padmore was young he had been engaged in the socialist movement since he was twenty-two years old as a Trinidadian student in Washington, DC, planning to attend Howard University to study medicine; he joined the Communist Party. Over the years he maintained contact with Du Bois and at the Pan African Congress introduced Du Bois as the chairman of the Congress and the Father of Pan Africanism. With the support of another young activist, Kwame Nkrumah, the three champions forged ahead with a Pan African socialist agenda. After the Manchester Congress the American government placed Du Bois under stricter surveillance, and it was with the support of African American socialist women that he was able to survive the agitations of the late forties and fifties.

Women such as Claudia Jones, Charlotta Bass, and Esther Cooper Jackson shored up his work and supported the octogenarian through the taking of his passport. Claudia Jones was born in Trinidad and raised in Harlem, New York. She graduated from high school and in 1936 joined the Young Communist

League after listening to a speech where the Communist Party defended the Scottsboro Boys who had been wrongly accused of attacking white girls on a freight train. Jones began speaking at rallies and in 1948 spoke to one thousand people in Phoenix about equal rights for black Americans. Jones was chosen to be the executive secretary for the Women's Commission of the Communist Party USA, eventually becoming the editor of *Negro Affairs*.

Jones saw herself as black nationalist and a feminist, and she was a member of the Communist Party. Jones made her name with the article "An End to the Neglect of the Problems of the Negro Woman!" published in *Political Affairs*. Running into trouble with the American government became a part of her life. She was arrested four times for her militancy and jailed in Ellis Island. Jones was one of the women who found Du Bois's work coinciding with her own mission.

Another woman, Charlotta Amanda Bass, was also among Du Bois's political friends. Bass championed protests for fair housing, voting rights, and labor rights. Bass founded the *California Eagle*, becoming the first African American woman to own and operate a newspaper in the United States. It operated from 1912 to 1951. In 1952 the Progressive Party nominated her for vice president. She was endorsed by Du Bois, Paul Robeson, and Ada B. Jackson, all progressive fighters for human rights. A third woman who stood out in the making of Du Bois's think tank was Esther Cooper Jackson who was an activist social worker and a strong civil rights campaigner. As one of the founding editors of *Freedomways*, a political and literary journal published from 1961 to 1985, she was in constant contact with Shirley Graham Du Bois and W. E. B. Du Bois as collaborators on bringing a progressive spirit of trade unionism, justice for Negro women domestics, and youth involvement in civil rights to the forefront.

Each of these women were both theoreticians and activists; they promoted the cause of socialism in their own way. Evidence reveals how the American government identified associates of Du Bois as agitators against the state. Indeed, these women, and Du Bois's male friends, were usually the courageous makers of a just society by agitating against the evils that were perpetrated by the officials of the nation. They did not fear talking about the abuses committed by the capitalists, imperialists, or routine officers in charge of maintaining the status quo; this was the bond that held them together. Because they were socialists, not all Communists, they attracted the attention of those whose purpose was to protect capital and capitalists even in the face of the exploitation of the masses.

As a socialist Du Bois felt that the intersections of race and class existed in a strange and distorted pattern where one could ask, "Whence comes this new wealth and on what does its accumulation depend? It comes primarily from the darker nations of the world — Asia and Africa, South and Central America, the West Indies and the islands of the South Seas. . . . Chinese, East Indians, Negroes and South American Indians are by common consent for governance by white folk and economic subjection to them."[16] While this was the reality, only in the Soviet Union had he seen the possibility of a difference where, at the Communist University for Eastern Peoples, he observed that the students were Russians, Ukrainians, Jews, Tatars, Roma, Caucasians, Armenians, and Chinese. Such diversity was unthinkable in the American universities of the time.

In a racist United States where white superiority was the doctrine of the day, he did not see any semblance of this type of diversity. So, filled with what was possible in human relations from what he saw in countries considered more progressive than the United States, he defended Bolshevism. Seeking to tie the role of black labor to the vast sea of workers of China, India, the South Seas, and Africa, Du Bois understood that the modern nations could not forever break the backs of the masses. As he observed, "Out of the exploitation of the dark proletariat comes the Surplus Value filched from human beasts which, in cultured lands, the Machine and harnessed Power veil and conceal. The emancipation of labor is the freeing of that basic majority of workers who are yellow, brown and black."[17] In this line of thinking Du Bois was supported by Paul Robeson, the reigning king of African popular and folk music in the twentieth century. In 1965, two years after Du Bois's transition, Paul Robeson wrote in *Freedomways*:

> My last memory of Dr. Du Bois is in London, in less happy circumstances, in 1962. The doctor, then 94 years old and very ill, had been brought to London for a very serious operation. He was tired and weak, and we worried about how he could stand the ordeal. I was ill in a London nursing home at the time and felt very sad and helpless about the Doctor's condition. So that when my wife, who visited him regularly in the hospital, told me that he wanted very much to see me and had asked especially for me, I got up and went to London University Hospital and we spent some time together. Ill as he was, he told me about his work on the *Encyclopedia Africana*; we talked about the progress of the Negro revolt at home in America, about the power and influence of the Socialist world, about the marvelous coming-of-age of the African people. I visited him once again in the hospital and was delighted and greatly relieved to find him miraculously improving. This was in August 1962. While I remained in the London nursing home, still ill, Dr. Du Bois recovered from his operation, got up and with Shirley traveled to Switzerland where he rested in the sun, went to Peking where they attended the October Celebration, on to Moscow where they attended the November Celebration, and back again to London in late November, where Dr. Du Bois visited me in the nursing home. He gave a fascinating account of his trip and experiences, which he had enjoyed immensely.[18]

Murali Balaji explored the depth of the relationship between Du Bois and Robeson in his book *The Professor and the Pupil*.[19] Du Bois, the elder, often reflected on Robeson, and Robeson the consummate singer and actor often demonstrated Du Bois's own wish for the soul of black folk. The love for the African people, who had suffered so much, was the hallmark of these two stellar individuals. While it was true that Robeson learned from Du Bois and respected him as the greatest scholar of his time, they were connected to the struggle for freedom by their commitment to see oppression defeated in all sectors of the world. They were not merely leaders in the African American arena; they were leaders in the larger world and held audiences with people in all parts of Europe, Asia, and Africa. Each in his own way produced the instruments, ideas, and concepts, both intellectual and spiritual, that were necessary for African and African Diaspora survival. In some way, because of their socialist leaning, and faith in the socialist idea of nonracialism, they became enamored with the possibilities of an America freed from the strictures of race. However, neither would see this development in their lifetime. Du Bois died in Ghana in 1963 and Robeson passed away in Philadelphia in 1976.

C. L. R. James had written his explosive analysis of the Haitian Revolution called *The Black Jacobins: Toussaint L'Ouverture and the San Domingo Revolution* in 1938 to further the revolt of the African masses against colonial powers.[20] Many observers, including the authors of this book, believe that James was influenced by Du Bois's work, which is proper in scholarship and research. Ideas, facts, and concepts are often traced to their genealogical intellectual origin and found to be connected because of good research. There is nothing wrong with this unless it is a direct taking of another's words.

Black Reconstruction was a bombshell of a work, based on the numerous arguments and discussions Du Bois had held with other scholars and students, and because of its powerful suggestions it was certain to have ramifications and reverberations outside of a small group of readers. However, reading Du Bois on socialism one must be certain to consider the implications of his work on authors in the Caribbean, the United Kingdom, and the African continent. Narrow-minded reading is not called for regarding Du Bois's socialism. Since the time Padmore invited Du Bois to support a Negro World Unity Congress they worked collaboratively for the development of a Pan African socialism. In our view, Padmore was the most valuable propagandist for the socialist position during the 1940s and for years later. However, it was Du Bois whose stature and endurance made *Black Reconstruction* the most important book of its kind for the socialist movement. Ultimately, for Du Bois, the Civil War, with all of its promise for a more egalitarian society, produced black workers and white workers with divergent views about capitalism. Instead of class playing the dominant role in the relationship of workers, the white workers saw themselves in a superior position to black workers. Nevertheless, Du Bois believed that socialism had clearer answers than capitalism to the plight of black workers.

When the conferees met at the historic Manchester Pan African Congress, Du Bois's books were widely displayed, and he was the dominant creator of Pan African socialism.

Reading Du Bois and socialism, one must always ask, "What question did he want to answer by proposing socialism as the answer?" He had to confront the problem of white racial domination and global imperial power. One was specifically local or national but had international reach; the other was international and interfered with African American domestic politics and economics. Therefore, by combining them, that is, extending the struggle of African Americans to the international arena he created a platform for socialism to answer both problems.

Ruthless exploitation to make surplus profit is the aim of imperialist powers and white racial domination. Du Bois, more than any other African American intellectual, saw resistance to both antlers of the raging antelope of capitalism to be the only way to bring about change. Black workers and farmers had to join with the workers of the world to transform their condition. He had articulated a doctrine where the strike and the boycott could be used effectively in organizing the masses. We believe that in this strategy, although he had seen it in Russia and India, he anticipated the monumental movement led by Martin Luther King Jr. a few years later. In 1957, two years after King had started the Montgomery Bus Boycott, Du Bois wrote to his protégé Nkrumah that he should try to build "a socialism on old African communal life, rejecting on the one hand the exaggerated private initiative of the West, and seeking to ally itself with the social programs of the Progressive Nations; with British and Scandinavian Socialism, with the progress toward the Welfare State of India, Germany, France and the United States; and with the Communist States like the Soviet Union and China, in peaceful cooperation and without presuming to dictate as to how Socialism must or can be attained at particular times and places."[21]

Chapter 5
Restorative Imagination in Du Bois's "The Comet"

Faced with the problematics created by the illusion of race, which was embedded in society as a cardinal principle held over from enslavement, during the dramatic period of the first quarter of the twentieth century, Du Bois felt obliged to imagine a new world. Energized by the newly announced victories of the socialists in the Russian Revolution of 1917, Du Bois felt that the time was coming for America to abandon its attachment to the faux doctrine of race. He had seen in the Russian Revolution the advancement of workers from all ethnic communities of the emerging Soviet Union as a harbinger of what was possible in the United States. Thus, in 1920 he wrote a science fiction short story built around Jim, a black man, and Julia, a wealthy white woman, after a comet hits New York City and unleashes toxic gas. They are the only people alive. At times, historical and science fiction lessons and creative works based on the past can inspire new ways to engage our present and prepare for the future. These potentially beneficial allegorical and archetypal references are replete in Du Bois's "The Comet."[1] In this chapter we interrogate the "The Comet" by applying an Afrocentric analytical lens to Du Bois's notion of the future.

Our evaluative mechanism, taken from the concept of Afrocentric Futurism, which Aaron X. Smith advanced in 2023 with the release of the edited book *Afrocentricity in AfroFuturism: Toward Afrocentric Futurism*, is a characterization of time and space centered on critiquing agency and accountability from within African culture.[2] Explaining and exploring the perspectives, theoretical scope, and intentions for the advancement of the methodological technique used when approaching and interpreting phenomena should prove helpful in navigating Du Bois's tropes and metaphors in his fictional account of "The Comet." By using fiction, as he often did, to advance his ideas about the dangers of race, Du Bois anticipated the strategic attraction between ethics and reality. The advent of race as a dominant discussion, largely predicted by Du Bois in his famous words about the color line and the twentieth century, makes his use of "The Comet" more important in relationship to blacks and whites.

When Theories Collide

Our approach to the reading of Du Bois's "The Comet" combines the fundamental elements of Afrocentricity with the technological lens appropriated from Afrofuturism to arrive at an analytical Afrocentric Futurism, which is described by Smith as follows:

> The study and implementation of the early ancient Kemetic techno-genesis of pioneering, cutting edge African cosmologies, creativity, and culture from an African/diasporic-centered perspective . . . Afrocentric Futurism analyzes phenomena through the foundational lens of Kemetic science, philosophy, spirituality, and related methodologies. . . . It is a self-defining liberation movement, which manifests an independently driven future through the utilization of lessons and connections to the tradition's deep structures of the ancient African past. Afrocentric Futurism is an effort to further anchor, connect, and reconnect contemporary consciousness and our Futuristic innovations with the immovable power of our African culture.[3]

While the underlying conceptual frame must be Afrocentricity, the idea of African agency in the context of historical time, the positioning of Afrocentric Futurism as a gathering of African cultural genres of art, science, and classical civilizations extends the Afrocentric lens. It is not so much that Afrocentric Futurism repeats Afrocentricity but rather that it enhances the speculative and predictive value of any ideology that seeks to speak in the interest of an African approach to the future. There are several ways that Afrocentric Futurism arrives at this analytical moment.

In the first place, the Afrocentric Futurism model represents *Nommo* and *Sankofa* personified. One term, *Nommo*, is derived from the Dogon culture of Mali, and the other, *Sankofa*, is an Akan word from Ghana. Through an appreciation for the power of the spoken and written word, which draws heavily from African values, customs, and worldviews retrieved from the past, we have endeavored to reinterpret "The Comet" beyond previous summaries, reviews, and interpretations, staking our claims for originality in the interpretation to the combination of the generative power of the spoken word as in *Nommo* in its most pervasive form and *Sankofa* as the retrieval element in the cultural memory that clarifies the future. Du Bois, without any indication of knowledge of these concepts, draws upon their foundation as a part of historical memory, and "The Comet" can be read as the logical thinking of African people faced with the enormity of a white supremacist environment. Du Bois had seen the same situations numerous times and by putting his story to print he was following the best tradition of African American storytellers and novelists. We see this Afrocentrically as a "what if" moment. Indeed, what if something like this would happen and the only people left on the earth are these two individuals?

Does the social order break down? Is race irrelevant? Would the classifications and categorizations built into the racial doctrine of white supremacy exist in this new order?

Afrocentricity

Afrocentricity, as we have shown, advances the notion of increasing African agency and seeing Africans throughout the Diaspora as centered subjects within their own stories, personal narratives, historiographies, and worldviews.[4] This approach to the self and phenomena differs greatly from the traditional depiction of African Americans as marginalized bit players who exist passively on the periphery of Eurocentric analysis. The early framework and functions of Afrocentric theory was developed by Molefi Kete Asante over the course of five theoretical works: *Afrocentricity: The Theory of Social Change*; *The Afrocentric Idea*; *Kemet: Afrocentricity and Knowledge*; *An Afrocentric Manifesto*; and *Malcolm X as Cultural Hero and Other Afrocentric Essays*.[5]

Through these works and a few other select articles and chapters, Asante explains the need for African people to move from the reduced status of dismissed objects to centered, sovereign subjects of our own historical, contemporary, and futuristic narratives. He declares that "Afrocentricity is a frame of reference wherein phenomena are viewed from the perspective of the African person. The Afrocentric approach seeks in every situation the appropriate centrality of the African person."[6] In education this means that teachers provide students the opportunity to study the world and its people, concepts, and history from an African worldview. "Afrocentricity is not a black version of Eurocentricity. Eurocentricity is based on White supremacist notions whose purposes are to protect White privilege and advantage in education, economics, politics, and so forth. Unlike Eurocentricity, Afrocentricity does not condone ethnocentric valorization at the expense of degrading other groups' perspectives."[7]

The Afrocentric theory emphasizes African agency, contextualizing identity and culture from an African historical lens, for example, Kemetic, Nubian, Yoruba, Akan, African Brazilian, African American, Afro–Puerto Rican, and Colombian; and urges a theoretical approach to reading Du Bois through what Asante refers to as location. Location theory is an approach that deals with outlooks, positionalities, place, ideological stances, and orientations as means of engaging with circumstances influenced by an acknowledgment of the power of subjectivity. The reader sees how this perspective shapes positioning and emanates from Du Bois's experiential knowledge as he writes "The Comet." One can understand how Du Bois uses ideas about identity, time, and place, as well as historical context, to make his point.

African people have strived to live in harmony with nature.[8] Contrarily, the imperial, colonial approach to life and reality that follows a more Eurocentric notion of purpose and power encourages the domination of the elements rather than cooperation with them.[9] The Afrocentric approach to reading Du Bois is thoroughly rooted in African history, and consequently presents a unique set of possibilities for the future.[10] Our reading of Du Bois demands that the nature of the subject and references indicative of African realities in "The Comet" be examined through the distinct lens of Afrocentric Futurism.[11]

Afrofuturism

Afrofuturism is a phrase first coined in 1993 by American cultural critic Mark Dery.[12] Since that time, several African American authors and academics have contributed creatively and analytically to the evolution and popularization of this evolving artistic and literary movement. The seminal work on the topic of Afrofuturism, *Afrofuturism 2.0: The Rise of Astro Blackness*, edited by Reynaldo Anderson and Charles E. Jones, provides a definition of Afrofuturism that Smith applied in his expansion of the concept. Anderson and Jones explain Afrofuturism as "speculative fiction that treats African American themes and addresses African American concerns in the context of 20th century techno-culture — and, more generally, African American signification that appropriates images of technology and a prosthetically enhanced future."[13]

Often referred to under the umbrella term the Black Speculative Arts Movement, Afrofuturism has gained exponential popularity through the works of several authors, including George Schuyler, Octavia Butler, Reynaldo Anderson, Ishmael Reed, Nalo Hopkinson, Y. L. Womack, Mark Dery, Isaiah Lavender, Nnedi Okorafor, and Sharise B. Moore.[14] The legacy of Afrofuturism has also been expanded through the work of musical creatives such as Janelle Monae, Erykah Badu, Betty Davis, C. L. Keyes, Sun Ra, Mother Moore, Meryem Saci, Sa Roc, Leif Womack, OutKast, and Howard Rambsy.[15]

The Gap Band, Parliament-Funkadelic, and Afrofuturist directors and producers have added to the movement through soundtracks and films such as *Space Is the Place*, *Brown Girl Begins*, *Afronauts*, *Supa Modo*, *The Sin Seer*, *They Charge for the Sun*, *Pumzi*, *The Last Angel of History*, *Crumbs*, *Robots of Brixton*, *Welcome to the Terror Dome*, and *The Black Panther* franchise. From a convergence of technology, film, music, and the digital movement one can see how Afrofuturism uses speculative fiction and science fiction as a global language and aesthetic platform to embrace many genres created by Afrodiasporic and African authors.[16] Using a combination of definitions and hints we see it as a process of reading where the images of technology and symbolism of space and time work together to form an arena of speculation about things, persons, and futures.

The combination of science fiction and the unique perspectives, challenges, and experiences of Africans throughout the Diaspora contribute to the creation of a fertile conceptual ground from which innovative theoretical approaches can emerge. Similarly, the intellectual and cultural climate increases opportunities for the synthesizing of existing methodologies for the sake of creating something altogether new as is the case with Afrocentric Futurism. We are interrogating "The Comet" with what might be considered an invention, but "The Comet" must be read as an integral part of the African American literary lineage open to both Afrocentric and Afrofuturist critiques.

Afrocentric Futurism

Afrocentric Futurism is a paradigm rooted in shared humanity and our greater potential for collective progress through mutual respect and cooperation. Toward the end of Du Bois's tale, the two wanderers each begin to see the other differently. They are recognizing the other as more human, that is, "a mother of all [future] life" and "as a man and a brother." Like the shackles, which the black man, Jim, mentions losing early in the story, the chains of class and race and the manacles of xenophobia and intolerance melt away in this rapturous cataclysmic moment, which resurrected dignity from the ashes of death and destruction. Du Bois was alluding to the eventual doom we as a human family are destined to experience if we do not acknowledge the dangers of rampant capitalism, classism, and racial discrimination before it is too late.

One hundred and three years after "The Comet" was first published, similarly fatalistic announcements can be heard on the same New York streets that Jim and Julia would frantically travel in search of life. Today's comets used to polarize, sensationalize, and stoke fear come in various forms. Whispers, rumors, publications, and dramatizations concerning multiple forms of imminent danger have become big business in this era of artificial intelligence, social media, and our twenty-four-hour news cycle. From warnings about racial tensions, the fall of the US dollar as the global reserve currency, or military threats from a foreign nation, we are compelled to wonder what the future holds.

No complete reading of Du Bois can take place without an acquaintance with the Afrocentric works that have advanced the alignment of society to the historical record. Scores of Afrocentric scholars have challenged the dominant narrative of white supremacy in ancient and current times. They have, in their quest to reconnect Africa to its classical traditions, raised the most important questions of culture and society.[17]

What we learn from the historians and scientists is that the Africans were the first progenitors of human futurism because for thousands of years the only *Homo sapiens* lived on the African continent. Du Bois's short story, "The Comet," reminds one that the first humans to gaze at the sky did it from the African continent. In this reading of Du Bois, we see that the star formations were subjects of human engagement relating to spirituality, math, science of time, creation stories, and predictions.

A Critical Yet Liberating Analysis of Du Bois

Understanding the foundational influences, sources, and cultural inspirations of the Afrocentric theory may cause curiosity for some who are familiar with Du Bois and his approaches to knowledge and African people. Du Bois and Afrocentricity, Afrocentric Futurism, or Afrocentric anything seems like an unlikely pairing on its face. Even those who acknowledge the immeasurably valuable nature of Du Bois's contributions to intellectualism and African American life would hardly consider him to be Afrocentric.[18] These critical clarifications have been advanced consistently by Afrocentric scholars who are also supporters of Du Bois's legacy. Asante expressed similar sentiments regarding Du Bois's theoretical and methodological positionality in his work *Afrocentricity: The Theory of Social Change*: "Du Bois was not Afrocentric. He studied African people but not so much from an African perspective as a European one."[19]

Scholar and author Sandra Van Dyke articulated and cited similar positions in her 1997 PhD dissertation, "Molefi Kete Asante's Theory of Afrocentricity: The Development of a Theory of Cultural Location." Van Dyke explains, "Du Bois became increasingly disillusioned with American politics and values. Asante sees Du Bois's Marxist connection as one that fails to take into account the realities of either racism or culture and binds him to essentially European frameworks of thought."[20]

"The Comet"

For Du Bois this delving into science fiction marked a peculiar departure from the nonfiction, quantitative, and historical work he is known for producing. The question remains what would encourage one of the most meticulous facts-rooted sociological scholars in American history to take a conceptual trip beyond the stars? He is drawing from the literary tradition of disaster stories while simultaneously rewriting the template for a more contemporary and expansive audience. We know that the seemingly preposterous found in science fiction or speculative literature is a part of the massive environmental and atmospheric possibilities for humans.[21] The stories appeal to modern Western readers because "they represent everything we most fear and, at the same time, perhaps, secretly desire: a depopulated world, escape from the constraints of a highly organized industrial society, [and] the opportunity to prove one's ability as a survivor."[22]

As Lisa Yaszek explains, "This is certainly true of Du Bois's story, which uses the natural disaster of a comet passing through Earth's atmosphere to explore whether there might be a future in which humans finally escape the constraints of a highly racist industrial society."[23]

"The Comet" is a challenging, compelling, and forward-thinking piece of literature that combines calamitous ecological and sociological elements brilliantly. Part dystopian nightmare, part ultimate critical analysis of race and class through the lens of an imaginary fallen metropolis, the comet roars with socioeconomic and racial nuance, which forces readers to see the best and worst in us while engaging worst-case scenarios.

The Story

The story takes place in New York City as rumors surrounding the potential impact of a comet swirl communities into various degrees of panic and preparation. The two unlikely costars of this dramatic fictional interpretation are an African American man described as "the messenger" named Jim Davis and a wealthy white woman of leisure named Julia who has been insulated by converging expressions of privilege and societal pressures to maintain a racialized economic status quo. Jim's role as messenger extends from the literal to the philosophical and theological as the story progresses. The focus on the negative elements of society that the comet stands a possibility of eradicating is ever present in Du Bois's telling of the story.

This comet was not able to be objectified for the amusement and exploitation of white society. On the contrary, this barreling ball of dust, rocks, and ice will come with clouds bringing travail like a scene straight out of the book of Revelation 1:7. "Unlike the friendly comet described by H.G. Wells in his novel *In the Days of the Comet* (1906), Du Bois's comet brings about a postapocalyptic world used for speculation on racial discrimination."[24] The heralded comet strikes the planet early in Du Bois's tale and a slew of events, tragic, revelatory, and inspirational, follow. The 1920 creation by Du Bois was originally presented as a chapter in *Darkwater: Voices from Within the Veil.*[25] It enjoyed a second issuance as part of *Dark Matter: A Century of Speculative Fiction from the African Diaspora.*[26]

This work is widely regarded as one of the many foundational precursors to the speculative arts movement known as Afrofuturism. Engagement with Afrofuturist content from an Afrocentric perspective gave birth to the Afrocentric Futuristic perspective.

Implementing this framework increases African American agency in the process of developing perspectives and meaning from various readings including historical, sociological, and religious texts. Thus, we can discern biblical images and themes in "The Comet" as Amaryah Armstrong wrote: "Against those who understand Du Bois as hostile to religion, scholarly examinations of W. E. B. Du Bois' relationship to religion and politics tend to read his use of religious and theological materials as either a sign of his adherence to heterodox notions of black Christianity or as a pragmatic religious naturalist."[27]

Throughout "The Comet" there are several subtle and at times overt references to religion and spirituality. The opening elements of fear, uncertainty, and mass hysteria are reminiscent of the biblical cities of the plagues. These locations, including Sodom and Gomorrah, Zeboiim, and Admah, were all said to be destroyed by God for the sinful lusts of Sodom and Gomorrah, while Zoar was spared. Biblical comparisons and the possibility of Du Bois being influenced by this notion of divine retribution provide additional layers of context to our reading of Du Bois's work. For example, a question of whether the comet was an act of God sent to rain down a modern version of fire and brimstone in the form of gaseous rocks emerges from this contextual paradigm. Could this event be just repayment for the racism, classism, and dehumanizing rampant capitalism that defined New York City in the roaring 1920s? In a twist of prophetic irony, we begin to see the comet as a cleanser, more than three decades before Proctor and Gamble created the popular scouring powder of the same name.

Julia looks toward her father and asks about the devastation that had befallen the world. She wanted to know the extent of the tragedy, and her father answered matter-of-factly, "Only New York." Was this a foretelling omen concerning the tragically fatalistic destiny of a nation refusing to acknowledge and respect the full humanity of others? The comet left the rest of the country unscathed, resulting in the destruction of the tentative union between the black man and the white woman by her racist father. A similar movement from hope to disappointment can be observed in Du Bois's *Black Reconstruction in America*, one of his most famous books. In the post–Civil War moment, Du Bois asserts, there was a possibility for an alliance between newly emancipated black people and poor whites, the two groups working together to forge an "abolition-democracy based on freedom, intelligence and power for all men."[28] "The tragedy of Reconstruction, as in 'The Comet', was the sundering of this coming together of black and white."[29]

Perhaps the most overt allegorical representation of religious overtones comes with Jim being referred to as "the messenger." We see this sobriquet appear eleven times throughout the story. The biblical savior Yeshua was said to be a messenger for God the Father. There is also an argument within scripture that the message has been corrupted and that adherence to the tainted distortion would result in men being accursed as seen in Galatians 1:8–9. Within this context we can look at America as a modern-day Egypt, with millions in bondage to their prejudices and biases. New York can be looked upon as a modern-day Galatia, or even Babylon, woefully misguided concerning the purpose and obedience to the messages of love and life while submerged, like the corpses in the vault, beneath leagues of lies and discrimination.

Du Bois encourages the reader to consider how religious symbolism, whether subtle or overt, influences his characters and his messaging as an author. The most pronounced use of this analogous, symbolic religious language came when Jim and Julia were being presented as the embodiment of a new Adam and Eve:

> An alternate interpretation of Jim and Julia as archetypal characters could also read them in a religious vein, as a post-apocalyptic Adam and Eve. Instead of a beautiful and peaceful "Garden of Eden" Du Bois places them in a world of death and ugliness, a world which metaphorically mirrors the one white folk imperially invented and orchestrated, especially considering the then recent bloodbath of World War One. However, Du Bois is quick to reveal, it is not a World War of utter desolation and asphyxiation karma so long as they free themselves from the vices and vulgarities of the former white supremacist world.[30]

Jim and Julia become unlikely progenitors of our new world giving birth to unprecedented degrees of empathy and respect as the toxicity of our current collection of negative social constructions dissipate in the stench of death. The stark contrast between the potential for new life while hollow symbols of its inevitable end are indiscriminately strewn throughout the city is undeniable. Du Bois makes a profoundly critical assessment of our nation in underlining the theme that our biases just may be stronger than our survival instincts and bear the possibility of outliving us as a species. Even after helping to save Julia's life according to her own accounts, Jim narrowly escapes being lynched moments later by a man that knows nothing else about him aside from the fact that he is a black man, not described in those words in the text yet a black man nonetheless. "They started backward with a cry and gazed upon each other with eyes that faltered and fell, with blood that boiled."[31]

Like a biblical narrative we find our protagonist standing "on the steps of the bank, watching the human river,"[32] which could allude to the banks of a river, providing an epic framing of the tale to be told. Like the infant Moses traveling down the Nile in a basket being discovered by Pharoah's daughter who arrived at the riverbanks to bathe, we repeatedly see biblical references to the riverbanks being the setting or playing an active role in biblical accounts. Some examples of the merging between the ecological and theological include the unfailing fruit and foliage by the riverbank, described in Ezekiel 47:12, and the seven cows emerging from the Nile in Genesis 41:3, thus taking their place along the riverbanks near the other cows gathered there.

The role and significance of riverbanks are also present in Genesis 41:17 as Pharaoh recounts his dream to Moses where he is located at the riverbank. Also, we find a similar symbolism in Ezekiel 47:6-7 where the son of man beholds several trees along either side of the river upon its banks. In "The Comet," we find Jim was outside the economic bank, perched on the symbolic bank watching a river of spirit, blood, and bone flowing frantically and unknowingly toward certain death. The indiscriminate yet collective nature of the havoc wreaked by the comet creates a powerful contrast to the segregated, economically discriminatory, and racially stratified society.

Being Seen and Seeing Yourself in the Other

The story includes a notion of invisibility as a protectant. Through Jim being rendered persona non grata to most of the white society, he was a prime candidate to run the potentially fatal errand that would eventually preserve his life. In a twist of fate, Jim was consequentially defended by the disregard of others. It was his invisibility that allowed him to see another day beyond the devastation that befell so many others. "Indeed, we are led to suspect that his sheer vertical depth in the vault is incidental to his being left alive compared to the darkness — the blackness — of the depth itself. It was blackness that put Jim beyond the world in the first place, rendering him immune in a most peculiar way to its effects, including those of the comet."[33]

The life of Du Bois involves similar dichotomies of invisibility and hypervisibility, which may mean that the author is writing elements of his lived experience into the role of the protagonist. Seeing Du Bois in Jim as the introduction opens with descriptions of being invisible and "outside the [white] world" was a theme that persisted throughout the tale and the life of Du Bois. The stinging gazes in the story are strangely like the feelings of being dismissed and disregarded shared by Du Bois when describing his own experiences. Similar notions of invisibility inspired author Ralph Ellison to write the novel *Invisible Man*, thirty-two years after the first publication of "The Comet."[34] Ellison details the battles black men engage in to be seen and viewed in a nuanced and more positive light. The other side of this invisibility described by Du Bois are these harmful looks, which were later defined by Toni Morrison as the white gaze.

Morrison popularized the *white gaze* as an idea that the lives of African Americans have no meaning and no depth without white people looking at them and defining their actions. The white gaze is present in innumerable ways in the workplace, with some manifestations being more prevalent than others. Nonwhite employees sometimes report experiences of the policing of their bodies within the workplace. Most African Americans have experienced the "white gaze" in some aspect of their lives, whether in the academy, the factory, or the corporation.

In "The Comet," one can see how Jim and the comet had some peculiar parallels between them. It can be argued that they each possessed qualities that could be viewed in the other. For example, the coldness and stiffness required to endure the subjugation Jim experienced are mirrored in the ice and rock comprising the comet. A notable set of distinctions and juxtapositions between our protagonist and the stellar object of mass obsession involves mobility and power.

The comet experienced a particularly liberating form of agency, soaring high above the clouds as Jim was descending into darkness in the bank's basement, under the earth. One moves from the sky to the earth while the other travels from the Earth's surface to the depths below. The comet was also capable of destructively barreling through the very city that served as a paralyzing prison of Jim's (and so many others) full potential. Perhaps Jim saw the comet as having superpowers in its ability to seemingly eradicate racial tensions, if only temporarily. To be a liberating force without regard for societal rules and discriminatory boundaries was a function of the comet yet a distant dream for Jim.

Safe in a Vault

One element of the story we chose to dive deeper into, while applying an Afrocentric Futuristic analysis, was the vault and the multifaceted interpretations of its presence and functions made manifest by Du Bois. "He started away. Then something brought him back. He was sounding and working again when suddenly the whole black wall swung as on mighty hinges, and blackness yawned beyond. He peered in; it was evidently a secret vault — some hiding place of the old bank unknown in newer times. He entered hesitatingly."[35] The apprehensions associated with the vault reflected a daily interplay for Jim as an African American attempting to navigate his job security and survival in a hostile and uncertain white world. There exists an abundance of rich symbolic meaning, with metaphors and similes throughout the story.

Many opportunities for multilayered interpretation come from the vault. Du Bois establishes this in the opening scenes where, in preparation for the comet's arrival, people throughout the city are found strategizing in preparation for the event. One of these precautionary measures involves Jim lowering himself into the bank's vault in the basement where he is currently serving at the will and pleasure of the bank's president in the face of imminent danger. While he is in the basement, there is a big boom outside that makes an earthquake inside the basement. Jim is worried, and he struggles to find a way to the surface. Outside then, he sees everyone is dead. The people are dead because of poisonous gas from the incoming comet as was told in the news a day before. This dynamic of a potential prison becoming a protectorate is a recurring theme in the story alongside darkness, dark skin, invisibility, and societal insignificance.

The vault can be interpreted historically and symbolically from several perspectives. For example, the vault became the unexpected sanctuary that not only brought Jim an odd sense of solace but preserved his life in the process. "Here with his dark lantern, he groped in the bowels of the earth, under the world. He drew a long breath as he threw back the last great iron door and stepped into the fetid slime within. Here at last was peace."[36]

The Vault as a Metaphor for the Heart of Capitalism

The most common association with a vault would typically be a place to store riches. Perhaps Du Bois was making an additional statement when he set a scene where many things are in the vault including sets of records, our protagonist, and a corpse. The bank president said to Jim, "I want you to go down into the lower vaults today. . . . Everything of value has been moved out since the water began to seep in."[37] The conflict between the elements of nature and material gain repeats from the microcosmic level of the water-stained vault to the macrocosmic, comet-wrecked city. Despite the pressing nature of the moment, Jim remains preoccupied with thoughts of what white people might think with his every move. "Then a new thought seized him: If they found him here alone — with all this money and all these dead men — what would his life be worth?"[38] Vaults are specifically designed to protect money and other things considered precious. Within capitalism, mortar, steel, and brick structures serve as symbols of financial stability, helping maintain the economic status quo.

Despite engaging with the collective reality of man's mortality and the threat of the annihilation of a significant segment of the species, money remains on the minds of many in this story. There is often a powerful magnetism between possessions and their owners. Status, identity, and ideas concerning self-worth can intersect to the extent that some people don't know who they are if they don't have their possessions and wealth. Du Bois skillfully alludes to the age-old adage *you can't take it with you* while characters in the tale appear to be prepared to take the approach that affords a materially prosperous afterlife popularized by ancient Egyptians.[39] The Afrocentric reader of the text will likely recognize the unfortunate racialized trope involving an African man considered expendable whose life is put at additional risk for a paltry price and therefore conjures up many discomforting historical parallels. African and African Diasporic men, women, and children have been relegated to the status of property with little to no ability to exercise the agency required to be self-determined.

Questions surrounding the value of black life are as old and American as the auction blocks utilized to provide inhumane answers.[40] In Jim's mind it seems that he was not at liberty to refuse his boss's request even if he desired to do so. Here we find him preparing for possible death rather than finally speaking and living his full truth and deciding not to take orders from anyone. Despite all the devastation, concerns about societal perceptions persisted. Not even a comet hurdling toward the Earth could free many people from the prison of their own minds, which disallowed them from leaving a toxic relationship or work environment. Jim is a cog in a great wheel of finance where some men and women are beneficiaries of the apparatus while most others remain among the less fortunate and are made to serve as the fuel for more efficient spinning to occur.

The wheel was spinning for Julia while spinning on Jim. For the benefit of a few at the expense of the masses has long been an unfortunate structure of capitalism. Du Bois spoke at length about the errors and dangers of rampant capitalism leading us to assess that the usage(s) of the vault were intentional in this regard. Having their time, safety, and sanity at stake, it is as if they are being fed to an insatiable monetary machine that specializes in extracting value without regard for the true human cost required. What is the future of any person or people willing to sacrifice their health, safety, or even their life for a job? In the event the employee died, the employer would typically replace them before the former workers were funeralized. Riches stored up and stacked up on the earth, worldly treasures that men kill for and have died over, contrast powerfully with Du Bois's presentation of the vault as symbolic of the proverbial pulmonary valve of the living, breathing superstructure of capitalism connected by the "human river that swirled down Broadway."[41] The breaking of the vault door as if torn off the hinges could be looked upon as foreshadowing the brief moments of consideration of a classless society that Jim and Julia later share. Du Bois lets us see what a conversation could have been for society. "Have you had to work hard?," she asked softly. "Always," he said. "I have always been idle," she said. "I was rich." "I was poor," he almost echoed. "The rich and the poor are met together," she began, and he finished: "The Lord is the Maker of them all. "Yes," she said slowly; "and how foolish our human distinctions seem — now."[42] A beautiful, precious dream of mutual humanity and the cherished possibilities of the rebirth of a more righteous and just civilization is abruptly aborted. The potential for a new way of being, thinking, and loving, torn off the hinges, gives way to past mores concerning our value, ignoring our equally priceless essence.

The Vault as a Metaphor for the Hull of a Ship

As Jim's character descends into the uncertainty of the darkness that envelops his ebony skin, visions of kidnapped Africans being forcibly lowered into slave ships may intrude on your thoughts. Could it be that an Afrocentric reading of this futuristic narrative is ambushed by jarring historical fact in a manner that makes the story more provocative for readers? The parallels between Jim descending into the vault while referring to his descending value in the eyes of his coworkers have undeniable unfortunate parallels to what conscious Afrocentric reading reveals. "Of course, they wanted *him* to go down to the lower vaults. It was too dangerous for more valuable men."[43]

This tragic acknowledgment plays into the age-old racist histories of arbitrarily devaluing African life and labor. This process was a mainstay during the Maafa, Marimba Ani's idea of the great tragedy of African capture and enslavement, where African men and women were often kept low on ships as they were being made to accept a condition even lower. "After the slaves received their last meal for the day they were driven below. If the sea was rough the slaves were unable to dance and whenever it rained hard they were kept below and the gratings were covered with tarpaulins which made it very hot below and nearly suffocated the slaves below the slave deck a horrible place."[44] Du Bois posits Jim in an unwanted dark and damp place at the beginning of his journey. The vault carries Jim through the tumult of the comet's fatal engagement with most of the city's citizens while he is preserved through his predicament due to his time spent in the vault. Black men who were imprisoned often speak of similar experiences. They claim that their time away safeguarded their lives as friends were killed on the outside due to dangerous lifestyles and conditions. Some version of the sentiment *I would have been with him/them that night had I been free* accompanies their wonder.

Jim emerges from the confines of darkness to greet a new world, familiar yet uncharted. Here we can see the vault as emblematic of a slave ship with its mix of wood, metal, and darkness holding death and wealth in the form of a black man/messenger. There exists a connection between alchemy and African American bondage. The mix of metals within the story of European commercial exploitation of Africans is a seldom studied element of the tragic tale of massive suffering. "Beginning in 1761, the British Royal Navy, which patrolled regularly in the tropics, experimented in copper sheathing with success. . . . In the last quarter century of the slave trade, from 1783 to 1808, one of the features most commonly emphasized in the sale of any given slave ship was its copper bottom."[45] So here we see the vault as a vessel, different from the *Good Ship Jesus* and other carriers of human cargo into a life of bondage,[46] but a proverbial *Amistad*, symbolizing the liberation of an archetypal black man, who becomes at once a sovereign authority, a savior, and a full human being due to his time spent within the submerged vessel.

The Vault as a Metaphor for Prison and Imprisonment

Like the stone castle-like structure of the Eastern State Penitentiary in Pennsylvania, which holds the distinction of being the world's first penitentiary, the sights witnessed by Jim resurrecting from the vault were jarring images of human forms crowded, lifeless, and seemingly discarded.[47] "In the great stone doorway, a hundred men and women and children lay crushed and twisted and jammed, forced into that great, gaping doorway like refuse in a can."[48] It is prudent to note that jails and prisons have long been referred to as *the can*. These references date back at least eight years before Du Bois released "The Comet." Donald Lowrie, a prisoner turned author, provided insights from inside when he penned his ordeals with the justice system in 1912, stating, "first thing I knew I was in th' can ag'in up against it f'r robbery, an' got this twenty-year jolt."[49] For decades, these facilities have been vaults of bondage, storing misguided and unrealized potential.

The vault in Du Bois's work also represented bondage, entrapment, boundaries, and imprisonment. As Jim stumbles in the darkness over a decayed corpse he is forced to wrestle with the potentially fateful nature of his present predicament. He could easily die in there and, even worse than that, he realizes that few would care if the truth of his demise were ever to surface. This prison is full of symbolism and secrets. A mix of decaying flesh and deferred dreams cloaked in darkness is a morbid yet accurate description of the bank vault that Du Bois vividly depicts. This unfortunate blend of descriptors could also be used to discuss Jim. Here we find a man being tolerated rather than celebrated in a position that fails to maximize his gifts or give life to his dreams, all the while being brutally steeped in the dark heartedness of disregard from a dismissive yet limiting white world. The vault can be viewed as a physical manifestation of the many mental prisons that appear throughout the tale. The metaphysical prison of limitations leads Jim and so many black people of his time to contort their minds, bodies, and wills to adjust and adapt to the soul-stealing stratifications of a racist society.

The twisted perversions of a people's purpose and potential fueled African enslavement, convict leasing, Jim Crow, lynching, segregation, redlining, police brutality, and racially disproportionate incarceration.[50] The vault represents physical and mental forms of bondage for the oppressed and oppressor alike. The visceral responses many readers experience while considering the uncertainty, darkness, and death Jim encounters behind heavy doors away from the awareness of the larger society presents several parallels to mass incarceration in America.

Although this story was being told within the context of America in the 1920s, the exponential increase in the prison population in recent decades adds additional elements of drama and relevance to the symbol of confinement used to open Du Bois's story.

> In less than thirty years, the U.S penal population exploded from around 300,000 to more than 2 million. . . . The United States now has the highest rate of incarceration in the world, dwarfing the rates of nearly every developed country, even surpassing those in highly repressive regimes like Russia, China, and Iran. In Germany, 93 people are in prison for every 100,000 adults and children living in the country. In the United States, the rate is eight times that, or 750 per 100,000. The racial dimension of mass incarceration is its most striking feature. No other country in the world imprisons so many of its racial or ethnic minorities. The United States imprisons a larger percentage of its black population than South Africa did at the height of apartheid.[51]

The Vault as a Metaphor for the Womb

We find the vault operating for Jim according to its objectives of the protection and preservation of that which is very valuable. Ironically, the inanimate vault engages with Jim in a manner that indicates his value to a greater extent than the interactions he previously had with his supervisor and colleagues. The vault for Jim was tantamount to the protection provided by the womb of a woman to a developing fetus into a baby. Equally ignorant and unaware of all the perils avoided by his presence there, Jim, like a child, was left to fumble in the dark within the bowels of his unknowing sustenance and salvation. The vault is preserving Jim's life simply by virtue of its structure and intended purpose to keep certain elements in while restricting others from entering. Within this protective darkness, time appeared to move slower than aboveground where countless lives were expiring in the blink of an eye.

Viewing Jim fighting to escape the vault within the symbolic context of a womb-like vessel summons thoughts of the biblical Jacob who struggled and wrestled in darkness with his twin brother Esau prior to entering the world. Rather than being bound with a sinister sibling, Jim finds himself in the dark with death in the form of the corpse of the vault clerk. Rather than a birthright being sold it is as if Jim's birthright to be regarded as fully human has been stolen. Just as Manhattan, where Jim emerges into a world anew, was originally occupied by the Lenape people and Central Park was originally the predominately African enclave known as Seneca Village, one reads "The Comet" with the awareness that white theft of African possessions and liberties is a tragic yet all too common national pastime.[52]

The overtones of birth and birthright have roots deeper than the nation where men and women who resembled Jim were the first to grace the shores of a world that was labeled *new* to others who arrived hundreds of years later.[53] Jim's emergence and assertion as hero and as human could be an optimistic omen speaking to the potential liberation and reclamation of a protagonist and of a people.

The Vault as Tomb/Pyramid

"There lay the body of the vault clerk, cold and stiff."[54] As Jim is becoming an unlikely recipient of blessings through his circumstances he is ironically face to face with death. The threat that the end met by the vault clerk would also be the fate of Jim is a possibility that makes Jim's descent into the basement and the vault ever more precarious and pensive. He could very well die in here, the reader is made sure to understand. Jim has already been devalued and intentionally put at greater risk than others in the building only to find out that he would not be the first to enter the vault, never to be seen alive again by his coworkers. Only this time death would strike asymmetrically and karmically.

"The stillness of death lay everywhere and everywhere bowed, bent, and stretched the silent forms of men."[55] The vault Jim enters could have easily become a mausoleum preserving his trapped remains had the poisonous gas from the comet entered his lungs, claiming his last breaths. From an Afrocentric Futuristic perspective, we find interesting connections to the tombs of ancient Kemet in Africa,[56] which forever hold messages like the way the vault threatened to hold Jim (the messenger) captive eternally. Interestingly, those Africans who constructed and adorned the tombs are some of the original Afrocentric Futurists.

Writing our history, secrets, and prophecies in stone requires ultimate forethought and a belief in the importance and expectation that these messages should and will be conveyed in perpetuity. The architectural aspects of these civilizations bear evidence of a forward-thinking orientation that Du Bois honors and maintains through his writings. The tomb itself is perhaps the epitome of Futuristic thought as men and woman were mummified in preservation and preparation for a future life in the underworld. These original people on the planet were people of the sun, melanin, and stardust — futuristic manifestations of intergalactic black excellence personified. Through stories such as "The Comet" and analyses like this, lessons and spiritual energies are being reawakened through the powers of *Nommo* and *Sankofa*. These expressions of creativity and innovative methodological approaches will continue streaking through roadblocks of revisionist history, devastating falsehood with the same transformative fury of the comet.

Chapter 6
Du Bois and the Color Line

Battling the Toxic Social Construction of Race

William Edward Burghardt Du Bois is one of the most prolific producers of African American scholarship in history. As a result, his interpretations and analytical assessments of a people emanate from a place of qualitative, quantitative, and experiential knowledge that is virtually unparalleled. As we argued in chapter 2, of all the concerns and problems (e.g., class, commerce, military conquest, justice) that Du Bois addressed over the years through activism, organizing, and literature, it was the color line that was one of the most defining challenges of his powerful legacy:

> In July, 1900, Du Bois declared the problem of the 20th century is the problem of the color line, the question as to how far differences of race, which show themselves chiefly in the color of the skin and the texture of the hair, are going to be made, thereafter, the basis of denying to over half the world the right of sharing to their utmost ability the opportunities and privileges of modern civilization.[1]

Long before Du Bois made his prophetic prediction concerning the legacy of racism and the racial caste system that has plagued the world, other scholars analyzed the dilemma at length.[2] One notable African American public intellectual (today these men and women would also be referred to as influencers) was Fredrick Douglass. Being born into bondage in February 1818 and having experienced plantation life as an enslaved person on the Eastern Shore of Maryland provided Douglass with unique insights into American separation and subjugation.[3] As he endeavored to advance the causes of abolition, suffrage, and a more perfect union of national powers and brothers of every creed and clime, a keen awareness of global challenges relating to race developed.[4]

Douglass took upon himself the role of standard bearer for African Americans in war and peace, in diplomacy and in women's rights, and in protest and rallies for peace.[5] James Oakes refers to Douglass as a radical and Abraham Lincoln as a republican, which surely he was, although it is difficult to see Douglass as a radical given his insistence on equal rights.[6] In 1881, Douglass recorded his assessment of the possibilities of eradicating this condition decades before Du Bois would make his defining declarations about the color line:

> Out of the depths of slavery has come this prejudice and this color line. It is broad enough and black enough to explain all the malign influences which assail the newly emancipated millions today. . . . the office of color in the color line is a very plain and subordinate one. It simply advertises the objects of oppression, insult, and persecution. It is not the maddening liquor but the black letters on the sign telling the world where it may be had . . . slavery, stupidity, servility, poverty, dependence, are undesirable conditions. When these shall cease to be coupled with color there will be no color line drawn.⁷

The unavoidable nature of racial oppression has led countless African Americans and other students of race and racism to consider what Du Bois and Douglass described as the color line. We are among that band of thinkers desirous of helping to resolve one of black America's most pressing concerns, the color line. One can imagine what it is like in a contemporary sense for a lone African American child to be in a camp, or at school, or on a picnic, playing games such as tug-of-war, a team of one against the rest. Sides matter and strength matters, but in some strange and bizarre way one feels forever a sense of aloneness, even amid scores of white children. Winners and losers are compelled in a cruelly rigged game, representative of a paltry imitation of life.

Of course, the simplicity and clarity of the game is reassuring. However, with growth, a deeper appreciation for nuance and complexity accompanies an affinity for the game's structure. A child might learn to assess its comparative value more adequately regarding sociological juxtapositions. The extreme aspects of the tug-of-war are analogous to the divisive competitive nature of racial stratification in America. In this competition two teams stay separated from each other, never touching, never talking, only communicating through screams and grunts. The pushing and pulling accompanying these visceral outbursts indicative of the competition is how we can view the racial dilemma we find ourselves facing. We are unnecessarily separated; we are limited in the directions we can take to achieve our goals. Although Africans are no longer in physical bondage, roped into the confines of a racialized subcaste, we remain bound by a cultural cable tow that confines our aspirations, energies, and abilities to be liberated from the weight of its binding ties.

Du Bois attempted multiple approaches at detangling the nation from the tragic traps and tricks of American racism, yet many of the knots persisted or grew tighter still. One of his observations involved the complexities around the color line that transcended race and racism and expanded to other areas of identity. Du Bois's interpretations of the color line displayed the importance of understanding the intersection of various forms of oppression and the need for simultaneous efforts of liberation. Du Bois's championing of women in "Of the Damnation of Women" precisely locates the problems of "the color line" and the "uplift of women" adjacent to one another rather than one after the other. In other words, chronologically, one movement for justice need not wait until another movement for justice has achieved its goals; rather, the two movements are simultaneously important and could prosper accordingly.

It seems logical to conclude following this statement that color liberation need not be pursued before gender liberation. Du Bois concludes, then, that the categories of race and gender matter simultaneously.[8] Recognizing the potential for interdisciplinary interactions (which have shaped our understanding of the color line) led Du Bois to expand his interpretations of the dilemma over time. Beyond the convergence of race and gender exist many elements that call for an international analysis of the color line. He notes the vast growth of the color line while interrogating the possibility of these multidirectional developments being problematic when attempting to grasp and resolve challenges presented by the color line:

> Du Bois attempted to imagine and reimagine his color line thesis as linked to and dependent upon an inclusion of the Asian world; it represents the secular cast of his political analysis that often accompanied his essays on Afro Asian religiosity and culture. The color line belts the world, first published in Collier's weekly on October 20th, 1906, asserts that the color line and race itself are in emergent crisis produced directly out of what he calls quote "the policy of expansion."[9]

Due to the convoluted nature of the problem, a man such as Du Bois, with supreme focus, consistently engaged in fastidious study, becoming an ideal candidate to tackle the national (and international) obstruction known as the color line. His willingness to confront the theoretical limitations of previously held positions and adjust accordingly helped to make Du Bois a more efficient scholar. Therefore, our reading of Du Bois on intersectionality places him at the head of the school of thought that seeks to understand the inevitable entanglement of gender, class, and race. One cannot study race or gender or class alone and probe the depths of oppression, persecution, and discrimination against African people in economic, social, and political circles.

Afrocentric reading demands an appreciation for his research methodology as well as his philosophical vision. An appreciation for the trial-and-error method of research, in combination with an open-mindedness concerning style of approach, organizational affiliations, and other alliances, fueled his important work beyond many of his intellectual contemporaries. Through his journey toward the development of a strategy to alleviate the painful realities of the color line, Du Bois attempted several approaches including third world allyship, communism, and intellectual assimilation. Perhaps most unique was his suggestion concerning intraracial segregation of an elite demographic within the African American community known as the Talented Tenth who would act as liberators, leaders,[10] and saviors of the other 90 percent.[11]

As a result of the complexity of Du Bois's investigations and his intellectual expressions, an equally sophisticated method of analysis and interpretation, involving race, class, gender, and geopolitics, must be employed in probing his legacy. Maulana Karenga is wise to say:

> When we engage W.E.B. Du Bois's work and thought to extract useful insights and develop intellectual and social initiatives based on these, we unavoidably must deal with his concept of the color line and the role he assigned it in African and human history. The concept of the color-line refers essentially to the role of race and racism in history and society. But of necessity, for Du Bois, it requires multidimensional analysis which identifies and seeks to understand the intersection of race and class as both modes of domination and modes of resistance on the national and international level.[12]

Du Bois was diligent in his targeted attempts to bring down this beast of supposed and imposed difference that impacted opportunities for upward mobility, optimal health, and other aspects of life's greater abundance. He was a man born in a time where the memory of racially codified enslavement was still fresh in the minds and on the lips of countless men and women. These were people capable of providing testimonial accounts of life on plantations, being considered property, who were forced to labor against their will under inhumane conditions. The notion of the color line within this context assumes additional layers of significance and urgency. Du Bois witnessed the deleterious effects of Jim Crow, the convict leasing system, and voter disenfranchisement (among other racialized barriers to black progress). He was a man who understood the dangers and detriment of a nation of citizens who would revel in making the murder of African Americans through lynching a treasured pastime.

Through Du Bois's *Crisis* magazine, the NAACP's chief organ, he worked to utilize journalism as a medium of resistance against the epidemic of extrajudicial murder that plagued black communities for decades. The campaign against lynching required organized propaganda. Russ Castronovo claims that "activists at the *Crisis* were not willing to wait for a solution that would bubble forth from aesthetic instincts. . . . Du Bois had long operated on 'a world scale,' and his attraction to propaganda rescued him from the instinctual beauty of nationalism backed by Langfield and other defenders of Western civilization."[13] At times, the color line appeared in the form of a rope with a noose on the end; at other times, it was made manifest in the form of signage denoting sundown towns, or as redlines on a map that adversely impacted the property value of African American–owned real estate. Various *color lines* could all be distilled to the dichotomous analytical framing of white and black. Du Bois witnessed the lasting elements and evolutionary aspects of the color line over time.

The length of his life provides added value to compendiums and readers, which highlight the evolving thoughts and strategies Du Bois employed throughout his ninety-five years of life.[14] It is important to note that deception preceded demarcation concerning the color line. There is a substantial amount of revisionist history, pseudoscientific propaganda, and willful ignorance that has contributed significantly to our collective conceptualizations of race. The origins of racial concepts, their value, and propensity are all informed by largely illusory yet consequential paradigms. We label the deceptive aspects of racial discrimination as *the color lie* that undergirds the popular notions of the color line. Like some twisted tornado, this deception wreaked havoc from mental region to cultural region and from continent to continent. We see its destructive impact, whether it is through historic segregation in the United States or apartheid that existed in South Africa.

How then can we who are widely less scholarly and less published than one who is one of the most productive and efficient intellectual luminaries in the history of our nation be successful concerning work he was not able to complete? *The color lie* is a global deception that has served to destroy economies, families, and communities through acts of racialized terror, genocide, miseducation, and exclusion.[15]

Out of this perceptually indeterminate phenotypical matrix backed by tangible impacts on resources, access, and opportunity, Aaron Smith theorized the self-deceiving racial concept of Euroblivousness. He describes it as a toxic mix of nationalistic racialized illusions that give birth to a denial of scientific, genetic, historical, and contemporary racial realities. These Euroblivious mythologies are perpetuated for the purpose of upholding false notions of whites being autochthonous on the continent and in the world and maintaining a sordid notion of preeminence among the peoples of the world. Despite the falsehoods and imagined elements of this obstructive zeitgeist, the ramifications of its perpetually problematic nature are often tangible and measurable. "The impact of perceived discrimination on the risk of hypertension in African Americans depends on their social class and coping style. Ignoring discrimination raises the risk of hypertension in high-income African Americans but lowers the risk in those with low incomes. Mortality rates in US states have been shown to be associated with the degree to which Whites disrespect Blacks."[16]

The color line has residual effects that could become a matter of life and death. Hatred and xenophobia and intolerance have overt and covert methods of decaying the moral fiber of a society and eating away at people on social, spiritual, and physical levels. Understanding the subtleties relating to the negative ramifications of the color line enabled Du Bois to compose analyses and suggestions that have endured beyond his life. Du Bois proposed timely solutions for a period that called for greater racial clarity, mixing bold candor with a sincere belief in potential progress along racial lines. There is no wonder that Du Bois, among others, could say that "Ideas of race and behavior were problematic in the late nineteenth century." Notions of "culture" and, especially, of anything like cultural relativism were rudimentary and not widespread at the time. "Race" itself carried biological connotations — connotations not entirely absent from Du Bois's discussion — that were troublesome, since biological notions of race served mainly to ground those beliefs concerning black inferiority which were accepted by whites. Thus, for good reason, black writers and intellectuals felt real ambivalence about the kinds of ideas about racial distinctiveness Du Bois was trying to portray."[17]

A reflection such as this demonstrates how certain ideas of Du Bois may have missed the mark or failed to resonate with the very people most in need of implementing his theories. It could be argued that Du Bois reached an influential ceiling in the United States at a point late in his life. Due to his age, the emergence of new political and intellectual voices, and cultural shifts that were making way for the unique cultural climate of the 1960s, Du Bois began to mean something different to most people in America.

He was a revered elder statesman certainly, but a driver of intellectual culture among the nation's most influential demographic, certainly not. At this stage in his career Du Bois was forced to incorporate ageism along with the previous list of challenges that included racism, elitism, and those who opposed him due to their hatred of communism. For these and other reasons, the final chapter of Du Bois's life being overseas was a fitting epilogue to the story of his life. What better place than Africa for Du Bois to finalize his journey and eternally rest (Accra, Ghana, August 29, 1963).

The trajectory of Du Bois's understandings, descriptions of, and engagements with Africa provide an interesting arc of his evolution from the class analysis that produced his Talented Tenth to his more geographically and intellectually Pan Africanist identity. We know from other scholars that "Du Bois's engagement with Africa was not merely connected to well-known political projects — the desire for decolonization and the emergence of a Pan-African consciousness — but was ultimately part of his search for a new way of thinking about the modern identity of the black subject through what has come to be known as the aesthetic ideology."[18]

Taking his mind (and later his body) beyond national borders served to internationalize Du Bois in a manner that exponentially expanded his outlook and influence. Du Bois utilized his international awareness concerning the vast connections between racial discrimination and power delegation. This color line, Du Bois would come to realize, belted the globe, being manifested in several ways on every continent. From Europe to America, Du Bois detailed a complicity concerning black subjugation that continues to reverberate through the ages. The foundations of these economic, spiritual, geographic, political, military, and ecological ramifications are securely fastened within a brutal historiography of bondage, brutality, thievery, and bloodshed. In lieu of the dark and daunting aspects of our collective racial historiography, Du Bois focused primarily on deconstructing and alleviating the impacts of racialized institutions and prejudices.

Du Bois was dexterous in his ability to convey the international elements of racial oppression, which could strike locally in such a profound manner that its targets fail to see the larger superstructure of oppression beyond their personal pain. Du Bois revealed how the access of the geopolitical ecosystem was firmly balanced on a foundation of racialized division and destruction. He notes key points in history where the color line was lengthened and etched deeper into the collective subconscious of the world. One key historical set of events took place in the Congo as imperial European forces brought genocidal disregard for human life in the interest of securing raw materials for the sake of profit, as Du Bois explains:

> The sinister traffic, on which the British Empire and the American Republic were largely built, cost black Africa no less than 100 million souls, the wreckage of its political and social life, and left the continent in precisely that state of helplessness which invites aggression and exploitation. "Color" became, in the world's thought, synonymous with inferiority, "Negro" lost its capitalization, and Africa was another name for bestiality and barbarism. Thus, the world began to invest in color prejudice. The "color line" began to pay dividends. For indeed, while the exploration of the valley of the Congo was the occasion of the scramble for Africa, the cause lay deeper.[19]

Some authors who have researched Du Bois and his theory about the future significance of the color line have questioned (in the short term) whether the famed scholar may have overemphasized the importance of the concept. Significant world events that happened soon after have influenced these critical opinions and assessments. So, although Du Bois may have accurately assessed the importance of the color line and prioritized it appropriately for the moment, no one could foresee many of the national and international crises that were to come in the ensuing months and years. One of the most prominent examples of this form of perceptual change in basic assumptions occurred because Du Bois lived and operated in times of crisis.

There is no question that the color line was one of the problems of the twentieth century, but calling it the central problem of the century happened before the Nazi Holocaust that was to occur years later. In fact, it is reported that Du Bois changed some wording and delivered the corrected page proofs of the manuscript of *Black Folk Then and Now* to his publisher on May 2, 1939, and had copies in his possession by May 29, and within four months Hitler had invaded Poland, and before that time, Jewish victims of Kristallnacht had already been shipped to the concentration camp at Dachau. The ensuing five years led Du Bois to reevaluate many of his perspectives on world history.[20] Du Bois adequately adapted to the changing international and national cultural climate, one of his greatest assets.

In Du Bois's personal pursuit of solutions and solace, he used travel, including relocation, to expand his consciousness and ideas about what is possible. At the age of ninety-three, Du Bois was still evolving and in motion figuratively. Elderly yet continually learning, Du Bois landed in Ghana upon an invitation from President Kwame Nkrumah to be lead editor for a project that would become the Encyclopedia Africana. The project was certainly in Du Bois's wheelhouse as he had done prior encyclopedia work and was fully capable of addressing issues ranging from racism to African philosophy.[21] This project mirrored his efforts to confront and combat the color line as both occupied a massive portion of his life and left much work to be done upon his passing.

Clarence Contee wrote about the meaning of Du Bois's passing in these words: "When Dr. W. E. B. Du Bois died in Accra, Ghana, on August 27, 1 was at work on one of the primary missions of his life, the Encyclopedia Africana. Scholar, polemicist, philosopher-prophet, and one of the founders of the National Association for the Advancement of Colored People, Du Bois had spent more than half a century at this unfulfilled dream."[22] One of the possibilities many famous African Americans have discovered overseas involves reinterpretations of race, racism, and themselves beyond the confines of the former. There is a consistent tradition of blacks pursuing an opportunity to express their full humanity and have it appreciated beyond our national borders. Several sought an escape from the harshest manifestations of the *color lie* by extending the color line through seeking a different type of colored life. Just as the great author James Baldwin sojourned to Paris and Istanbul or the incomparable Josephine Baker, Nina Simone, and Tina Turner relocated to Paris, to France and the Netherlands, and to Switzerland, respectively, Du Bois similarly left his home in search of a greater sense of all that home is expected to provide (e.g., safety, encouragement, recognition, appreciation). "In America, there's always this fear of unpacking race, unpacking sexism, unpacking classism."[23]

As a result of the limitations on the domestic expansions of African consciousness generally and Pan African consciousness specifically, many scholars since Du Bois have studied and relocated abroad. The differences in economy, human relationships, governmental systems, and religious practices all inform curious travelers. However, there is much to learn through analyzing consistent themes that persist despite geographic, linguistic, and demographic differences existing in nations visited versus America. Du Bois's understandings about what makes America's color line, racial history, and expressions of racial oppression unique were complemented significantly through the opportunity to step outside of these systems and to analyze them as a conscientious observer (and sometimes objector).

One example of the value of this comparative analysis came in gaining a sounder understanding of the intersections between race and class. In taking a global approach to this problem, Du Bois adds a layer of depth and lasting accuracy that make many of his observations and color line theory continuously relevant, flexible, and evolving. Looking at South Africa with an awareness of Nazi as well as southern American racial intolerance is just one example of what makes Du Bois's outlook special. He writes, "In both the United States and the Union of South Africa it has been the organized white laborers who have systematically by vote and mob opposed the training of the black worker and the provision of decent wages for him. In this respect they have ranged themselves with exploiting investors and disseminators of race hatred like Hitler.... Only the Communists and some of the C.I.O. unions have ignored the color line as a significant fact."²⁴

There is immense value in developing an international historical perspective in our quest to read the subtleties of Du Bois's work in the racial climate of his time. There may have been those who saw the atrocities against the Jewish people, the Roma, Afro-Germans, and LBGTQ communities as the demonic actions of the Third Reich, but Du Bois understood the complexities of color consciousness and was a capable communicator in terms of expressing these realities so that the masses could understand. Through effective contextualization and applicable clear analogies, Du Bois drew a direct connection between the racial politics of Germany and Germantown, Pennsylvania:

> In the case of Jews one meets something different, which an American Negro does not readily understand. Prejudice against Jews in Germany comes nearer being instinctive than color prejudice. For many centuries Germans have disliked Jews but the reasons have varied and are not at all analogous to white dislike of blacks in America. There has been no tragedy in modern times equal in its awful effects to the fight on the Jew in Germany. It is an attack on civilization, comparable only to such horrors as the Spanish Inquisition and the African slave trade; it has set civilization back 100 years and has made the settlement and understanding of race problems more difficult and more doubtful.²⁵

In a similar evolutionary conceptual expansion as Malcolm X making a shift from civil rights to human rights, Du Bois would gradually extend his localized sociological analysis of Philadelphia into a geopolitical, ethnographic critique of military engagements, cultural underpinnings, and the power of propaganda. Thoughts about racial division were an early focus of Du Bois by virtue of his keenly inquisitive intellect and the nature of his adolescent experiences.

He recognized and articulated the sentiments that President Lyndon Baines Johnson would concede decades later:

> But rarely in any time does an issue lay bare the secret heart of America itself. Rarely are we met with a challenge, not to our growth or abundance, or our welfare or our security, but rather to the values and the purposes and the meaning of our beloved nation. The issue of equal rights for American Negroes is such an issue.... There is no Negro problem. There is no Southern problem. There is no Northern problem. There is only an American problem.²⁶

As the president identified in his conversation around voting rights, the color line is a true divider of peoples, cultures, and resources.

This lasting concept has been established and deeply etched in the proverbial sands of time and represents an act of social scarification that has left an indelible mark of exploitation, inferiority, divisive polarization, self-hatred, and destruction in its wake. This whirlwind of division has swept through the impoverished and the Harvard graduate turned successful professional alike. The effects were powerfully popularized by the Kerner Report, which resulted from the National Advisory Commission on Civil Disorders, an initiative created by President Johnson in 1967 to help quell civil unrest stemming from racial discrimination. The report clearly revealed to some and affirmed for others that "our nation is moving towards two societies: one white, one black — separate and unequal."[27] Today, we are left to endure the aftermath of many discriminatory storms. We are currently in a situation where we are responsible for cleaning up the proverbial debris of past transgressions.

Prior to rebuilding back better, our ability to access previous plans that assist in our understandings of current challenges can prove to be of critical importance. Today there exists a plethora of ongoing debates around critical race theory and inclusive curricula. As many strive to involve and give added power and value to black voices and perspectives, others are taking a more adversarial and reprobate approach to the seemingly inevitable shifts within previously whitewashed academic spaces. As an intellectual and educator, Du Bois was keenly aware of the transformative potential that proper education could have upon a generation whose starting line in the race of life was also the color line.

Linda Darling-Hammond argues that "the problem of the color line follows us into the twenty-first [century], especially regarding education. The color line divides us still. In recent years, one visible evidence of this in the public policy arena has been the persistent attack on affirmative action in higher education and employment. A mere fifty years after *Brown* v. *Board of Education* many Americans who believe the vestiges of discrimination have disappeared take the position that affirmative action now provides an unfair advantage to minorities."[28] Attacks on the potential for uplift and black progress have long included rampant hyperbolic and xenophobic mongering designed to stimulate deep-seated white fears of the declining functionality of white racial supremacy as a doctrine of this era. These narratives do not require factual evidence or ethical positions, but rather trigger exaggerated rhetoric that serves to mobilize insecure and power-hungry whites along with collaborative elements of black society against the notion of equality and equity.

These combined factors required Du Bois to be courageous and well-studied to undertake the arduous task before him. Simply explaining the color line within a historical context contrasted with its modern manifestations during the time Du Bois wrote was a struggle within itself prior to beginning to deconstruct and potentially nullify the effects of the color line. Like an African intellectual version of the classical Atlas, one man stood with the weight of the willfully deceived world upon his shoulders and through the sincere ignorance and disingenuous claims feigning the same, he worked to utilize his intellectual gifts to leave a presence of peace behind for the world that followed. The depth of Du Bois's analysis revealed layers or additional lines within the readily observable color line. As Du Bois asserts, "Suddenly now there loomed plain and clear the shadow of a color line within a color line a prejudice within a prejudice."[29]

Du Bois was forced to attempt to reconcile the sordid obsessions of a race of men who would consistently imitate the very people they worked so feverishly to subjugate and exterminate. As a result of his studies, he accurately assessed the lasting power of our racial problem. According to Lewis Gordon, "Deny it as we may, therefore or cause of a multitude of evils, the problem of the color line is a persisting problem, a problem that, in the eyes of some, is here to stay.... Born from the divide of black and white, it serves as a blueprint of the ongoing division of humankind."[30] Upon his trestle board of intellectual contemplation, Du Bois strived to map out a strategy to address the perceptually stagnated aspects of our understanding regarding racism and the color line. Du Bois's knowledge of history led him to view education as the primary means of avoiding oppression. Herman Beavers says, "As Du Bois insists, lack of education creates a community ripe for exploitation and prone to squander its political resources, which are birthrights in a mighty nation in exchange for spoils that have little value in the public sphere."[31]

Scholars today continue to struggle with the societal knotting that Du Bois was tasked to disencumber us from. As a self-appointed advocate and voice for the race, Du Bois took seriously his role as advocate, educator, and embodiment of intellectualism and African American poise under pressure. Some would assess our current condition and assume a critical position toward the work that Du Bois and others attempted to conduct throughout their lives in efforts to improve racial conditions for future generations. The opinion is typically accompanied by a perception that little has changed for African Americans over the past century. Despite the popularity of such positions, it is a perspective that runs contrary to much empirical evidence in many regards including voting, opportunities for upward mobility, and the adjustments and evolution of policies designed to increase equity in society along racial lines.

Others supportively suggest that although Du Bois was not fully successful, he left behind tracings of a path that could potentially be used as a productive template to emulate his diligence and productivity in service to humanity by carefully raising the veil of color in America. Despite the abundance of positive aspects of Du Bois's scholarship, there are also opportunities for readers to critique some of his proposals for racial uplift. One cause for consternation is the use of the term *color line*. These comments may have more to do with the ways the term is interpreted and applied than with the actual concept and its initial intent. The terminology can give the impression that separation is somehow an inevitable distinction based upon the reality of racial difference. These separations and acts of exploitation and dehumanization are occurring by design. Demarcation is a product of massive intentionality, consistently applied and strategically manipulated to achieve maximum levels of racial stratification.

A prime example of destructive racialized demarcation can be observed on the island of Hispaniola:

> Today many Haitians have been socialized in a political climate that has at least rhetorically celebrated the African cultural elements of Haitian society. On the other side of the island, the national discourse has been very much the opposite, where national identity has been consolidated through an embracement of the Hispanic roots of the country and a marked rejection of everything African, as well as Blackness more generally. Thus, Haitians who migrate to the Dominican Republic find that, in addition to crossing a territorial line, they are also crossing a color line.[32]

When many people envision a dividing line, they conceive of it being down the middle, creating equal parts on either side of the line.

The color line divides black poverty and white privilege, black economic exploitation, and white unearned wealth. There is no equality to speak of in this arrangement. The color line could be understood as a solid floor through which whiteness will never fall and an opaque limiting ceiling blocking light and opportunity for black people. To operationalize Du Bois's theories, analysis, and temperament can assist future generations to mimic the standards that the father of American sociology modeled for our benefit in eradicating the negative impacts of the color line. Reading the sociological and academic bones of Du Bois's work can also help to deconstruct the power dynamics that deceive and constrict through the modern manifestation of the color line. One of the most valuable takeaways from the work of Du Bois involves his optimism relating to our ability to transcend the negative structures that have plagued our communities for years. "Yes, Du Bois was a universalist, and he did imagine individuals transcending the color line, with its out-of-group tensions and in-group obligations."[33]

The solution-based optimism of Du Bois is consistently tempered with unabashed candor and at times scathing critiques of the racial status quo. The belief in possibilities for positive change through reality-based educated analysis rather than delusional denial of racial realities represents an optimistic worldview and approach to phenomena. For Du Bois, "the program of systematic popular education was one of two prongs of his strategy for eliminating racial antagonism."[34] He believed in the power of information to uplift and improve people and societies. Thus, reading Du Bois from this angle means that the reader must meet the challenges of a racially infused society with the kind of determination a person seeks out troublesome weeds that must be uprooted, rather than simply pruned for the sake of temporary convenience and aesthetic value. To reiterate, we must not prune racial problems that need to be completely uprooted. Du Bois was seeking to uproot racism; he certainly was no problem pruner.

This level of deflection, self-deception, or putting off necessary engagements with issues around race and racism (pruning) recalls the game children played at camps like Frost Valley at recess called hot potato. Each generation conveniently inconveniences the next generation by handing them a laundry list of issues that their cohort was unable or unwilling to adequately face on their own. Favorites include health care, our national debt, and inflation, and near the top (if not at the top) of many lists consistently is the issue of the color line.

In the first quarter of the twenty-first century, we see the color line in our debates about police brutality after the murder of George Floyd, which prompted national and international protests coordinated on unprecedented scales. These uprisings fit interestingly into

> the annals of twentieth-century Black uprising against police violence that scholars use to classify protest events such as the inciting incident, e.g., police violence against a Black civilian, acquittal of perpetrating officers, target of protest and purpose of protest (e.g., achieve justice/accountability, address systemic racism and police violence, promote reform). Additionally, from the vantage point of the concept of "most likely" cases . . . several of the attributes of the Floyd protests that make it unique (e.g., scale and media coverage) also arguably render it more likely than other episodes of protest to exert the broad effects on public opinion suggested by theories of activated public opinion and focusing events.[35]

Activist groups like Black Lives Matter and the Proud Boys can be viewed as existing on opposing sides of the metaphoric moat of racial strife, racial denial, and potential racial progress.

In this contemporary scenario the color line is emblematic of the rope that is constantly being pulled back and forth while expecting a different result than the last series of pulling created. Hopefully through engaging with sound reality-based and optimistic conceptualizations like those promoted by Du Bois we can avoid wasted exertion of energy on repetitive cycles of polarization and blame. If we can avoid the collective dangers that the depths of the metaphoric moat concealed, while preventing our modern color line from becoming a noose to us all, perhaps then we can recognize the potential connectivity of the color line rather than the opportunity for perpetual competition. For you, the reader, the message of Du Bois and the color line is clear: there is still work to be done and our reading of Du Bois must be assertively Afrocentric in analysis and critique. There can be no children's games in our endeavor to fulfill the destruction of the color line; it is work that must be done.

Chapter 7
The Evolution of Du Bois into a Pan African Race Organizer

Du Bois is the definitive model of Pan Africanism in African American history. No other intellectual or activist can be said to share the same dominant position as Du Bois.

This chapter is an exercise in reading Du Bois's Pan African organizing through the lens of race. When one reads Du Bois on Pan Africanism it is necessary to see that he brought a freshness, a clarity, and an energy to a discourse that permeated much of the political conversation of people of African descent. Therefore, we explore how Du Bois's Pan African creativity, persistence, and organization in pursuit of a consequential ethnographic and political adventure made sense to his contemporaries.[1]

What are the most enduring contributions of Du Bois to Pan Africanism? This critical analysis will navigate the literary labyrinth of Du Bois's writings while centering on what could perhaps be considered the crown jewel of Du Bois's Pan African consciousness, the convening of his own Pan African Congress in London in 1919. Already by the first part of the twentieth century W. E. B. Du Bois, who had attended H. Sylvester Williams's Pan African Conference in 1900, was consistently heralded as one of the most productive and consequential African American intellectuals. His convening of the postwar congress in London was a bold assertion of his leadership role in the African world.

Afrocentric Methodology

Molefi Kete Asante argues that Afrocentricity places African people at the center of their own experiences and understanding as opposed to relegating them to the margins of Eurocentric ideologies.[2] Afrocentricity views/analyzes/defines and critiques phenomena centering blacks as subjects, rather than marginalized objects on the conceptual periphery of European analysis. Asante advances this revolutionary intellectual and cultural concept to encourage the agency and full humanity of African people as actors in all historical contexts. This means that any study of Africans must seek to locate the people squarely in the center of their own experiences and perspectives. In pursuit of the Pan African experiences and influences that helped prompt Du Bois to organize the First Pan African Congress, it is of critical importance to recognize and clearly articulate the distinguishable characteristics of the methodological lens necessary for our analysis.

Asante's book *Race, Rhetoric and Identity: The Architechton of Soul* is one of the seminal works in reevaluating various phenomena (including, but not limited to, the political organization of culture, politics, education, and identity) within the milieu of African life and history.[3] In fifteen chapters he provides an in-depth treatment of the greater universe of communication, media, and rhetoric advantageous to agency in the Afrocentric perspective.

In this work, the author navigates through the constant discourse of race and identity while displaying how the two realities are inextricably interwoven with racial oppression. The societal, spiritual, structural, and symbolic suppression of African self-determination that Du Bois courageously sought to disrupt with the organizing of the Pan African Congresses is manifested through the many subjects that fuel the varied chapters of Asante's text. The implications of racial oppression are deciphered in each chapter as the author demonstrates that various individuals in society are conflicted by the social context although they are often well-meaning individuals.

Du Bois had formulated the idea of double consciousness long before he organized the First Pan African Congress. Du Bois, speaking of African Americans, posed a dilemma. He saw the African American person on the cross between death and life, hanging by a thread between Americanness and blackness, without ever being able to reconcile them. To us, it was Du Bois's wish to be accepted as an American that created his conflicted state. For him, to be American was the same as being accepted as white, that is, not in color but in privileges. To be black in a racist society was truly to be given death, as the lynching of blacks in the South proved that Africans were not really a part of the America created for whites.

We assert, as Asante had claimed in his work, that double consciousness was not a psychic problem but a political one.[4] We are plagued not by a double consciousness but by a tug between supporting the government as our best hope for ending discrimination and loving the country for which many have died, as opposed to social nihilism, alienation, and anarchy.

Afrocentricity allows for an authoritative agency that asserts an African viewpoint to combat many of the misconceptions and negative effects of rhetorical marginalization. From this vantage point African people can properly locate themselves. One of the most powerful components of Asante's text is his constant acknowledgment of the reciprocal nature of rhetoric as it relates to race, identity, and the interplay between culture and politics.[5] African people are not simply dormant receptacles of propaganda and other rhetorical messaging emanating from different segments of society.[6] There is a steady conversation taking place (whether it is consciously acknowledged or not) between the media, schools, political institutions, corporations, and the people they service or subject. The interplay between institutions and individuals is bridged by the roads of rhetoric on which these messages respond and travel.

The First Pan African Congress

A series of congregations and assemblies, generating conversations around issues of liberation from a Pan African perspective, helped to define the first half of the twentieth century. The Pan African Congress in 1919 organized by W. E. B. Du Bois begins a period of Pan African intellectual collaboration that has no equal, and is distinguishable from related prior conventions, and from most that followed, by the strong attempt to connect all African peoples. In a personal correspondence to the congress, Du Bois's desire to distinguish the congress from other movements is plainly apparent. Du Bois was engaged in actively asserting the goals and purposes of the congress, while decidedly disassociating the movement from the political engagement of his rival Marcus Garvey or his followers and supporters within (or sympathetic to) the efforts of the United Negro Improvement Association and African Communities League (UNIA-ACL).[7]

Local disagreements from within the African community were only a small segment of the forms of opposition Du Bois would face when attempting to organize the congress. As the vision for liberation became more expansive and sophisticated so did the enemies of Du Bois's progress. Numerous tactics were employed by those who sought to minimize, stagnate, and in all ways stifle the momentum and desired outcome of the First Pan African Congress. Du Bois would later document various subversive tactics employed by those in opposition to black cooperation and liberation.

The Pan African Congress would eventually include fifty-seven delegates, including sixteen African Americans, twenty West Indians, and twelve continental Africans, suggesting, from the very beginning, a Pan African character to the First Pan African Congress. France, Belgium, and Portugal were represented by officials.[8] Du Bois was tasked with syndicating the messaging while maintaining the momentum of the movement around Pan Africanism and the critical need for an increase in international networking and political strategizing. One of the ways in which Du Bois was extremely effective was through his consistency and awareness about many of the critical perspectives and inaccurate anecdotes of information that he would regularly motion to correct, rebuff, or convey clarity concerning the congress, mostly by writing articles in *The Crisis* and other publications.

When discussing the 1919 conference in retrospect, Du Bois found it relevant to contribute to the efforts to dispel myths and misunderstandings about the movement: "I am writing to appraise [apprise] you of these facts because of some public misapprehension of our aims and purposes. The Pan-African Congress is for conference, acquaintanceship, and general organization. It has nothing to do with the so-called Garvey movement and contemplates neither force nor revolution in its program. We have had the cordial cooperation of the French, Belgium and Portuguese governments and we hope to get the attention and sympathy of all colonial powers."[9] Du Bois articulated the intention of the congress, which emanated from an increased understanding of the intersectionality between race and class in relation to his conceptualization of Pan Africanism. Du Bois posits his evolving personal political perspectives within the larger analytical context and scope of international Pan African politics, understanding the relationship between local, national, and broader challenges.

The discussions, plans, strategizing sessions, and presentations of the congress dealt primarily with ways to deconstruct and destabilize the international manifestation of imperial Western colonial domination over many African peoples scattered throughout the Diaspora without agitating for revolution or physical violence. Later, throughout the seven sessions of the congress the body evolved to include the role of mediator between colonial factions and the indigenous populations they exploited in the West Indies and Africa.[10]

The context for the Pan African Congress was fraught with political ripeness. After the First World War in 1918, the Allied forces claimed/reclaimed victory and gained control of the lands that were previously under the control of enemy powers as articulated through the Paris Peace Conference. This conference to many at the time represented a culmination of Du Bois's understanding and ability to overcome the strategies and tactics implemented to manipulate his brilliance and minimize his progressive impact in the Pan African world. This congress stands as a shining symbol of the ability to grow, redeem, and resurrect through the appreciation of pragmatic political realities in conjunction with the aspirations and direction of our revolutionary African ancestors.

Thus, Du Bois's desire and intention to work toward further internationalizing the potential solution(s) to the problem of the color line had taken on a global African outlook. This international identification exponentially increased the collective network of individuals and nations who were now in closer alignment with their respective brothers and sisters on various continents simply through choosing to locate themselves within a more expansive and potentially farther-reaching political classification. The organizational direction that resulted from the First Pan African Congress can be evidenced by a perusal of the list of needs that developed by the time subsequent meetings were organized.

Classified as *immediate needs*, this organizational international agenda expresses a hunger for greater degrees of Pan African agency, greater access to education and natural resources, and a call to demilitarize the colonies while creating more equitable distributions of wealth.[11] Although there was a Second Pan African Congress in 1921, it was at the Third Pan African Congress in 1925 where the immediate needs of Africa became important and urgent.

Third Pan African Congress

The Third Pan African Congress demonstrates the momentum that was unleashed by Africans from the Americas, the Caribbean, and the Continent meeting to chart the future of the Black World. Among the conclusions and demands adopted by the delegates were the following:

> A voice in their own government.
> The right of access to land and its resources.
> Trial by juries of their peers under established forms of law.
> Free elementary education for all; broad training in modern industrial technique; and higher training of selected talent.
> The development of Africa for the benefit of Africans, and not merely for the profit of Europeans.
> The abolition of the slave trade and of the liquor traffic.
> World disarmament and the abolition of war; but failing this, and if White folk bear arms against Black folk, the right of Blacks to bear arms in their own defense.
> The organization of commerce and industry to make the main object of capital and labor the welfare of the many, rather than the enriching of the few.[12]

The power and agency necessary for producing a clear-cut empowering agenda were considerable. Du Bois asserted an African will, consonant with the intersection between aggressive rhetoric and stoic resistance, as he launched his Pan African movement. Here we find gathered some of the most capable minds concerning enacting change among black people, of a similar accord. From the title of the event to the location of the conference, to its guest list and stated agenda there are consistent elements and overtones of African unity and liberation that powerfully counter the colonial agenda. The anticolonialist rhetoric of the First Pan African Congress holds contemporary relevance on two fronts. First, it suggests an overt resistance to a history of exploitation and, second, allows for a more nuanced cultural critique of the ways major European and American events such as world's fairs with exhibitions of exotic peoples preserve the tradition of subjugating the global majority.

Du Bois on Pan Africanism

"Pan Africanism has been bandied about in recent years with disturbing inaccuracy. . . . the time has surely arrived when historians should come to the aid of synoptic students of Africa, the 'Pan-Africanism' of whose academic approach has become so individual that it distorts out of all recognition the Pan-African movement and the Pan-African movements."[13] Du Bois expressed an expansive vision of the Pan African movement that would benefit exponentially from recognizing how those who seek to exploit the labor of the masses of people (white and black) are manipulated:

> The Pan African movement when it comes will not, however, be merely a narrow racial propaganda. Already the more far-seeing Negroes sense the coming unities: a unity of the working classes everywhere, a unity of the colored races, a new unity of thinking men. The economic solution of the Negro problem in Africa and America has turned the thoughts of Negroes towards a realization of the fact that the modern White laborer of Europe and America has the key to serfdom of Black folk in his support of militarism and colonial expansion.[14]

To analyze an unparalleled African American intellectual such as Du Bois through the honest Afrocentric lens of his early flashes of dislocation proves to be an extremely beneficial exercise in relation to the powerful Pan African scholar he became over the years. There were multiple opportunities throughout his life for Du Bois to occupy the position of educator/promoter as related to the Pan African movement. "A Black Newspaper conducted an open discussion of the usefulness of the Pan African Movement, and Du Bois was moved to reply in two letters."[15] On one occasion Du Bois is cited in a response to an inquiry by Bishop C. S. Smith concerning Pan Africanism. "Dr. Du Bois replies to Bishop C.S. Smith [of Detroit] *New York Age* June 25, 1921. This letter is of particular interest, for in it Du Bois is at pains to distinguish the Pan-African Movement."[16] The fact that Du Bois's journey to his eventual international, Pan African perspective was decidedly gradual in nature and well documented in fact creates the opportunity for an amazingly rich case study on the effects of Pan Africanism in the life of Du Bois and through Du Bois to black people. In this way, the life of Du Bois is what can be critically described as a later blooming Pan Africanist proves uniquely informative. Like the need for a control and a variable in the world of experimental scientific study, an ethnographic, candid critical analysis can yield interesting contrasts between Du Bois at earlier stages in his political and cultural development (e.g., anti-Garvey rhetoric) to what became more prominently Pan African expressions.

Scholars studying Du Bois are lucky to draw from almost a century of context and contributions. Successfully identifying and replicating the Pan African strategies, effectiveness, examples, and literature that helped to transform Du Bois could potentially transform the world. The evolution of Du Bois's Pan African consciousness speaks to the potential to awaken otherwise dormant degrees of similar capabilities within the masses of African people. Exposure to an Afrocentric political perspective, combined with related travel and lived experiences, can prove positively transformative in the quest for a conscious Pan African critical mass capable of international revolutionary change.[17] A study of Du Bois provides an opportunity to conduct a rich case study because of his popularized early attention to class and the role of what he considered to be the Talented Tenth.

Late in his life, the writings of Du Bois reflect an integrated evolution of various political approaches and worldviews once held prominently, and now a fusion of prior and contemporary thoughts and organizational perspectives enhance the later developed Pan African stance. This acknowledgment of the necessity for a multifaceted approach to the problems of racism, imperialism, capitalism, and militarism displayed the sophisticated, layered Pan Africanist approach Du Bois expressed in relation to the congress.

In the Pan African implementation of Du Bois's rhetoric, cultural expressions, and political strategy, he found a clear voice that decidedly marked his furthest departure from any vestiges of elements of his previous theory of double consciousness. Despite the significant growth and rhetorical and geopolitical phases of refinement, one constant underlining assertion remained with Du Bois: the lasting relevance of the color line.

Confronting Race and Pan Africanism

The denial of present impacts of past racial injustices, coupled with the exaggerated belief in progress that the nation has made concerning its racist core, is taxing to conscious minds and righteous spirits.[18] The psychological suppression of the realities of racism has grown to define much of the international colonial worldview. The color line has stretched into a new century with equally problematic racial ramifications that require reflective and contemplative thinking and tactical engagements. Such actions and analyses and potential solutions must be rooted in the harsh yet optimistic balance of historical context while being fueled by the fearlessness and posture of expectancy that has often defined the Afrocentric and Pan Africanist expressions that Molefi Kete Asante describes as a victorious consciousness.

Throughout history there exists significant documentation concerning the effectiveness of dividing opposition in efforts to weaken and leave them as prime targets for economic, political, intellectual, and cultural manipulation and exploitation. The rule of divide and conquer throughout the African Diaspora has been a tactic employed to create confusion, dissension, and sometimes violent conflict.[19] The potentially tragic and fatal costs of these manipulations can be examined in the lives and interactions between Martin Luther King Jr. and Malcolm X.

The First Pan African Congress in 1919 would face opposition from outside forces attempting to dictate the nature and components of the proceedings. Held in Paris during the time of the Versailles Conference of victorious states over Germany and its allies, the Pan African Congress was Du Bois's first attempt to mobilize the African intellectuals to demand what was needed for Africa and Africans. Blaise Diagne, the Senegalese thinker who served in the French government, was able to assist Du Bois in gaining space to hold the congress. Two years later they would convene the 1921 Pan African Congress in August in London. A month later they met in Brussels to complete the congress.

Belgian pressures were so strong and their exploitation of the differences among the participants so astute that they not only virtually dictated the resolutions of the session but they also dampened the radical trend adopted by the congress in London. As J. Ayodele Langley argues, "W.E.B. Du Bois's Pan-African crusade 'never recovered its élan after Brussels'."[20] There exist numerous examples of manipulative division in areas of Diasporic existence that extend far beyond the traditionally political medium including the media (reporter April Ryan and former White House aide Omarosa Manigault Newman; rappers Tupac Shakur and Biggie Smalls) or the world of cultural critical leadership.[21]

One of the more salient critical perceptions of Du Bois exists in the idea that he became the personification of anti–Pan African intellectual realities at certain periods of his personal, political, and academic life. This critique of Du Bois is fueled greatly through an analysis of his criticism and opposition to Marcus Garvey and what came to be known as the Garvey-led Back to Africa movement. During this postwar decade, two prominent leaders, W. E. B. Du Bois and Marcus Garvey, clashed in their separate plans to establish an African state and an international organization of Negroes. Both men were propagandists. Du Bois was editor of *The Crisis*, the official magazine of the NAACP, and Garvey owned the *Negro World*.[22]

The rifts between Du Bois and Garvey can be truly instructive in displaying ways to potentially resist the manipulative designs of outside forces. An apparent key to avoiding or minimizing the effectiveness of the divide and conquer strategy from a Pan African perspective as evidenced through the continued revelatory evolution of Du Bois's cultural consciousness involves an internal declaration to refuse to be used.

Du Bois evolved into this cultural, personal stance, rising above being used at times as a political pawn (by early NAACP leader Joel Spingarn and others according to many of his critics) to a place where he was displaying flashes of potential to eventually become a Pan African organizing juggernaut. Beyond Garvey there were other public figures who were highly esteemed and possessed differing opinions and political strategies regarding what was the best path toward liberation for African people throughout the Diaspora. Another more popular public figure who was a major factor in the crafting of elements of Du Bois's early political strategy was Booker T. Washington.

As described in greater detail earlier in the book, Du Bois held a firm understanding and often critical opinion of Booker T. Washington's strategy and perspective on the most beneficial methods of progressing black people. The cultural contributions of Booker T. Washington provided Du Bois with inspiration and cautionary tales concerning the dangers of detrimental optics and aligning too intimately with positions and politics of respectability and perceived subservience.

Du Bois on the "Tuskegee Machine"

An assessment of Booker T. Washington leadership capabilities and institutional impacts was offered Du Bois's sociological innovative text, *Souls of Black Folk*

> In 1903,* Andrew Carnegie made the future of Tuskegee certain by a gift of $600,000. There was no question of Booker T. Washington's undisputed leadership of the ten million [blacks] in America, a leadership recognized gladly by the Whites and conceded by most African Americans. But there were discrepancies and paradoxes in this leadership. It did not seem fair, for instance, that on the one hand Mr. Washington should decry political activities among [blacks], and on the other hand dictate [black] political objectives from Tuskegee. At a time when [black] civil rights called for organized and aggressive defense, he broke down that defense by advising acquiescence or at least no open agitation.[23]

Ironically, despite Du Bois's assessment of Booker T. Washington acting as a primary manifestation of manipulated black leadership, Du Bois would not escape critiques from those who viewed him through a similarly disconnected, disingenuous lens. The sometimes sordid and antagonistic history between men like Du Bois and Garvey reinforces the importance of recognizing an extremely destructive yet effective tactic that has been implemented in the war to suppress and distract from the internationally transformative potential of Pan Africanism, which is to divide and conquer. Never be manipulated into becoming a tool of oppression against your own people. This mantra resonated powerfully with us throughout our studies of Du Bois and his journey to more significant Pan Africanist perspectives.

Du Bois in Ghana

Perhaps being the only African American in numerous settings throughout his adolescence fueled a greater desire for African intellectual camaraderie for Du Bois. The growing hunger for greater degrees of Afrocentric location initially appeared to lie dormant within the recesses of Du Bois's double consciousness, occasionally finding sparks at places like Fisk before fully blooming in Ghana.[24] Many leaders have traveled long distances to get closer to themselves. The tendency for prominent African Americans and others to choose to return to the Continent because of various political, cultural, and security concerns has a long-standing history. Like Du Bois in Ghana, activists like Stokely Carmichael, creative artists such as Josephine Baker and James Baldwin, and others would change their geographic location in attempts to modify their condition and relationship to the larger society.[25]

These seekers were determined while representing expressions of cultural creativity and agency and fomenting a theme of resistance to the binding, limiting bitterness of delusional American racial hypocrisy.* These activists, authors, and performers experienced a greater sense of freedom after taking the brave leap to a place other than the geographical ground zero of their immediate oppression or obstacle. They sought and often found refuge in places where they acquired and appreciated a greater degree of racial agency and political and creative autonomy.

It is important to note that in many instances, however, these attempts to outrun racism were later recognized as only temporary fixes to an international and systemic issue of racial oppression. This reality is emblematic of Du Bois and his relocation to Africa. The intellectual and cultural blossoming brought Du Bois into a different space ideologically as he relocated his personhood. The potential for becoming more culturally *located* through the act of relocation continues to generate significant interest among Pan Africanists who often view themselves as global citizens and feel at home in various parts of the Diasporic community. The appeal to gain perspective through creating distance may be of particular interest to African Americans who believe that the presidency of Donald Trump created (and continues to create) an increasingly hostile environment toward supporters of Pan Africanist perspectives.[26]

As the United States of America becomes increasingly and openly hostile toward Pan African, Afrocentric concepts of African self-determination and organization, certain questions must be asked. To what extent should physical, continental separation be considered and championed as an instrument of liberation?[27] Could a Pan African Congress or conference receive government support in the United States during the same time period? These questions show the critical importance of time and place regarding the effectiveness of organizations and events and strategy.

Pan Africanism and Applied Strategy

To effectively organize the African world throughout the Diaspora, it is necessary to organize various expressions of our collective consciousness. This tactic should not be confused with any delusional desires of complete agreement with or a uniformity of the Afrocentric, methodological approach.

It is, however, imperative that communication remains open, common goals are put in their proper place, and various forms of struggle are appreciated. By the end of the First World War, the name of William Edward Burghart Du Bois was highly respected and esteemed among Africans and peoples of African descent throughout the world. Having contributed to the founding of an effective propaganda organization through which the struggle for Negro political, economic, and social emancipation in America could be conducted, Du Bois turned his attention to the African aspect of the Colonial Question and the formation of the Pan African Congress.[28]

A peculiar paradox exists between the worldview and politics of Du Bois prior to the First Pan African Congress and sometime afterwards as his political location grew increasingly Pan Africanist. While Du Bois was attacking prominent Pan Africanist leaders such as Garvey he was consistently being praised, awarded, and rewarded. One of the recognitions that illustrated Du Bois's openness to an American sense of integration early in his career was the acceptance of the Spingarn Award named for one of the original leaders of the NAACP, Joel Spingarn. In 1920, Professor Du Bois was awarded the Spingarn Medal for his outstanding contribution to his race. It was awarded annually to the man or woman of African descent and American citizenship who during the year attained the highest achievement in any field of human endeavor.

One of the primary messages that Du Bois and the fifty-seven delegates promoted at the First Pan African Congress involved the African people on the Continent exercising agency in a leadership capacity concerning the future of the politics of the Continent. Du Bois felt strongly that it was the right and the responsibility of the African people to determine Africa's destiny and that the surrounding supporters throughout the Diaspora should be there to undergird their efforts accordingly. Du Bois planned to gain direct insights into the nuanced elements of the challenges faced in various capacities. One of the outlets of inside information from which Du Bois planned to extract testimonies that could inform strategy was from African American military men.

The hypocrisy evident in the lived experiences of men who were willing to sacrifice 100 percent for a country that would often continue to view them as three-fifths of a man despite their courage and valor was a paradox of particular interest to Du Bois. The opportunities provided to black soldiers and the negative treatment experienced when in contact with their white superiors provided peculiar parallels between military experience on base and abroad when compared to the ongoing racial battles being fought by countless civilian blacks back home. The delegates were prominent men and women who were either already in Europe or could afford to make the journey. They included the principal of Tuskegee, Robert Moton; Charles D. B. King, president of Liberia; and Blaise Diagne, French legislator from Senegal.

Upon his return trip from Europe, Du Bois seemed to possess a renewed vigor on issues of equality and protection for the constitutional rights of African Americans. This is the same type of reinvigorating energy and expanded perspective that could have given rise to the concept described by Du Bois in the context of an emerging *New Negro.* This notion was culturally compounded by many African Americans who were active in the military and later returned from service. Upon arrival, these courageous Africans were determined to transform northern cities in a way that would fit racial pride, dignity, and determined will. Du Bois was provided intimate access to observe and chronicle the lives of African American servicemen.

When he was afforded the opportunity to observe, it ignited a renewed, revolutionary spark in Du Bois that contributed to his rhetorical vigor and the vastness of his approach to interconnected issues throughout the Diaspora at home and abroad. In an editorial for the NAACP's official publication, *The Crisis*, Du Bois wrote, "But, by the God of Heaven, we are cowards and jackasses if, now that the war is over, we do not marshal every ounce of our brain and brawn to fight a sterner, longer, more unbending battle against the forces of hell in our own land."[29] The recruitment and incorporation of African American military personnel was a driving force of the new nomenclature, developing publications and even institutions as Du Bois himself described when discussing the primary directive of the Phylon Institute, an organization for economic development of the black community.

The primary purpose of the congress was said to be in line with the direction of the Phylon Institute. Du Bois was desirous of organizing African Americans after the war. Many others were in favor of seeing these efforts come to fruition. Despite wide-ranging support for Du Bois as an intellectual and political strategist, he was not without his critics. Communist affiliations and self-identifications did not prevent accusations by some who derided Du Bois as a tool of capitalist control. One of the bedrocks of these critiques typically classified Du Bois as the quintessential anti–Pan Africanist who was woefully out of touch with the lives and needs of the poor and working-class masses of black people. "The presumed bourgeois, overly academic distraction from sincere, productive methods of liberation struggle is how many detractors would come to define Du Bois. Black agents of international capitalism like Du Bois . . . are all offering their services to their imperialist masters. . . . Du Bois, the ideological leader of the middle-class Negro intellectuals, is trying to take away the lead from the revolutionary movement by playing with 'left phrases.' . . . What stupidity! What demagogy!"[30]

One of the personal characteristics of Du Bois that allowed him to remain focused on his goals despite an abundance of obstacles and opposition throughout his life was his unwavering confidence in the authority of his perspective and rhetoric. Du Bois rooted himself in an extraordinary self-confidence that has been described as condescending arrogance by his critics. This self-assuredness played a key role in the Pan African shifts in Du Bois's consciousness and the continuation of the Pan African Congress. Du Bois's confidence persisted even when numerous voices from outside and within were not supportive of the continuation of the political gathering or promotion of the related Pan African concepts.

Members of the NAACP attempted to dissuade Du Bois from internationalizing the black struggle and implementing a Pan Africanist approach rather than simply remain concentrated on local and national hindrances to black freedoms and human dignity. Du Bois says, "I had come back with the idea that we were going to carry on the work that I had been doing about the Pan African Congress, and I held one Congress after I came back there. But many people in the NAACP said that we had enough trouble in the United States without seeking problems in Africa."[31] In the face of doubt and attempted discouragement, Du Bois remained steadfast in his quest to promote Pan Africanism through vehicles such as the Pan African Congress. Other conferences had been convened prior to the organizing of the First Pan African Congress. However, one of the primary concerns of Du Bois and others can be found in a comparative analysis regarding the extent to which African people and participants present at other conferences were afforded any degree of agency that could be legitimately considered self-determinative.

One such problematic conference that included black agenda points without the necessary black agency to ring authentic with scholar organizers such as Du Bois was the 1919 Paris Peace Conference. This conference, which Du Bois attended, presented a void in potential organizational effectiveness that Du Bois sought to fill with his contribution. Regarding a suspected lack of agency at the peace conference, Du Bois interrogated questions of the color line while juxtaposing challenges faced by Africans with the conditions of Negros in America.[32] Even as Du Bois moved further along the continuum toward more Pan Africanist perspectives, he continued to display remnants of Communist and Marxist influences as other earlier influential aspects of his identity were complemented but not erased with the onset of increased Pan Africanist consciousness.[33] The focus on economic equity and the fair treatment of the laboring class clearly traced evidence of the lasting effects of the models and of desired societal structuring. In a strong speech called "The Niagara Movement Address to the Nation," Du Bois said:

> We want the laws enforced against rich as well as poor; against Capitalist as well as Laborer; against White as well as Black. We are not more lawless than the White race, we are more often arrested, convicted, and mobbed. We want justice even for criminals and outlaws. We want the constitution of the country enforced. We want Congress to take control of the Congressional elections. We want the Fourteenth Amendment carried out to the letter and every State disenfranchised in Congress which attempts to disenfranchise its rightful voters. We want the Fifteenth Amendment enforced and no State allowed to base its franchise simply on color.[34]

Du Bois's reformist rhetoric reveals an optimism that is rooted in his wealth of knowledge and his trust in his own personal capabilities. This leads him to a rhetorical and organizational strategy spurred on by his confidence in the ability to reform many systemic problem areas in society that are largely connected with inequality and the denial of the full humanity of African people.

The arc of Du Bois's Pan African experiences and expressions bend powerfully in the direction of concretely validating the value, legitimacy, and geopolitical advancement of African people, to employ Pan Africanist strategies and consciousness to achieve liberation and African agency/self-determination throughout the Diaspora.

Without international cooperation, Du Bois recognized that he would be putting his people at a significant disadvantage concerning their ability to tackle international systemic challenges while utilizing only a limited local or nationalist approach to the analysis and opposition to enemies of African empowerment and self-sufficiency. From the Talented Tenth to later traveling almost 10,000 miles (about 16,093.44 kilometers) to Ghana and strategizing with Pan Africanist giants like Kwame Nkrumah and others,[35] Du Bois displays the ability for all Africans to awaken our inner Pan Africanist spirit. For Du Bois, Africa marked a new level of awakening to the importance of Pan African consciousness:

> I think it was in Africa that I came more clearly to see the close connection between race and wealth. The fact that even in the minds of the most dogmatic supporters of race theories and believers in the inferiority of colored folk to White, there was a conscious or unconscious determination to increase their incomes by taking full advantage of this belief. And then gradually this thought was metamorphosed into a realization that the income-bearing value of race prejudice was the cause and not the result of theories of race inferiority; that particularly in the United States the income of the Cotton Kingdom based on Black slavery caused the passionate belief in [black] inferiority and the determination to enforce it even by arms.[36]

Despite Du Bois's wrestling with cultural dislocation, adherence to Marxism, Communist, or black petty bourgeois values and worldviews, his heart always bent toward the unity of Africans. Above all the theoretical and political static that was fed to the mind of a young Du Bois and young Africans throughout the Diaspora is the sweet song of Sankofa, returning to fetch what was forgotten or lost. Mother Africa continues to passionately pound the psycho-spiritual drum of Pan African victorious consciousness, leading active minds to higher levels of Pan African awareness. W. E. B. Du Bois is now among those many African American ancestors leaving behind a legacy of disciplined, diligent struggle and continued revelation. Our goal was to complexify Du Bois just enough so that you, the reader, will be able to see both the value of and the contradictions in this great intellect.[37]

Chapter 8
The Afrocentric Corrective at the Crest of Victory

Afrocentricity is fundamentally an interrogative science. It questions as it proceeds to inform the reader.[1] In the work of Du Bois, one must be careful to canvas the intellectual ground that he covers with an eye toward his vision. The reason for caution is that his scholarly capabilities were instrumental in the foundational shaping of American sociology, Pan Africanism, and inspiring countless individual achievers in society. Between his birth, five years after the signing of the 1863 Emancipation Proclamation, and his death ninety-five years later, on the eve of the historic March on Washington for Jobs and Freedom on August 28, 1963, Du Bois left an incomparable legacy of scholarship and intellectual thoughts.[2] However, the question remains, in what ways does this impressive academic resume serve to inspire and assist with current studies, societal challenges, and lapses in motivation for the contemporary moment and for future generations?

This chapter is designed to serve as an inspirational epilogue for those who will continue to read Du Bois Afrocentrically, especially as we engage the evolution of the color line, history, sociology, or any topics that fall under Du Bois's research umbrella.[3] Understanding where Du Bois should be located on the continuum of Afrocentricity, that is, Afrocentrically *located, dislocated, lynched, or culturally decapitated*, is a subject of great debate among scholars examining Du Bois's first publications.[4] We will investigate various takes on this subject and look at supporters and detractors in the fields of academia and organizational leadership. It is clear to us that there are elements in Du Bois's work that need to be seen as expressing nuances that are often missed when he is studied or read strictly as a historian or sociologist. Our thrust is to make educated assessments and informed predictions for the world to come, while appreciating the role Africans play in its shaping. Du Bois spent his years seeking to advance the understanding of African people being in time and space from the beginning of human history; although, as we have shown, he did not call himself an Afrocentrist, President Nkrumah encouraged him to produce an "Afrocentric" Encyclopedia Africana.

One approaches the reading of Du Bois with apprehension, not because he is difficult reading, but because his thematic work is complex. He was one of the leading thinkers on the issue of education for African people, along some of the same paths as in Carter G. Woodson's work.[5]

Afrocentrists write and speak of the power of victorious consciousness as opposed to the defeatist attitudes that exist in some circles. Du Bois had a composure about himself that allowed him to move expertly through the attacks by his staunchest critics. This ability, to keep his vision clear, was at the heart of his purpose. Reading Du Bois assures the reader that it is possible to demonstrate courage and intellect simultaneously.

Let us access the Du Boisian legacy in a manner that resurrects the promises of his scholarship through replicating more students of life, science, government, and art and culture. Here we posit Du Bois as an illuminated template for future greatness. Let these new expressions of intellectual and human conquest continue to streak through the skies like a comet, reflecting the light of glowing minds against the dark waters of poverty, ignorance, racism, and despair. If we were to connect a benedictory statement tying the past and the present, we would like to infuse the vast legacy of W. E. B. Du Bois from the cobblestone streets of Germantown in Philadelphia to the falls of Niagara and overseas in Ghana.[6]

We ask the reader to take a socially transformative approach to Du Bois's strong will and witness how he viewed personal and educational development as qualities to be shared to change the conditions of society. There was always, particularly after the Manchester Pan African Congress in 1945, a deliberate attempt on his part to speak of Africa as one. His Pan African consciousness was designed to grow vineyards of productive liberating thought, bearing fruits of wisdom, righteousness, and justice powerful enough to eradicate the destructive energies of Eurocentric distortions of African history. This was all connected to his drive to see transformation on the African continent. Toward the end of his life, Du Bois quickly moved in the direction of being more concerned with the proper development of economies on the continent of Africa. Much of his previous attention to social realities became focused upon systems of government and African unity, rather than the ego-driven competitiveness we witnessed from Du Bois against Marcus Garvey.[7]

Du Bois's departure from a solely black leadership structure concerning progressive organizations of his era was a major point of contention among him and his contemporaries. There was a strong sense of commonality with the working people of many nations in his writings. Increasingly influenced by socialist thinking, Du Bois could not omit the common suffering of millions of people in other parts of the world. However, this did not keep him from paying primary attention to the plight of his own long-suffering community. Concerning group politics this difference was powerfully illustrated in the friction between William Monroe Trotter, the head of the National Equal Rights League, and Du Bois, heading up the National Association for the Advancement of Colored People.[8] The interplay between the two organizations was contentious at times despite the similarities of their stated objectives and their ultimate agreement to line up against the Tuskegee Machine led by Booker T. Washington. One matter of concern for many was the demographics relating to the integration of black organizations and those who were viewed as fit to occupy positions of leadership. These are challenges that continue to stifle the growth and efficiency of several modern organizations.

Many black leaders sought a *for us by us*, Black led organization when the NAACP was formed. Many were wary of the organization working with whites. The most important black leaders of this period, including Washington, Trotter, and Garvey, criticized white dominance of the NAACP. Du Bois must be read as believing that any whites who supported the interests of African Americans had to be seen as worthy to be allies. In fact, he was one of the leaders of the National Association for the Advancement of Colored People during the time it was headed by a white person.

Personal contentions have regularly seeped into scholarly and organizational critiques of the early black human rights movement. One of the primary differences within the tradition of black leaders and organizations is the propensity for government agencies to dedicate exorbitant amounts of energy and tax dollars exaggerating existing conflicts and differences within the black community.[9] Groups such as the Office of Strategic Services spent time and money tracking Du Bois's activities.[10]

Du Bois perhaps most clearly represented his adherence to the beneficial aspects of the critical literary tradition when he submitted a review of his own work, analyzing *The Souls of Black Folk* as part of a special assignment in 1904 for the *Independent*.[11] The weekly magazine out of New York, edited primarily by Hamilton Holt, offered a rare opportunity to read Du Bois's thoughts on his own writings from the vantage point of literary criticism.

Although Du Bois displayed what many may perceive as a defensive posture toward previous critiques of the text, in the grand tradition of artists being sensitive about their work, he offered greater insight into the mind of the man beyond the pages.[12] The column in the *Independent* is called "Every Man His Own Reviewer." Du Bois felt that although there were a few who criticized the subjective nature of the review, it was, after all, his experiences that made the work important.

Du Bois continues his defense strategy through explaining some of the motivations and cultural contextualizations that influenced his method of expression and why others may have difficulty reading Du Bois's text. The Afrocentric tradition emphasizes agency, ancestral connections, and differences between cultures; Du Bois similarly emphasizes African agency.[13] The value of cultural grounding and the power of perspective are each on full display throughout Du Bois's review.

His cultural lens also functioned as a symbolic shield against inapplicable notions of Eurocentric acceptability as he strove to rupture literary and educational glass ceilings. The style can be characterized as African. Richard Rath says Du Bois "made no apology, contending that 'the blood of my fathers, spoke through me and cast off the English restraint of my training and surroundings.'"[14]

Du Bois articulately explained the essence of the timeless adage that purports that it was *a black thing*, and they wouldn't understand, long before this colloquialism became a mainstay within black culture. Some scholars refer to Du Bois as moderately Afrocentric in his writings and worldview.[15]

There exist legitimate critiques, however, regarding Du Bois's African cultural defenses given the fact that he praised and deferred to several European thinkers to whom he attributed much of his intellectual inspiration.[16] Due to the changes in Du Bois's political and ideological stances and focus, which could be viewed as a product of his evolution or inconsistency (depending upon the perspective of the beholder), a wide range of descriptions of Du Bois have arisen over the years.

Some of these labels are integrationist, Pan Africanist, Hegelian, social scientist, mystic, Communist, elitist, Spencerian, Marxist, romantic, sociologist, ethnographer, Roycean, intellectual puppet of hegemonic corporate conglomerates, and even an anarchist.[17] The fact that some of these depictions are diametrically opposed to others while describing the same man represents an accurate reflection of the wide-ranging expressions of thought vis-à-vis the contradictions that are often affiliated with Du Bois's legacy.

The allegations of inconsistency as a major flaw in Du Bois's scholarly legacy plagued him in life and today. Authors such as Richard Cullen Rath appear to agree with Eric J. Sunders, attributing the creation of an Afrocentric, philosophical historiography to Du Bois. Although Rath subscribes to the definition of Afrocentricity advanced by Molefi Kete Asante, he branches away from Asante concerning the application of the concept as it relates to Du Bois's scholarly Afrocentric location. We disagree with Rath's reading because Du Bois never outlined any theoretical position that could be seen to apprehend knowledge. He was much more thematic and practical in his approach to African American history and culture.

If he had an ideology, even then it was based on an eclectic set of facts and ideas instead of being a highly developed theoretical treatment of the black condition and an avenue for liberation from that situation as we see with Afrocentricity. Of all Du Bois's achievements, he never developed a theoretical position. In fact, to a large degree we must credit Kwame Nkrumah with encouraging Du Bois to work toward an Afrocentric approach.

Rath explains his position thusly:

> Du Bois created an Afrocentric philosophy of history. Recognition of his Afrocentric vision ties disparate strands of his thought together with a cogent and compelling whole; I use the definition of "Afrocentric" proposed by Molefi Kete Asante, who coined the term. To adopt an Afrocentric outlook "is to place Africans and the interest of Africa at the center of our approach to problem solving" and to give "agency, subject positions, to Africans." But Asante explicitly denies that Du Bois was Afrocentric. Du Bois, he maintains, simply added African

references to his essentially Eurocentric scholarship. He dismisses the possibility of multiple perspectives — what Du Bois famously called "double consciousness" — as inauthentic.[18]

If Du Bois ever appeared dismissive and defensive in his retorts it is worthy of noting that there were popular media outlets with white journalists who took their critical assessments of Du Bois's work to the extent of claiming that exposure to the content in his books would have a devilish impact and incite blacks to sexually violate white women.

Racist and xenophobic reactions to African Americans were pervasive in the early part of the twentieth century. Such vitriol would later plague debates around guns, abortion, and marijuana. Yet Du Bois found numerous supportive voices from within and from outside his community. Most of them came from African American reviewers including public intellectuals and political activists. J. E. Casely-Hayford viewed works like *The Souls of Black Folk* as an example of the type of literature that could help to remedy our national racial quandary. Casely-Hayford is an example of someone who saw the value in Du Bois's reflective and contemplative style.[19] A very notable white exception to the demographic makeup of Du Bois's most ardent supporters was Max Weber, the famed German political economist and sociologist.[20]

Weber pushed for *Souls of Black Folk* to be translated into German, believing that there were enough parallels concerning the expressions of humanity in the face of oppression that (although described in a local context) could have positive international implications. Weber also commissioned Du Bois to write an article that detailed his perspectives and possibilities for improvements around North American and German race relations. The working relationship between Du Bois and Weber powerfully illustrated the balance between the value of the uniqueness and nuance of a racialized perspective while illustrating the connective sociological tissues that tend to transcend demographic distinctions. The correspondence between these two great sociological minds reveals the mutual appreciation and respect for the wide-reaching, transformative potential for scholarship that they shared.

Weber had written "I am quite sure to come back to your country as soon as possible and especially to the South, because I am absolutely convinced that 'the color line' problem will be the paramount problem of the time to come here and everywhere in the world."[21] Furthermore, he writes, "And above all consider one thing: the day of the colored races dawns. It is insanity to delay this development; it is wisdom to promise us in light and hope for the future."[22] The relationship between the two displays how the study of the race paradigm/problems could be conducted in efforts to eradicate its impacts. Intellectual connections that supersede geographical distance, language barriers, and racial differences effectively illustrate the inclusive nature of scholarship whether it emanates from a sociological, Pan Africanist, or Afrocentric perspective. For Weber, Du Bois represented a long sought after American voice that included the knowledge, candor, and careful consideration for accuracy in research that, until discovering Du Bois, Weber struggled unsuccessfully to find.

As a result of this appreciation for the uniqueness of the opportunity before him, Weber was forthright and persistent in expressing the need for collaboration with Du Bois. Weber's difficulty in searching for and appreciation in locating Du Bois comes across in correspondence between the two. Weber writes:

> I failed in finding in the American (and of course any other) literature an investigation about the relations between the (so called) "race-problem" and the (so called) "class-problem" in your country, although it is impossible to have any conversation with white people of the South without feeling the connection. We must meet today in Germany not only the *dilettantic littérature* but a "scientific" race-theory, built up on purely anthropological fundaments, too, — and so we must accentuate especially those connections and the influence of social-economic conditions upon the relation of races to each other. I saw that you spoke some weeks ago about this very question and I should be very glad if you would find yourself in a position to give us, for our periodical, an essay about that object.[23]

This form of cross-promotion and production of scholarship is a primary component to the victorious intellectual crescendo of Afrocentric thought. A tipping point for many philosophies, products, and other expressions typically occurs when there is an exponential increase in visibility/consumption, which results in multiple communities or demographics having access to or interest in the aforementioned. We as scholars within the Afrocentric tradition cannot be desirous of being perpetually siloed to the extent that our concepts, ideas, and subjects of study are relegated only among the community or communities that currently fall under our ideological canopy. For these historiographies' ideas and methodologies to take hold on an increased level in the future, a greater emphasis on expansion and exposure must be part of the overall strategy.

To have maximum impact we must magnify contact and leave lasting, positive, and transformative impressions upon those we engage. Understanding this, it is the duty of contemporary scholars who study and write about Du Bois to do so in a manner that makes him as relatable, attractive, illuminating, challenging, and intriguing as possible. This is achieved through the ways we read and convey his academic and personal legacies.

Many African scholars find themselves in a similar position to Du Bois, evolving toward a more Afrocentric, more Pan Africanist mindset. Like a Bennu bird rising out of the sand and dust to be seen in the clear light of day, those scholars move ever closer to their own sense of agency based on their historical narratives. Most of us fall somewhere along the continuum between the most unaware dislocated Eurocentric African and the fully centered Afrocentric scholar. As a result of the fluidity of African consciousness, which exists throughout the world, Du Bois in all his evolution, contradictions, and expressions of brilliant and flawed humanity becomes exponentially more relatable than what readers may look upon as an infallible intellectual.

Today, our task is to read Du Bois while remembering two things: one, that we are not standing in his shadow but are basking in his literary light; and, two, that within his incomparable legacy we will find nuggets of truth, contradiction, and inspiration as we continue to read his work Afrocentrically. One can read Du Bois this way without isolating him as a singular phenomenon among African people. His individual gifts were outstanding and, in many ways, immeasurable, but he was a product of a people who had reflected on many attributes of human life during and after the enslavement and had begun the task of analyzing our condition. Du Bois was aware of the intellectual tradition of Alexander Crummell and Frederick Douglass, for example, and his writings must be seen as reflecting the accumulated wealth of philosophical and social knowledge from our traditions.

The Afrocentric tradition involves reflection on classical traditions of the African world to reinforce certain values, ethical positions, and historical practices. It is not religion, but culture in the sense that it is separated from any act of divinity or closed belief system, but rather Afrocentricity is connected in an actual material way to what we know and have known. Thus, our relationship Afrocentrically to Du Bois is one that is decorated with the tropes and metaphors of cultural maintenance.[24] But respect does not necessitate a lack of criticism; it is the reason for critiquing. In the tradition of cultural maintenance, the preservation of a balance between the physical and ethereal worlds is required. Recognizing this, we offer our readers their own roles and responsibilities in this continuous cycle of generation and regeneration of spirit and mission as a solemn hermeneutic matter. Our reading of Du Bois will open new channels, interests, and concepts that can add to the educational, aesthetic, and commemorative infusions of intellectual communities.

Much of Du Bois's intellectual endeavors could be viewed retrospectively as trial-and-error exercises due to his ability to adapt with changing times while utilizing lessons presented through past research and publication. There are also cultural and socioeconomic shifts that occurred regularly throughout Du Bois's life, which could also contribute to shifting approaches and perspectives on certain issues. Eric Porter, for one, saw this clearly regarding Du Bois and race:

> Common to the failures of left and liberal projects alike was a belief that new scientific research debunking the category would tear away the veil separating black and non-black bodies and minds. But racial inequities clearly persisted into the first post racial moment, and Du Bois feared they might even be enhanced in the future if the promise of color blindness supported by these findings turned into a refusal to see race (and racism) in its various manifestations or enabled its morphology to change. So, Du Bois insisted on remaining attuned to the persistence and complexity of race, which remained a central

"problem of the future world."[25]

Porter's assessment of Du Bois's attraction to race was correct. It was a historical attraction since Frederick Douglass had written the following in "The Color Line" in 1881:

> The slave master had a direct interest in discrediting the personality of those he held as property. Every man who had a thousand dollars so invested had a thousand reasons for painting the black man as fit only for slavery. Having made him the companion of horses and mules, he naturally sought to justify himself by assuming that the negro was not much better than a mule. . . . they belittle our virtues and magnify our vices and have made us odious in the eyes of the world. Slavery had the power at one time to make and unmake Presidents, to construe the law, and dictate the policy, set the fashion in national manners and customs, interpret the Bible, and control the church, and naturally enough the old masters set themselves up much too high and they set the manhood of the negro too low. Out of the depths of slavery has come this prejudice and this color line. It is broad enough and black enough to explain all the malign influences which assail the newly emancipated millions today. . . . The office of color in the color line is a very plain and subordinate one. It simply advertises the objects of oppression, insult, and persecution. It is not the maddening liquor, but the black letters on the sign telling the world where it might be had. . . . Slavery, stupidity, servility, poverty, dependence, are undesirable conditions. When these shall cease to be coupled with color, there will be no color line drawn.[26]

Douglas as a maestro of protest and agitation set the table from which Du Bois would dine on the analytical depths of the color line. Upon reading Du Bois, therefore, we must feel the emotional attachment to Douglass in the background, making all the noises necessary for Du Bois to thoroughly examine the color line. Douglass was to Du Bois as Du Bois has been to several generations of African scholars: the model of excellence that disproved all negativities that came with the division of humans into races.

By engaging in interdisciplinary research, Du Bois pushed forward on explanations of the great divide between white privilege and black poverty. He was able to combine history, sociology, and predictive analytics in his research program. In the early twentieth century he inherited the mantle of the men and women who had traveled this road before him, and tackled the American question of what was to become of the millions of former servants and field hands who were drastically impacted by the end of enslavement. This was a most pressing national concern, but a constant worry for those who had personally navigated the terrain between freedom and unfreedom.

Today, the scholarship Du Bois produced on these topics could be described as a merger between history, sociology, and predictive analytics. At the time of the production of his 1906 analysis, "The Economic Future of the Negro," the fate of Africans recently freed was of national concern. Du Bois would regularly take on national racial burdens, curiosities, and quandaries as a scholar immersed in the study of African American life, challenges, and potential. One advantage to Du Bois's observations was his ability to frame the conversation in a way that encourages the reader to confront potential biases and avoid observational inaccuracies relating to reductionist interpretations of African American life.

In writing about the economic situation of African Americans, Du Bois made it clear that he had not forgot about the abiding difficulties confronting the black population:

> When now we discuss the economic future of this group of ten million, we must first not fall into the prevalent error of speaking of these persons as though they formed one homogeneous group. This was not true even in slavery times, and it is so false today that any theories built on such a conception are false from the start. The Negro American after slavery made four distinct and different efforts to reach economic safety. The first effort was through the preferment of the selected house servant class; the second was by means of competitive industry; the third was by means of landholding and the fourth by means of what I am going to call the group economy.[27]

Here, by identifying the four avenues of economic development (preferment of the selected house servant class; competitive industry; landholding; and group economy), Du Bois set the discussion terms. We can follow him up this path, expand upon it, or reject it, but we have a plan from him. There are numerous instances of Du Bois's ability to frame conversation and analysis by creating a set of boundaries and descriptors that allow diverse populations from various perspectives to engage in conversation about certain topics with mutual understanding. Two further examples of this structuring could be found in the sociological format provided in *The Souls of Black Folk* and the creative criteria advanced in Du Bois's 1926 contribution, "Criteria of Negro Art," a transcript from a speech provided in honor of Carter G. Woodson who was being awarded as the twelfth recipient of the Spingarn Medal for African-descendant people displaying high achievement as part of the NAACP's national conference.[28]

The scholarship of Du Bois, like his organizational efforts, struck at the heart of the illusory propped up image of power that is white supremacy. For example, *The Philadelphia Negro* tore away the veil of a hegemonic, monolithic set of negative depictions of African Americans. This and other scholarly efforts served to dispel false notions of inherent criminality and revealed a diversity of thought and expression that brought the true diversity and humanity of a people to the fore. Du Bois was intentionally disruptive to the educational traditions of his day, which he believed were inadequate to effectively address the needs of his people. "His writings are a brilliant sociological record of the 19th and 20th centuries, but largely ignored by sociology until the last two decades. Today, his work is regularly included in sociology syllabi, usually only partially as he was a prolific writer throughout his long adult life — historian, novelist, political commentator as well as sociologist. Du Bois's work interweaves all four knowledge practices — professional, policy, public, and critical. He poses a serious challenge to the conventional canon."[29]

It is time to embrace the unconventional and the innovative aspects of thought and society. The hour is nigh where we will see the implementation of Du Bois's scholarship extend far beyond sociological borders. Du Bois openly objected to what he felt was Booker T. Washington's suggestion that African Americans acquiesce to a subordinate status within the racially tiered caste system of the American experiment.

He demolished the altruistic veneer of European international initiatives, revealing a calculated quest for control over a vast array of raw materials and related resources of foreign nations. Today, we are utilizing the work of Du Bois to similarly promote greater hope, understanding, and potential concerning black empowerment and scholarly engagement with attention to the national and international implications in the tradition of the great scholar in the spirit of his work. In the future, we may enjoy fully immersive academic experiences where students of tomorrow utilize technology likened to the ways libations (spiritual technology) are implemented.

The ability to transcend space and time and merge the earthly and after (or other) life is a source of great hope. We must abandon the fears of those who remain frightfully engaged in conversations and debates about robots coming to take their jobs and instead focus more on the positive ways technology can be used to improve society. There are many ways to skillfully implement new uses of emerging artificial intelligence. I envision holograms of Du Bois projected before students of all ages discussing his ideas and contrasting them with current events and trends courtesy of artificial intelligence, holographic projections, and machine learning. This type of access to new forms of engagement and relevance relating to Du Bois and other scholars expands the definition of computer update.

Scholars of today continue to wrestle with race and racism, simultaneously appreciating both the socially constructed foundation and the empirically measurable outgrowths in a variety of sectors of society (e.g., education, health care, employment, imprisonment). Afrocentric scholars read Du Bois's sociological studies with an eye toward African agency; therefore, we seek in our reading the action-place, the subject position, of the African person regardless of the sector of society we are evaluating. What are the Africans doing and thinking? Is it possible for African people to solve some of their most immediate problems? Du Bois understands the complexity of these questions although we have no record that he was asked these questions by his peers. Porter provides us with some appreciation for his analysis:

> Through his complicated engagement with race and science, Du Bois suggests an ethos that contemporary investigators can deploy when looking at race and racism in all their complex manifestations, even as popular and political common sense argues that science impels us to move on to other subjects. Du Bois's project signals the way that an anti-racist intellectual project must be attuned to the potential racist power, as well as through different kinds of instructional configurations. In other words, it is not merely that discourses of color blindness and racial transcendence mask the existence of racial hierarchies. Rather these orientations are potentially the ideological mechanisms upholding white supremacy.[30]

Parsing the subtle delineations between racial progress and the denial of racial realities continues to be a precarious balance to maintain in our lived experiences. Afrocentrists understand that race is biologically a false notion, but the evidence of racial thinking is all around us in the outcomes of institutions and the practices of people. Racial hierarchy developed and maintained by those who believe in white racial domination remains a major part of our social reality; thus, reading Du Bois, with an eye on the contemporary situation, is necessary.

Du Bois has provided intellectual road maps, blueprints, and compelling timelines, suggesting sociological, ethnographic, and philosophical possibilities for a society deeply entrenched in racial thinking. His studies, stories, and testimonials can be effectively used to illuminate the route he saw for a true humanity. Du Bois's comprehensive arsenal of twenty-one books, collections of essays, letters, pamphlets, and unfinished writings, numbering in the thousands, have been digitized by the University of Massachusetts at Amherst and made usable through a grant from the National Endowment for the Humanities. In our estimation, Du Bois recognized, as we have written, that his life was a performance for the elevation of black people, and he understood precisely where he was in that process. He would claim that there were hurdles that had to be overcome. In fact, he wrote, "Two great obstacles to this consummation are apparent: A. The lack of unity, want of harmony, absence of self-sacrificing spirit, and no well-defined line of policy seeking definite aims; and B. the persistent, relentless, at times covert opposition employed to thwart . . . at every step of his upward struggles to establish the justness of the claim to the highest physical, intellectual, and moral possibilities."[31]

Du Bois also observed an intimate connection between the economic structures of a given society and the types of life lessons members of that community received. This systemic socialization strategy was a departure from his previous Talented Tenth approach to solving massive problems among black people. Moving from a more individualistic to a structural systems analysis and approach to a more practical problem-solving approach motivated critics of the theory including Booker T. Washington.

> Washington accuses [Du Bois's Talented Tenth] of being able to understand only theories and ideas. He asserts that they have crammed their heads full of book knowledge; in so doing they have lost contact with the real world and real people. [32]

Let us consider, finally, the possibility of building new concepts and intellectual paradigms informed by the work of Du Bois that seek to elevate humanity beyond the racial paragon that plagued his people throughout his life. We do not view these newly proposed frameworks as a departure or betrayal of Du Bois's thoughts and theories. This elevation will reflect the goals both clearly stated and implied through researching Du Bois's extensive commentary. Despite predicting the lasting effects of the color line, I believe we could conclude with a substantial degree of certainty that Du Bois's predictions were expressed in efforts to have us eventually freed from the grip of the racial disregard he so eloquently described rather than being perpetually bound by the limitations and challenges he articulated. The process of identifying and articulating these conditions will eventually lead to their deconstruction and destabilization, which in turn will create opportunities for the development of newer, more equitable means of engaging humanity. The power of a legacy such as the one established by Du Bois is rooted in its ability to continue through generations while expanding in appreciation, understanding, and practical application of the lessons therein.

Notes

Chapter 1

1. Du Bois stands alongside other African American historians of the twentieth century as iconic figures: Carter G. Woodson, John Henrik Clarke, John Hope Franklin, Darlene Hines, Charles Wesley, and Merle Epps. But none of these outstanding scholars reached the height of Du Bois in the national imagination as an academic, activist, philosopher, and productive scholar. His reputation as the major force in African American history remains unrivaled although Carter G. Woodson is a close second.

2. Manning Marable, "A Conversation with John Hope Franklin," *Souls* (Summer 1999): 73–87. Manning Marable, an important intellectual, interviewed John Hope Franklin at Columbia University after Franklin's retirement from Duke University. One is struck by Marable's astute questioning of the historian and impressed by how much of Franklin's conversation had to do with the practice of being a good mentor. Somewhere buried in his memory seemed to have been parts of Du Bois's trajectory that he wanted to avoid, although there was no doubt that he admired Du Bois.

3. John Hope Franklin was named after the first African American president of Atlanta University, John Hope, who was one of W. E. B. Du Bois's most loyal supporters and friends. Indeed, the parents of John Hope Franklin, Buck Colbert Franklin, an attorney, and Mollie Parker Franklin, a teacher, were active in the civil rights arena in Oklahoma and became famous for defending African Americans after the Tulsa Riots of 1921. Franklin was born in 1915 and died in 2009 after achieving recognition as a Presidential Medal of Freedom holder for his immense historical contributions. His book *From Slavery to Freedom* is one of the most read history books in the American curriculum.

4. Marable, "A Conversation with John Hope Franklin," 77.

5. Marable, "A Conversation with John Hope Franklin," 77.

6. Marable, "A Conversation with John Hope Franklin," 77.

7. Performativity, for Afrocentrists, is the act of exhibiting behaviors and staging actions that can denote or connote emotions, interests, attitudes, or futures. Denoting refers to signs that stand for something specific while connoting refers to signs and performances that imply different emotions, interests, and attitudes toward futures.

8. Cedric Robinson, *Black Marxism: The Making of the Black Radical Tradition* (Chapel Hill: University of North Carolina Press, 2000), 185.

9. W. E. B. Du Bois, *Darkwater: The Givens Collection* (New York: Washington Square Press, 2004), 6.

10. W. E. B. Du Bois, *Darkwater: Voices from Within the Veil* (Rahway, NJ: Harcourt, Brace and Howe, 1920), 11.

11. Du Bois, *Darkwater: Voices from Within the Veil*, 11.

12. Daniel Agbeyebiawo, *The Life and Works of W.E.B. Du Bois* (Accra, Ghana: W.E. B. Du Bois Center, 1998), 12.

13. There was neither fear nor fondness for whites since he had seen and known them all his life in Great Barrington as the town's regular folk. Thus, it was not unusual for him to feel at home in the company of Europeans or Asians throughout his life. He was equally well prepared in European ways as he was later to become by his southern experience in the ways of his own people.

14. Du Bois, *Darkwater: Voices from Within the Veil*, 13.

15. W. E. B. Du Bois, "A Negro Student at Harvard at the End of the 19th Century," *Massachusetts Review* 1 (Spring 1960): 455.

16. Michael Tillotson, *Invisible Jim Crow: Contemporary Ideological Threats to the Internal Security of African Americans* (Trenton, NJ: Africa World Press, 2011), 60.

17. Fisk University in Nashville, Tennessee, was one of the institutions that sought to assert African American culture as a world-class product. Organized in 1871, the Jubilee Singers were an established ensemble of student vocalists who traveled the world promoting African American culture. Among the songs they popularized were "Swing Low, Sweet Chariot" and "Steal Away," both composed by Wallace Willis, the Choctaw freedman, while living in Indian Territory between 1850 and 1870.

18. Shamoon Zamir, *Dark Voices: WEB Du Bois and American Thought, 1888-1903* (Chicago: University of Chicago Press, 1995), 62.

19. Zamir, *Dark Voices*, 63.

20. Clarence A. Bacote, *The Story of Atlanta University: A Century of Service, 1865–1965* (Atlanta: Atlanta University Publications, 1969), 134–36; see also W. E. B. Du Bois, *The Autobiography of W. E. B. Du Bois: A Soliloquy on Viewing My Life from the Last Decade of Its First Century* (New York: International Publishers, 1968), 210–18.

21. Jonathan Grossman, "Black Studies in the Department of Labor, 1897–1907," *Monthly Labor Review*, June 1974, 12.

22. Numerous other competitions for the masses of the African American people have been explained or studied in connection with the Du Bois–Washington controversy. People want to know if Malcolm X and Martin Luther King could be seen in the light of this epic debate about the future of black people. Neither Du Bois nor Washington sought this controversy; it was heaved upon them by the positions they took regarding the education of the black masses, the political aspirations of the elites, and the objectives for the black community.

23. *Phylon* remains a peer-reviewed academic journal covering culture in the United States from an African American perspective. Du Bois founded it in 1940 and it is still housed at Clark Atlanta University.

24. Elliott M. Rudwick, "The Niagara Movement," *Journal of Negro History* 42, no. 3 (1957): 177.

25. Booker T. Washington, "Atlanta Compromise Speech" (1895), in *Encyclopedia of Race and Racism*, by Patrick L. Mason (New York: Macmillan, 2013), 280–82.

Chapter 2

1. See W. E. B. Du Bois, *The Autobiography of W. E. B. Du Bois: A Soliloquy on Viewing My Life from the Last Decade of Its First Century* (New York: International Publishing, 1968).
2. This thinking derived from his 1899 study of the Philadelphia African American community, which started his six decades of research into the quantifiable nature of racial inequality.
3. Patricia Reid-Merritt, *A State-by-State History of Race and Racism in the United States* (New York: Praeger, 2017).
4. W. E. B. Du Bois, *The Souls of Black Folk* (1903), is the most popular book written by Du Bois.
5. Priscilla Bawcutt, ed., *The Poems of William Dunbar* (Glasgow: Association for Scottish Literary Studies, 1999).
6. W. E. B. Du Bois, *The Philadelphia Negro: A Social Study and History of Pennsylvania's Black American Population, Their Education, Environment and Work* (New York: Pantianos, 1899).
7. Matthew Wills, "Constructing the White Race," *JSTOR Daily*, September 12, 2016.
8. Karen Brodkin, *How Jews Became White Folks and What That Says About Race in America* (New Brunswick, NJ: Rutgers University Press, 1998).
9. Jennifer Guglieimo and Salvatore Salerno, *Are Italians White? How Race Is Made in America* (New York: Routledge, 2004).
10. Matthew Wills, "Constructing the White Race," *JSTOR Daily,* September 12, 2016, 2. https://daily.jstor.org/constructing-the-white-race/.
11. Du Bois, *Souls of Black Folk*, 8.
12. Ibram X. Kendi, *How to Be an Anti-Racist* (New York: One World, 2019), 11.
13. Kendi, *How to Be an Anti-Racist*, 230.
14. Michael Omi and Howard Winant, *Racial Formation in the United States* (New York: Routledge, 2014).
15. D. W. Griffith, *Birth of a Nation* (1915), Student Digital Gallery, accessed August 8, 2023, https://digitalgallery.bgsu.edu/student/items/show/11113.
16. William Julius Wilson, *The Declining Significance of Race* (Chicago: University of Chicago Press, 2012).

17. Booker T. Washington, "The Atlanta Exposition Speech," September 18, 1895. https://iowaculture.gov/sites/default/files/history-education-pss-areconstruction-atlanta-transcription.pdf.

18. Washington, "Atlanta Exposition Speech."

19. https://www.hoplofobia.info/wp-content/uploads/2022/05/PG-Manifesto.pdf.

20. W. E. B. Du Bois, *The Ordeal of Mansart* (New York: Mainstream Publishers, 1957), 198.

21. Du Bois, *Ordeal of Mansart*, 197–99.

22. David Levering Lewis, W. *E. B. Du Bois: Biography of a Race, 1868–1919* (New York: Henry Holt, 1994), 198.

23. W. E. B. Du Bois, "On Christianity," in *W. E. B. Du Bois: Writings*, ed. Nathan Huggins (New York: Library of America, 1986), 2.

24. Anthony B. Pinn, "Reading Du Bois through Religion and Religious Commitment," *Journal of Religion* 94, no. 3 (2014): 382.

25. Reiland Rabaka, *W. E. B. Du Bois and the Problems of the Twenty-First Century: An Essay on Africana Critical The*ory (London: Lexington Books, 2007), 293.

26. William Matthew Flinders Petrie, *Letter from Sir William Matthew Flinders Petrie to W.E.B. Du Bois* (New York: Crisis Publishing, 1912), 1–4.

27. Du Bois, *Letter from W.E.B. Du Bois to Sir William Matthew Flinders Petrie*.

28. Du Bois, *Souls of Black Folk*, 41.

29. Ruth Reviere, "Toward an Afrocentric Research Methodology," *Journal of Black Studies* 31, no. 6 (2001): 709–28.

30. Reviere, "Toward an Afrocentric Research Methodology," 710.

31. Michelle Taylor, "Black Mamas on the Screen: African Matriarchy and African American Motherhood," PhD diss., Temple University, 2023, 31.

32. Du Bois, *Souls of Black Folk*, 76.

33. Du Bois, *Dusk of Dawn: An Essay Toward an Autobiography of a Race Concept* (New York: Schocken, 1940), 7.

34. Du Bois, *Souls of Black Folk*, 1903, 76.

Chapter 3

1. Unquestionably, the publication of *The Philadelphia Negro,* a data-driven, urban-based study of the condition of the African American community, thrust Du Bois into the forefront of social science practice.

2. See Reiland Rabaka, *Du Bois Dialectics: Black Radical Politics and the Reconstruction of Critical Social Theory* (New York: Lexington Books, 2008), 64–66.

3. Henry Lyman Morehouse, "The Talented Tenth," *American Missionary* 50, no. 6 (June 1896).

4. Booker T. Washington, "The Atlanta Exposition Address," 1895, in *The Booker T. Washington Papers*, vol. 3, ed. Louis R. Harlan (Urbana: University of Illinois Press, 1974), 583–87.

5. W. E. B. Du Bois, "The Talented Tenth Memorial Address," in *The Future of the Race*, ed. Henry Louis Gates Jr. and Cornel West (New York: Knopf, 1996), 162.

6. Du Bois, "Talented Tenth Memorial Address," 162.

7. Morehouse, "Talented Tenth."

8. Morehouse, "Talented Tenth."

9. Morehouse, "Talented Tenth."

10. W. E. B. Du Bois, *The Souls of Black Folk* (1903), chapter 6, "On the Training of Black Men," 73.

11. Du Bois, "Talented Tenth Memorial Address," 162.

12. Booker T. Washington, "Speech to the Atlanta Cotton States and International Exposition" (1895), *American RadioWorks*.

13. W.E.B. Du Bois Collection, JWJ MSS 8, Box 3, Folder 57, pp. 15–16, Beinecke Rare Book & Manuscript Library, Yale University.

14. Kelly Miller, "The Education of the Negro," *U.S. Dept. of Interior Annual Report, FY Ending 1901; Report of the Commissioner of Education* (1902), vol. 1, chapter 16.

15. Miller, "Education of the Negro."

16. W. E. B. Du Bois, "The Twelfth Census and the Negro Problems," *The Southern Workman* 29, no. 5 (May 1900): 305–9.

17. W. E. B. Du Bois, "To the Nations of the World," quoted in Alexander Walters, *My Life and Work* (New York: Fleming H. Revell, 1917), 257–60, http://docsouth.unc.edu/neh/walters/walters.html#walt257.

18. David Hume, "Part I, Essay XXI: Of National Characters," in *The Philosophical Works of David Hume, Including All the Essays, and Exhibiting the More Important Alterations and Corrections in the Successive Editions Published by the Author: Essays, Moral, Political, and Literary*, vol. 3 (Edinburgh: Adam and Charles Black; Boston: Little, Brown and Company, 1854), 217–36, 228–29.

19. Robert Bernasconi and Anika Maaza Mann, "The Contradictions of Racism: Locke, Slavery, and the Two Treatises," in *Race and Racism in Modern Philosophy*, edited by Andrew Valls (Ithaca: Cornell University Press, 2005), 89–91.

20. Thomas Jefferson, *Notes on Virginia*, 1834, 146.

21. James R. Forman, *Self-Determination and the African-American People* (Seattle: Open Hand Publishing, 1981).

22. Du Bois, "Talented Tenth Memorial Address," 168.

23. Rabaka, *Du Bois Dialectics*, 64–66.

24. Molefi Kete Asante, *Afrocentricity: Theory of Social Change* (Chicago: African American Images, 2003).

Chapter 4

1. John Henrik Clarke, *My Life in Search of Africa* (Chicago: Third World Press, 1999), 4.

2. Amir Jaima, "Historical Fiction as Sociological Interpretation and Philosophy," *Transaction* 53, no. 4 (2017): 586.

3. Ta-Nehesi Coates, *Between the World and Me* (New York: Spiegel and Grau, 2015), 10.

4. Molefi Kete Asante and Nah Dove, *Being Human Being: Transforming the Race Discourse* (New York: Universal Write Publications, 2021).

5. Du Bois, *Souls of Black Folk*, preface.

6. W. E. B. Du Bois, *Black Reconstruction in America, 1860–1880* (New York: Harcourt and Brace, 1935), 367.

7. Du Bois, *Black Reconstruction in America*, 367.

8. W. E. B. Du Bois, "The African Roots of War," *The Atlantic*, May 1915.

9. Jennifer D. Keene, "W. E. B. Du Bois and the Wounded World: Seeking Meaning in the First World War for African Americans," *Peace and Change* 26, no. 2 (2001): 135–52.

10. Chad L. Williams, *The Wounded World: W.E.B. Du Bois and the First World War* (New York: Macmillan, 2023), 148.

11. Rabaka, *W. E. B. Du Bois and the Problems of the Twenty-First Century*, 92–93. Here Rabaka expands on the notion of an Africana anticolonial theory.

12. W. E. B. Du Bois, *The Souls of Black Folk*, with an introduction by Manning Marable (New York: Routledge, 2004), 119.

13. W. E. B. Du Bois, "Why I Won't Vote," *The Nation*, October 20, 1956.

14. Du Bois, "Why I Won't Vote."

15. Bill V. Mullen, "W.E.B. Du Bois Was the Father of Pan African Socialism," *Jacobin*, May 2, 2022, 187.

16. Michael Murphy, "Climate Change and the Color Line," *Class, Race, and Corporate Power* 1, no. 1 (2013): 4.

17. Du Bois, *Black Reconstruction in America*, 16.

18. Paul Robeson, "The Legacy of W. E. B. Du Bois," *Freedomways* (first quarter, 1965), 39.

19. Murali Balaji, *The Professor and the Pupil: The Politics and Friendship of W.E.B. Du Bois and Paul Robeson* (New York: Nation Books, 2007).

20. C. L. R. James, *The Black Jacobins: Toussaint L'Ouverture and the San Domingo Revolution* (New York: Vintage, 1989).

21. Letter from W. E. B. Du Bois to Kwame Nkrumah, February 7, 1957; originally published in *Freedomways* (first quarter, 1965), 8.

Chapter 5

1. W. E. B. Du Bois, *The Comet* (New York: Graphic Arts Books, 2021).

2. Aaron X. Smith, ed., *Afrocentricity in AfroFuturism: Towards an Afrocentric Future* (Jackson: University Press of Mississippi, 2023).

3. Smith, *Afrocentricity in Afrofuturism*, 17.

4. Molefi Kete Asante, *An Afrocentric Manifesto: Toward an African Renaissance* (Cambridge: Polity Books, 2007).

5. See Molefi Kete Asante, *Afrocentricity: The Theory of Social Change* (Chicago: African American Images, 2003); Molefi Kete Asante, *The Afrocentric Idea* (Philadelphia: Temple University Press, 2004); Molefi Kete Asante, *Kemet, Afrocentricity, and Knowledge* (Trenton, NJ: Africa World Press, 1990); Asante, *Afrocentric Manifesto*; and Molefi Kete Asante, *Malcolm X as Cultural Hero and Other Afrocentric Essays* (Trenton, NJ: Africa World Press, 1993).

6. Molefi Kete Asante, "The Afrocentric Idea in Education," *Journal of Negro Education* 60, no. 2 (1991): 170–80; quote, 171.

7. Asante, "Afrocentric Idea in Education," 172.

8. Tsenay Serequeberhan, *The Hermeneutics of African Philosophy: Horizon and Discourse* (London: Routledge, 1994).

9. Christopher Columbus Baldwin, *Diary of Christopher Columbus Baldwin* (Worcester, MA: American Antiquarian Society, 1901).

10. Jan Vansina, "A Comparison of African Kingdoms," *Africa* 32, no. 4 (1962): 324–35. Vansina was one of the most important thinkers on the issue of African oral traditions, and he established the greatness of African kingdoms outside of the gaze of Europe.

11. Aaron X. Smith, ed., *Afrocentricity in AfroFuturism: Towards an Afrocentric Future* (Jackson: University Press of Mississippi, 2023). Although Aaron X. Smith had identified the term prior to the publication of the book, it is in the text where one finds his unique emphasis on Afrocentric Futurism.

12. Mark Dery, "Black to the Future: Interviews with Samuel R. Delany, Greg Tate, and Tricia Rose," in *Flame Wars: The Discourse of Cyberculture*, ed. Dery (Durham: Duke University Press, 1994), 179–222.

13. Reynaldo Anderson and Charles Jones, *Afrofuturism 2.0: The Rise of Astro-Blackness* (New York: Lexington Books, 2017), viii.

14. Reynaldo Anderson and Clinton R. Fluker, eds., *The Black Speculative Arts Movement: Black Futurity, Art+Design* (New York: Lexington Books, 2019); George S. Schuyler, *Black No More* (New York: Penguin, 2018); Octavia E. Butler, *Bloodchild and Other Stories* (New York: Seven Stories Press, 2011); Reynaldo Anderson, "Future Movements: Black Lives, Black Politics, Black Futures — an Introduction," *TOPIA: Canadian Journal of Cultural Studies* 39 (2018): 5–21; Ishmael Reed, *Yellow Back Radio Broke-Down* (Dallas: Dalkey Archive Press, 2022); Nalo Hopkinson, *Brown Girl in the Ring* (Aspect, 2001); Ytasha L. Womack, *Afrofuturism: The World of Black Sci-Fi and Fantasy Culture* (Chicago: Chicago Review Press, 2013); Mark Dery, *Escape Velocity: Cyberculture at the End of the Century* (New York: Grove Press, 1997); Isiah Lavender III, ed., *Black and Brown Planets: The Politics of Race in Science Fiction* (Jackson: University Press of Mississippi, 2014); Nnedi Okorafor, "Organic Fantasy," *African Identities* 7, no. 2 (2009): 275–86; B. Sharise Moore, "Alla Our Stuff," *Journal of Pan African Studies* 4, no. 2 (2010): 415–19.

15. See, for example, Janelle Monáe and Erykah Badu, *The Electric Lady*, 2013; Cheryl L. Keyes, "'She Was Too Black for Rock and Too Hard for Soul': (Re)Discovering the Musical Career of Betty Mabry Davis," *American Studies* 52, no. 4 (2013): 35–55; John Szwed, *Space Is the Place: The Lives and Times of Sun Ra* (Durham: Duke University Press, 2020); Akala Daley, Meryem Saci, Sa Roc, and Leif Womack, "International Hip Hop Afterparty," 7th Annual African and African Diaspora Studies Student Research and Engagement Conference, March 19, 2015, https://digitalcommons.kennesaw.edu/aadsstucon/7thAnnual/HipHopAfterParty/1/; and Howard Rambsy, "Beyond Keeping It Real: OutKast, the Funk Connection, and Afrofuturism," *American Studies* 52, no. 4 (2013): 205–16.

16. These are some of the works that enlighten the speculative reading of historical and contemporary works. Cheryl L. Keyes, "'She Was Too Black for Rock and Too Hard for Soul': (Re)Discovering the Musical Career of Betty Mabry Davis," *American Studies* 52, no. 4 (2013): 35–55; Szwed, *Space Is the Place*; Akala Daley, Meryem Saci, Sa Roe, and Leif Womack, "International Hip Hop Afterparty," 7th Annual African and African Diaspora Studies Student Research and Engagement Conference, March 19, 2015, https://digitalcommons.kennesaw.edu/aadsstucon/7thAnnual/HipHopAfterParty/1/; Rambsy, "Beyond Keeping It Real"; "Parliament/Funkadelic," in *Encyclopedia of Recorded Sound*, ed. Frank Hoffmann (New York: Routledge, 2004), 1590–93; Ian Bourland, "Afronauts: Race in Space," *Third Text* 34, no. 2 (2020): 209–29.

17. Among the writers who have examined these questions and dedicated their careers to correcting the historical record are Cheikh Anta Diop, The *African Origin of Civilization: Myth or Reality*, ed. and trans. Mercer Cook (Chicago: Chicago Review Press, 2012); Asante, *Afrocentric Manifesto*; Maulana Karenga, *Introduction to Black Studies* (Los Angeles: University of Sankore Press, 1993); Nah Dove, "The Emergence of Black Supplementary Schools: Resistance to Racism in the United Kingdom," *Urban Education* 27, no. 4 (1993): 430–47; Ivan Van Sertima, "Death Shall Not Find Us Thinking That We Die," *Présence africaine*, n.s., nos. 149–50 (1989): 321–30; Jon Henrik Clarke, "Africa and the American Negro Press," *Journal of Negro Education* 30, no. 1 (1961): 64–68; Chancellor Williams, *Destruction of Black Civilization: Great Issues of a Race*

from 4500 BC to 2000 AD (Morrisville, NC: Lulu Press, 2020); Anthony T. Browder, *Nile Valley Contributions to Civilization: Exploding the Myths*, vol. 1 (Washington, DC: Institute of Karmic Guidance, 1992); and Martin Bernal, *Black Athena: The Afroasiatic Roots of Classical Civilization*, vol. 1, *The Fabrication of Ancient Greece 1785–1985* (New Brunswick, NJ: Rutgers University Press, 2020).

18. See these works: José Itzigsohn and Karida L. Brown, "The Sociology of WEB Du Bois," in *The Sociology of W. E. B. Du Bois: Racialized Modernity and the Global Color Line*, ed. Itzigsohn and Brown (New York: New York University Press, 2020); Du Bois, *Dusk of Dawn*; W. E. B. Du Bois, *W. E. B. Du Bois on Sociology and the Black Community* (Chicago: University of Chicago Press, 2013); Aldon Morris, *The Scholar Denied: W.E.B. Du Bois and the Birth of Modern Sociology* (Berkeley: University of California Press, 2015).

19. Molefi Kete Asante, *Afrocentricity: The Theory of Social Change* (Buffalo: Amulefi, 1980), 20.

20. Sandra Van Dyk, "Molefi Kete Asante's Theory of Afrocentricity: The Development of a Theory of Cultural Location," PhD diss., Temple University, 1998, 60.

21. Readers should see Lisa Yaszek, "Afrofuturism, Science Fiction, and the History of the Future," *Socialism and Democracy* 20, no. 3 (2006): 41–60, and Adriano Elia, "W. E. B. Du Bois's Proto-Afrofuturist Short Fiction: 'The Comet,'" *Il Tolomeo* 18 (2016): 173.

22. Yaszek, "Afrofuturism, Science Fiction," 59–60.

23. Yaszek, "Afrofuturism, Science Fiction," 51.

24. Elia, "W. E. B. Du Bois's Proto-Afrofuturist Short Fiction," 178.

25. W. E. B. Du Bois, *Darkwater: Voices from Within the Veil* (Rahway, NJ: Harcourt, Brace and Howe, 1920).

26. Sheree Renée Thomas, *Dark Matter: A Century of Speculative Fiction from the African Diaspora* (London: Hachette, 2014).

27. Amaryah Shaye Armstrong, "The Apocalyptic Theology of W. E. B. Du Bois: Black Culture at the End of the World," *Black Theology* 20, no. 1 (2022): 25.

28. W. E. B. Du Bois, *Black Reconstruction in America: Toward a History of the Part Which Black Folk Played in the Attempt to Reconstruct Democracy in America, 1860–1880* (New York: Routledge, 2017), 182.

29. Joe P. L. Davidson, "Ugly Progress: WEB Du Bois's Sociology of the Future," *Sociological Review* 69, no. 2 (2021): 386.

30. Reiland Rabaka, "WEB Du Bois's 'The Comet' and Contributions to Critical Race Theory: An Essay on Black Radical Politics and Anti-Racist Social Ethics," *Ethnic Studies Review* 29, no. 1 (2006): 25–26.

31. Du Bois, "The Comet" (1920), 60.

32. Du Bois, "The Comet" (1920), 54.

33. Darryl A. Smith, "Droppin' Science Fiction: Signification and Singularity in the Metapocalypse of Du Bois, Baraka, and Bell," *Science Fiction Studies* 34, no. 102 (2007): 201–19, quote at 209.

34. Ralph Ellison, *Invisible Man* (New York: Penguin, 2016).

35. Du Bois, "The Comet" (1920), 54.

36. Du Bois, "The Comet" (1920), 54.

37. Du Bois, "The Comet" (1920), 54.

38. Du Bois, "The Comet" (1920), 55.

39. Steven Snape, *Ancient Egyptian Tombs: The Culture of Life and Death* (New York: Wiley-Blackwell, 2011).

40. George Francis Dow, *Slave Ships and Slaving* (Mineola, NY: Dover, 2002).

41. Du Bois, "The Comet" (1920), 55.

42. Du Bois, "The Comet" (1920), 59.

43. Du Bois, "The Comet" (1920), 55.

44. Dow, *Slave Ships and Slaving*, 178.

45. Marcus Rediker, *The Slave Ship: A Human History* (New York: Penguin, 2008), 71.

46. Randall Kenan, "The Good Ship 'Jesus': Baldwin, Bergman, and the Protestant Imagination; or, Baldwin's Bitter Taste," *African American Review* 46, no. 4 (2013): 701–14.

47. Donald Lowrie, *My Life in Prison* (Createspace Independent Publishing Platform, 1912), 123.

48. Lowrie, *My Life in Prison*, 124.

49. Lowrie, *My Life in Prison*, 125.

50. A multitude of scholars have documented the abuses against African people. See, for example, Christopher Muller, "Freedom and Convict Leasing in the Postbellum South," *American Journal of Sociology* 124, no. 2 (2018): 367–405; Arthur F. Raper, *The Tragedy of Lynching* (Chapel Hill: University of North Carolina Press, [1933] 2017); John R. Logan and Mark Schneider, "Racial Segregation and Racial Change in American Suburbs, 1970–1980," *American Journal of Sociology* 89, no. 4 (1984): 874–88; Gregory D. Squires, ed., *Redlining to Reinvestment* (Philadelphia: Temple University Press, 2011); Jill Nelson, ed., *Police Brutality: An Anthology* (New York: Norton, 2001); Michelle Alexander, "The New Jim Crow," *Ohio State Journal of Criminal Law* 9 (2011): 7.

51. Michelle Alexander, *The New Jim Crow: Mass Incarceration in the Age of Colorblindness* (New York: Free Press, 2010), 6.

52. Teresa McGuire, "African Antiquities Removed During Colonialism: Restoring a Stolen Cultural Legacy," *Detroit College of Law Review* (1990): 31.

53. See Ivan Van Sertima, *They Came Before Columbus* (New York: Random House, 1976); Lerone Bennett, *Before the Mayflower* (Chicago: Colchis, 2018); and Joseph H. Gaines, "An Indelible Imprint of Literacy: The Olmec and African Presence in Pre-Columbian America," *International Journal of Learning* 14, no. 4 (2007).

54. W. E. B. Du Bois, *The Comet* (New York: Graphic Arts Books, 2021), 55.

55. W. E. B. Du Bois, *The Comet* (New York: Graphic Arts Books, 2021), 55.

56. Snape, *Ancient Egyptian Tombs*.

Chapter 6

1. Juguo Zhang, *W.E.B. Du Bois: Quest for the Abolition of the Color Line* (New York: Routledge, 2001), 141.

2. Keene, "W.E.B. Du Bois and the Wounded World."

3. Frederick Douglass, *Narrative of the Life of Frederick Douglass: An American Slave, Written by Himself* (Cambridge: Harvard University Press, 2009).

4. David Levering Lewis, *W.E.B. Du Bois: Biography of a Race, 1868–1919* (New York: Henry Holt, 1993).

5. S. J. Walker, "Frederick Douglass and Woman Suffrage," *Black Scholar* 4, nos. 6–7 (1973): 24-31.

6. James Oakes, *The Radical and the Republican: Frederick Douglass, Abraham Lincoln, and the Triumph of Antislavery Politics* (New York: Norton, 2011).

7. Frederick Douglass, "The Color Line," North American Review 132, no. 295 (1881): 567–77. 573

8. Ange-Marie Hancock, "WEB Du Bois: Intellectual Forefather of Intersectionality?," *Souls* 7, nos. 3–4 (2005): 74–84.

9. W. E. B. Du Bois, *WEB Du Bois on Asia: Crossing the World Color Line*, ed. Bill V. Mullen and Cathryn Watson (Jackson: University Press of Mississippi, 2005). 212

10. W.E.B. Du Bois, *The Talented Tenth* (New York: James Pott and Company, 1903), 102–4.

11. W.E.B. Du Bois, *The Souls of Black Folk* (Chicago: A.C. McClurg, 1903).

12. Maulana Karenga, "Du Bois and the Question of the Color Line: Race and Class in the Age of Globalization," *Socialism and Democracy* 17, no. 1 (2003): 141–60. 141

13. See Michele Langfield, "The Welsh Patagonian Connection: A Neglected Chapter in Australian Immigration History," *International Migration* 36, no. 1 (1998): 67–91, and Russ Castronovo, "Beauty Along the Color Line: Lynching, Aesthetics, and the Crisis," *PMLA* 121, no. 5 (2006): 1443–46. 1443

14. W. E. B. Du Bois, *Writings* (New York: Library of America, 1986); Eric J. Sundquist, ed., *The Oxford W.E.B. Du Bois Reader* (New York: Oxford University Press, 1996); Meyer Weinberg, ed., *W.E.B. Du Bois: A Reader* (New York: Harper & Row, 1970); Philip S. Foner, ed., *W.E.B. Du Bois Speaks: Speeches and Addresses 1890–1919* (New York: Pathfinder Press, 1970).

15. Readers who are unfamiliar with the evidence of the damage that the color lie rooted in white supremacist rhetoric and logic has caused might refer to the many works referenced here: William F. Holmes, "White-Capping: Agrarian Violence in Mississippi, 1902–1906," *Journal of Southern History* 35, no. 2 (1969): 165–85; Neil R. McMillen, "The White Citizens' Council and Resistance to School Desegregation in Arkansas," *Arkansas Historical Quarterly* 30, no. 2 (1971): 95–122; Christa A. Boske, "'I Wonder if They Had Ever Seen a Black Man Before?' Grappling with Issues of Race and Racism in Our Own Backyard," *Journal of Research on Leadership Education* 5, no. 7 (2010): 248–75; Carter G. Woodson, *The Miseducation of the Negro* (New York: Penguin, [1933] 2023); Jawanza Kunjufu, *Countering the Conspiracy to Destroy Black Boys* (Chicago: African American Images, 1985); Birgit Brander Rasmussen, "'Attended with Great Inconveniences': Slave Literacy and the 1740 South Carolina Negro Act," *PMLA* 125, no. 1 (2010): 201–3; Howard N. Rabinowitz, "From Exclusion to Segregation: Southern Race Relations, 1865–1890," *Journal of American History* 63, no. 2 (1976): 325–50.

16. I. Janssen, M. Hanssen, M. Bak, R. V. Bijl, R. Graaf, W. Vollebergh, and J. Van Os, "Discrimination and Delusional Ideation," *British Journal of Psychiatry* 182, no. 1 (2003): 71–76; and Dickson D. Bruce, "WEB Du Bois and the Idea of Double Consciousness," *American Literature* 64, no. 2 (1992): 299–309. 2999

17. Bruce, "W.E.B. Du Bois and the Idea of Double Consciousness, *American Literature*, *64*(2), 299-309. 305.

18. Gikandi, "W.E.B. Du Bois and the Identity of Africa," *GEFAME Journal of African Studies* 2, no. 1 (2005); https://quod.lib.umich.edu/g/gefame/4761563.0002.101/--w-e-b-dubois-and-the-identity-of-africa?rgn=main;view=fulltext

19. Du Bois, "African Roots of War" (1915), in Weinberg, *W.E.B. Du Bois: A Reader*, 360–71. 362

20. W.E. Burghardt Du Bois, *Black Folk Then and Now: An Essay in the History and Sociology of the Negro Race* (New York: Henry Holt & Company, 1939).

21. Clarence Contee, "The Encyclopedia Africana Project of WEB Du Bois," *African Historical Studies* 4, no. 1 (1971): 77–91.

22. Contee, "Encyclopedia Africana Project of WEB Du Bois." *African Historical Studies*, *4*(1), 77-91.77

23. Christina Turner, "How Racism Pushed Tina Turner and Other Black Women Artists Out of America," *Canvas Arts*, PBS News, April 22, 2021, 1–3.

24. W. E. Burghardt Du Bois. (1944). Prospect of a World Without Race Conflict. *American Journal of Sociology*, *49*(5), 450–456. http://www.jstor.org/stable/2770481. 454,

25. W. E. B Du Bois, "What of the Color-Line? Travels in the Reich, 1933–1945," in *Travels in the Reich, 1933–1945: Foreign Authors Report from Germany*, ed. Oliver Lubrich (Chicago: University of Chicago Press, 2012), 135.

26. Johnson, L. B. (1965). Remarks of the President to a Joint Session of the Congress: The American Promise. United States: U.S. Government Printing Office, 2.

27. Fred Siegel, Stephan Thernstrom, and Robert Woodson Sr., "The Kerner Commission Report" (Washington, DC: Heritage Foundation, 1998), https://www.heritage.org/poverty-and-inequality/report/the-kerner-commission-report.

28. Linda Darling-Hammond, "The Color Line in American Education: Race, Resources, and Student Achievement," *Du Bois Review: Social Science Research on Race* 1, no. 2 (2004): 213–46. 214

29. W. E. B. Du Bois, *Dark Princess*, repr. ed. (Jackson: University of Mississippi Press, [1928] 1995). 43

30. Lewis R. Gordon, "Du Bois's Humanistic Philosophy of Human Sciences," *Annals of the American Academy of Political and Social Science* 568, no. 1 (March 2000): 265–80, 265.

31. Herman Beavers, "Romancing the Body Politic: Du Bois's Propaganda of the Dark World," *Annals of the American Academy of Political and Social Science* 568, no. 1 (March 2000): 250–64. 252

32. Mark Q. Sawyer and Tianna S. Paschel, "'We Didn't Cross the Color Line, the Color Line Crossed Us': Blackness and Immigration in the Dominican Republic, Puerto Rico, and the United States," *Du Bois Review: Social Science Research on Race* 4, no. 2 (2007): 303–15, quotation at 308.

33. Sawyer and Paschel, "'We Didn't Cross the Color Line,'" 308.

34. Adolph L. Reed Jr., *WEB Du Bois and American Political Thought: Fabianism and the Color Line* (New York: Oxford University Press, 1997), 50.

35. Tyler T. Reny and Benjamin J. Newman, "The Opinion-Mobilizing Effect of Social Protest Against Police Violence: Evidence from the 2020 George Floyd Protests," *American Political Science Review* 115, no. 4 (2021): 1499–1507, 1500.

Chapter 7

1. See the following works, for example, W. E. B. Du Bois, *The Talented Tenth* (New York: James Pott and Company, 1903), 102–4; Donna Y. Ford, Brian L. Wright, Christopher Sewell, Gilman Whiting, and James L. Moore III, "The Nouveau Talented Tenth: Envisioning W.E.B Du Bois in the Context of Contemporary Gifted and Talented Education," *Journal of Negro Education* 87, no. 3 (2018): 294–310; Dan S. Green, "W. E. B. Du Bois' Talented Tenth: A Strategy for Racial Advancement," *Journal of Negro Education* 46, no. 3 (1977): 358–66; Juan Battle and Earl Wright, "W.E.B. Du Bois's Talented Tenth: A Quantitative Assessment," *Journal of Black Studies* 32, no. 6 (2002):

654–72; and Joy James, "The Profeminist Politics of W.E.B Du Bois: With Respects to Anna Julia Cooper and Ida B. Wells Barnett," in *WEB Du Bois on Race and Culture*, by Bernard W. Bell, Emily R. Grosholz, and James B. Stewart (New York: Routledge, 2014), 141–60.

2. Asante, *Afrocentric Idea*.

3. Molefi Kete Asante, *Race, Rhetoric, and Identity: The Architecton of Soul* (Amherst, NY: Humanities Press, 2005); Molefi Kete Asante, "Racism, Consciousness, and Afrocentricity," in *The Lure and Loathing: Essays on Race, Identity, and the Ambivalence of Assimilation*, ed. G. Early (New York: Penguin, 1993), 127–43.

4. Asante, "Racism, Consciousness, and Afrocentricity."

5. Asante, "Racism, Consciousness, and Afrocentricity."

6. We are relying on these authors for our understanding of propaganda: Edward L. Bernays, *Propaganda* (New York: Ig Publishing, 2005); Jason Stanley, "The Problem of Propaganda," in Jason Stanley, *How Propaganda Works* (Princeton: Princeton University Press, 2015), 1–21; Robert Jackall, ed., *Propaganda* (New York: New York University Press, 1995); Dustin Kidd and Christina Jackson, "Art as Propaganda: Bringing Du Bois into the Sociology of Art," *Sociology Compass* 4, no. 8 (2010): 555–63.

7. Marcus Garvey, *Selected Writings and Speeches of Marcus Garvey* (New York: Courier Corporation, 1991); Judith Stein, *The World of Marcus Garvey: Race and Class in Modern Society* (Baton Rouge: Louisiana State University Press, 1991); Mark Christian, "Marcus Garvey and the Universal Negro Improvement Association (UNIA): With Special Reference to the 'Lost' Parade in Columbus, Ohio, September 25, 1923," *Western Journal of Black Studies* 28, no. 3 (2004); David Van Leeuwen, "Marcus Garvey and the Universal Negro Improvement Association," teachers service homepage (Washington, DC: National Humanities Center, October 2000).

8. Martin O. Ijere, "W.E.B. Du Bois and Marcus Garvey as Pan-Africanists: A Study in Contrast," *Présence africaine* 1 (1974): 188–206.

9. W. E. B. Du Bois to Charles Evans Hughes, U.S. Secretary of State, New York, June 23, 1921, https://www.international.ucla.edu/asc/mgpp/sample09.

10. Michael Craton, *Testing the Chains: Resistance to Slavery in the British West Indies* (Ithaca: Cornell University Press, 2009); R. B. Sheridan, *Sugar and Slavery: An Economic History of the British West Indies, 1623–1775* (Chicago: Canoe Press, 1994).

11. Kyle D. Logue, "Reparations as Redistribution," *Boston University Law Review* 84, no. 5 (2004): 1319–74; and Melvin L. Oliver and Thomas M. Shapiro, "Disrupting the Racial Wealth Gap," *Contexts* 18, no. 1 (2019): 16–21.

12. Resolutions of the Executive Committee of the Third Pan African Congress. December 1923. https://credo.library.umass.edu/view/full/mums312-b022-i417 (downloaded 12-23-24)

13. Resolutions of the Executive Committee of the Third Pan African Congress. December 1923. https://credo.library.umass.edu/view/full/mums312-b022-i417 (downloaded 12-23-24)

14. Quoted in Patrick Anderson, "Pan-Africanism and Economic Nationalism: WEB Du Bois's Black Reconstruction and the Failings of the 'Black Marxism' Thesis," *Journal of Black Studies* 48, no. 8 (2017): 732–57. 739

15. Herbert Aptheker, Ed., The Correspondence of W.E.B. Du Bois, Volume I

16. W. E. B. Du Bois, Reply to Bishop C. S. Smith, New York Age June 25, 1921

17. Jerome H. Schiele, "Organizational Theory from an Afrocentric Perspective," *Journal of Black Studies* 21, no. 2 (1990): 145–61; Jerome H. Schiele, "An Afrocentric Perspective on Social Welfare Philosophy and Policy," *Journal of Sociology & Social Welfare* 24, no. 2 (1997): 21.

18. Robert Chrisman and Nathan Hare, *Contemporary Black Thought: The Best from the Black Scholar* (Indianapolis: Bobbs-Merrill, 1973).

19. Stephen R. Weissman, "What Really Happened in Congo: The CIA, the Murder of Lumumba, and the Rise of Mobutu," *Foreign Affairs* 93, no. 4 (July/August 2014): 14–24; Georges Nzongola-Ntalaja, *Patrice Lumumba* (Columbus: Ohio University Press, 2014).

20. M. W. Kodi, "The 1921 Pan-African Congress at Brussels: A Background to Belgian Pressures," *Transafrican Journal of History* 13 (1984): 48–73, 48.

21. Omarosa Manigault Newman, *Unhinged: An Insider's Account of the Trump White House* (New York: Simon and Schuster, 2018); Jeff Weiss and Evan McGarvey, *2pac vs. Biggie: An Illustrated History of Rap's Greatest Battle* (New York: Voyageur Press, 2013).

22. Eliott M. Rudwick, "Du Bois Versus Garvey: Race Propagandists at War," *Journal of Negro Education* 28, no. 4 (Autumn 1959): 421–29.

23. W. E. B. Du Bois, "Of Mr. Booker T. Washington and Others," in *The Souls of Black Folk*, with introduction by Manning Marable (New York: Routledge, 2015), 23-32, http://sageamericanhistory.net/reconstruction/documents/duboisonbtw.html (downloaded 12-23-24)

24. Nasar Meer, "WEB Du Bois, Double Consciousness, and the 'Spirit' of Recognition," *Sociological Review* 67, no. 1 (2019): 47–62.

25. Stokely Carmichael, *Stokely Speaks: From Black Power to Pan-Africanism* (Chicago: Chicago Review Press, 2007); Robert F. Williams, *Negroes with Guns*, ed. Marc Schleifer (Mansfield Center, CT: Martino Publishing, [1962] 2013), 39; James Baldwin, *Conversations with James Baldwin* (Jackson: University Press of Mississippi, 1989); and Mary L. Dudziak, *Exporting American Dreams: Thurgood Marshall's African Journey* (Princeton: Princeton University Press, 2011).

26. Donald J. Trump and Tony Schwartz, *Trump: The Art of the Deal* (New York: Ballantine Books, 2009).

27. Richard Gibson, *African Liberation Movements: Contemporary Struggles Against White Minority Rule* (Oxford: Oxford University Press, 1972).

28. George Padmore, *Pan-Africanism or Communism* (New York: Doubleday, 1971), 94.

29. W.E.B. Du Bois, "Returning Soldiers," *The Crisis*, July 1918, editorial.

30. Manning Marable, *W.E.B. Du Bois: Black Radical Democrat* (Woodbridge, CT: Twayne, 1986), 99.

31. Du Bois, W. E. B. (1940). *Dusk of Dawn: An Essay Toward an Autobiography of a Race Concept. With a Tribute to Dr. Du Bois*. Kraus-Thomson Organization Limited, 218

32. Du Bois, W. E. B. (2014). *The World and Africa and Color and Democracy (The Oxford WEB Du Bois)* (Vol. 9). Oxford University Press

33. See also Du Bois, " Negro and Communism"; Saman, "Du Bois and Marx."

34. Du Bois, "Address to the Country," delivered at the second annual meeting of the Niagara Movement, Harpers Ferry, West Virginia, August 19, 1906, *The Broad Ax* 11, no. 44 (August 25, 1906): 1, available online at the Library of Congress: https://chroniclingamerica.loc.gov/lccn/sn84024055/1906-08-25/ed-1/seq-1.pdf.

35. Robert Chrisman, "Black Studies, the Talented Tenth, and the Organic Intellectual," *Black Scholar* 43, no. 3 (2013): 64–70; Daryl Zizwe Poe, *Kwame Nkrumah's Contribution to Pan-African Agency: An Afrocentric Analysis* (New York: Routledge, 2004); W. E. B. Du Bois, "Marxism and the Negro Problem," in *Capitalism vs. Collectivism: The Colonial Era to 1945*, ed. M. Pohlmann (New York: Routledge, 2003), 223–30.

36. Harald Bauder and Salvatore Engel-Di Mauro, eds., *Critical Geographies: A Collection of Readings* (Praxis ePress, 2008), 284.

37. W. E. B. Du Bois, "Returning Soldiers," The Crisis 18 (May 1919), 13.

Chapter 8

1. Molefi Kete Asante, *The Pyramids of Knowledge* (New York: Universal Write Publications, 2020).

2. Martin Luther King, A. Philip Randolph, Roger Wilkins, Anna Arnold Hedgeman, Norman Hill, March on Washington for Jobs and Freedom, *Speech at the Lincoln Memorial, Washington, DC*, 1963, August 28. Stanford University Martin Luther King, Jr. Research and Education Center, King Papers.

3. John Hope Franklin, *The Color Line: Legacy of the Twenty-First Century* (Columbia: University of Missouri Press, 1993).

4. Molefi Kete Asante, "Afrocentricity, Race, and Reason," in *Dispatches from the Ebony Tower: Intellectuals Confront the African American Experience*, ed. Manning Marable (New York: Columbia University Press, 2000); see also Molefi Asante, "Analytic Afrocentricity," *Current Perspectives in Social Theory* 22 (2003).

5. W. E. B. Du Bois, *The Education of Black People: Ten Critiques, 1906–1960* (New York: New York University Press, 2001).

6. Acheompong Frank and Kwaku Bright Amevor, "The Impacts of Microfinance on the Entrepreneurial Activities of Artisans at Abossey Okai in Accra," *Research Journal of Commerce and Behavioral Science* 5, no. 1 (2015): 116–23.

7. Rudwick, "Du Bois Versus Garvey: Race Propagandists at War."

8. Charles K. Ross, *Outside the Lines: African Americans and the Integration of the National Football League* (New York: New York University Press, 2000).

9. Mel King, *Chain of Change: Struggles for Black Community Development* (New York: South End Press, 1981).

10. George C. Chalou, ed., *The Secrets War: The Office of Strategic Services in World War II* (Washington, DC: National Archives and Records Administration, 1992).

11. See W. E. B. Du Bois, *The Souls of Black Folk: Essays and Sketches* (Chicago: McClurg, 1903); Stephanie J. Shaw, *W. E. B. Du Bois and the Souls of Black Folk* (Chapel Hill: University of North Carolina Press, 2013).

12. James L. Conyers Jr., ed., *Afrocentric Traditions*, vol. 1 (Piscataway, NJ: Transaction, 2011).

13. Conyers, *Afrocentric Traditions*.

14. Richard C. Rath, "Echo and Narcissus: The Afrocentric Pragmatism of W. E. B. Du Bois." *Journal of American History* 84, no. 2 (September 1997): 461–95; quote at 461.

15. Victor Molobi, "Ancestral Veneration of the Core of African Spiritual Renewal Among the AICs in South Africa," *Studia Historiae Ecclesiasticae* 31, no. 1 (2005): 111–26; Michael E. Nowlin, "To Wake the Nations: Race in the Making of American Literature by Eric J. Sundquist," *Canadian Review of American Studies* 24, no. 1 (1994): 128–31.

16. See Karl Marx, *Karl Marx: A Reader*, ed. Jon Elster (Cambridge: Cambridge University Press, 1986).

17. See the various discussions and depictions of Du Bois in this wide variety of writings: Steve Valocchi, "The Emergence of the Integrationist Ideology in the Civil Rights Movement," *Social Problems* 43, no. 1 (1996): 116–30; Brandon Kendhammer, "Du Bois the Pan-Africanist and the Development of African Nationalism," *Ethnic and Racial Studies* 30, no. 1 (2007): 51–71; Robert Stern, *Hegelian Metaphysics* (New York: Oxford University Press, 2009); R. W. Williams, "The Early Social Science of WEB Du Bois," *Du Bois Review: Social Science Research on Race* 3, no. 2 (2006): 365–94; Ralph W. Hood Jr., "Study of Mysticism," in *Where God and Science Meet: How Brain and Evolutionary Studies Alter Our Understanding of Religion*, by Patrick McNamara (Westport, CT: Praeger, 2006), 119; Richard Handler, "Boasian Anthropology and the Critique of American Culture," *American Quarterly* 42, no. 2 (1990): 252–73; Du Bois, "Negro and Communism"; Lauren Cameron, "Spencerian Evolutionary Psychology in *Daniel Deronda*," *Victorian Literature and Culture* 43, no. 1 (2015): 63–81; Reiland Rabaka, "WEB Du Bois and/as Africana Critical Theory: Pan-Africanism, Critical

Marxism, and Male-Feminism," *Africa and the Academy: Essays on Theory and Practice*, ed. J. L. Conyers (Jefferson, NC: McFarland, 2003): 67–112; Juguo Zhang, *WEB Du Bois: The Quest for the Abolition of the Color Line* (New York: Routledge, 2001); Madhumita Lahiri, "World Romance: Genre, Internationalism, and WEB Du Bois," *Callaloo* 33, no. 2 (2010): 537–52; Morris, *Scholar Denied* ; Jack Katz, "On Becoming an Ethnographer," *Journal of Contemporary Ethnography* 48, no. 1 (2019): 16–50; Gary Herstein, "The Roycean Roots of the Beloved Community," *Pluralist* 4, no. 2 (2009): 91–107.

18. Rath, "Echo and Narcissus," 462.

19. W. E. B. Du Bois, *Souls of Black Folk*, introduction by Manning Marable (New York: Routledge, 2015).

20. Max Weber, *Max Weber: A Biography* (New York: Routledge, 2017).

21. Max Weber to W. E. B. Du Bois, November 17, 1904, in N. D. Chandler, "The Possible Form of an Interlocution: WEB Du Bois and Max Weber in Correspondence, 1904–1905," *CR: New Centennial Review* 6, no. 3 (2006): 193–239,198

22. W. E. B. Du Bois, "*Die Negerfra Vereinigten Staaten*," in Nahum Dimitri Chandler, "WEB Du Bois and Max Weber in Correspondence, 1904–1905," *CR: New Centennial Review* 6, no. 3 (2006): 193–239. 193

23. Max Weber to W. E. B. Du Bois, November 17, 1904, in Nahum Dimitri Chandler, "The Possible Form of an Interlocution: WEB Du Bois and Max Weber in Correspondence, 1904–1905," *CR: New Centennial Review* 6, no. 3 (2006): 193–239, 196.

24. Asante, *Afrocentric Idea*.

25. Eric Porter, *The Problem of the Future World: W. E. B. Du Bois and the Race Concept at Midcentury* (Durham: Duke University Press, 2010), 22.

26. Frederick Douglass "The Color Line," *North American Review* 132, no. 295 (1881): 567–77. 573

27. W. E. B. Du Bois, "The Economic Future of the Negro," *Publications of the American Economic Association* 7, no. 1 (1906): 219–42, 219.

28. W. E. B. Du Bois, *The Problem of the Color Line at the Turn of the Twentieth Century: The Essential Early Essays*, ed. Nahum Dimitri Chandler (New York: Fordham University Press, 2020). Originally published in *The Crisis* 32 (October 1926): 290–97.

29. Michael Burawoy, "Decolonizing Sociology: The Significance of WEB Du Bois," *Critical Sociology* 47, nos. 4–5 (2021): 545–554., 546.

30. Porter, *Problem of the Future World*, 22.

31. Du Bois, *Problem of the Color Line.*, 62.

32. Battle, J. & Wright, E. (2002). WEB Du Bois's talented tenth: a quantitative assessment. Journal of Black Studies, 32(6), 654-672, 656.

Bibliography

Agbeyebiawo, Daniel. *The Life and Works of W.E.B. Du Bois.* Accra, Ghana: W.E.B. Du Bois Center, 1998.

Alexander, Michelle. "The New Jim Crow." *Ohio State Journal of Criminal Law* 9 (2011).

Alexander, Michelle. *The New Jim Crow: Mass Incarceration in the Age of Colorblindness.* New York: Free Press, 2010.

Anderson, Patrick. "Pan-Africanism and Economic Nationalism: W. E. B. Du Bois's *Black Reconstruction* and the Failings of the 'Black Marxism' Thesis." *Journal of Black Studies* 48, no. 8 (2017): 732–57.

Anderson, Reynaldo. "Future Movements: Black Lives, Black Politics, Black Futures — An Introduction." *TOPIA: Canadian Journal of Cultural Studies* 39 (2018): 5–21.

Anderson, Reynaldo, and Clinton R. Fluker. *The Black Speculative Arts Movement: Black Futurity, Art+Design.* New York: Lexington Books, 2019.

Anderson, Reynaldo, and Charles E. Jones, eds. *Afrofuturism 2.0: The Rise of Astro-Blackness.* New York: Lexington Books, 2017.

Aptheker, Herbert, ed. *Against Racism: Unpublished Essays, Papers, Addresses (1887–1961) of W.E.B. Du Bois.* Boston: University of Massachusetts Press, 1985.

Armstrong, Amaryah Shaye. "The Apocalyptic Theology of WEB Du Bois: Black Culture at the End of the World." *Black Theology* 20, no. 1 (2022): 25–40.

Asante, Molefi Kete. *The Afrocentric Idea.* Rev. ed. Philadelphia: Temple University Press, 1998.

Asante, Molefi Kete. "The Afrocentric Idea in Education." *Journal of Negro Education* 60, no. 2 (1991): 170–80.

Asante, Molefi Kete. "Afrocentricity, Race, and Reason." In *Dispatches from the Ebony Tower: Intellectuals Confront the African American Experience*, edited by Manning Marable. New York: Columbia University Press, 2000.

Asante, Molefi Kete. *Afrocentricity: The Theory of Social Change.* Chicago: African American Images, 2003.

Asante, Molefi Kete. *An Afrocentric Manifesto: Toward an African Renaissance.* Cambridge: Polity, 2007.

Asante, Molefi Kete. *Race, Rhetoric, and Identity: The Architecton of Soul.* Amherst, NY: Humanities Press, 2005.

Asante, Molefi Kete. "Racism, Consciousness, and Afrocentricity." In *Lure and Loathing: Essays on Race, Identity, and the Ambivalence of Assimilation*, edited by Gerald Early, 127–43. New York: Penguin, 1993.

Asante, Molefi Kete, and Nah Dove. *Being Human Being: Transforming the Race Discourse.* New York: Universal Write Publications, 2021.

Bacote, Clarence Albert. *The Story of Atlanta University, A Century of Service, 1865–1965*. Atlanta: Atlanta University Publications, 1969.

Baldwin, Christopher Columbus. *Diary of Christopher Columbus Baldwin*. Worcester, MA: American Antiquarian Society, 1901.

Bauder, Harald, and Salvatore Engel-Di Mauro, eds. *Critical Geographies: A Collection of Readings*. Praxis (e)Press, 2008.

Beavers, Herman. "Romancing the Body Politic: Du Bois's Propaganda of the Dark World." *Annals of the American Academy of Political and Social Science* 568, no. 1 (March 2000): 250–64.

Bell, Bernard W., Emily R. Grosholz, and James B. Stewart. *W.E.B. Du Bois on Race and Culture*. New York: Routledge, 2014.

Bennett, Lerone. *Before the Mayflower*. Chicago: Colchis, 2018.

Bernal, Martin. *Black Athena: The Afroasiatic Roots of Classical Civilization*. Vol. 1, *The Fabrication of Ancient Greece 1785–1985*. New Brunswick, NJ: Rutgers University Press, 2020.

Bernasconi, Robert, and Anika Maaza Mann. "The Contradictions of Racism: Locke, Slavery, and the Two Treatises." In *Race and Racism in Modern Philosophy*, edited by Andrew Valls, 89–107. Ithaca: Cornell University Press, 2005.

Bernstein, J. M. *The Fate of Art: Aesthetic Alienation from Kant to Derrida and Adorno*. College Station: Penn State University Press, 1991.

Bourland, W. Ian. "Afronauts: Race in Space." *Third Text* 34, no. 2 (2020): 209–29.

Browder, Anthony T. *Nile Valley Contributions to Civilization: Exploding the Myths*. Vol. 1. Washington, DC: Institute of Karmic Guidance, 1992.

Bruce, Dickson D. "W. E. B. Du Bois and the Idea of Double Consciousness." *American Literature* 64, no. 2 (1992): 299–309.

Burawoy, Michael. "Decolonizing Sociology: The Significance of WEB Du Bois." *Critical Sociology* 47, nos. 4–5 (2021): 545–54.

Butler, Octavia E. *Bloodchild and Other Stories*. New York: Seven Stories Press, 2011.

Castronovo, Russ. "Beauty Along the Color Line: Lynching, Aesthetics, and the Crisis." *PMLA* 121, no. 5 (2006): 1443–59.

Chalou, George C., ed. *The Secrets War: The Office of Strategic Services in World War II*. Washington, DC: National Archives and Records Administration, 1992.

Chandler, Nahum Dimitri. "The Possible Form of an Interlocution: W. E. B. Du Bois and Max Weber in Correspondence, 1904–1905." *CR: The New Centennial Review* 6, no. 3 (2006): 193–239.

Chrisman, Robert, and Nathan Hare. *Contemporary Black Thought: The Best from the Black Scholar*. Indianapolis: Bobbs-Merrill, 1973.

Christian, Mark. "Marcus Garvey and the Universal Negro Improvement Association (UNIA): With Special Reference to the 'Lost' Parade in Columbus, Ohio, September 25, 1923." *Western Journal of Black Studies* 28, no. 3 (2004).

Clarke, John Henrik. "Africa and the American Negro Press." *Journal of Negro Education* 30, no. 1 (1961): 64–68.

Clarke, John Henrik. *My Life in Search of Africa*. Chicago: Third World Press, 1999.

Conyers, James L., Jr., ed. *Afrocentric Traditions*. Vol. 1. Piscataway, NJ: Transaction Publishers, 2011.

Craton, Michael. *Testing the Chains: Resistance to Slavery in the British West Indies*. Ithaca: Cornell University Press, 2009.

Darling-Hammond, Linda. "The Color Line in American Education: Race, Resources, and Student Achievement." *Du Bois Review: Social Science Research on Race* 1, no. 2 (2004): 213–46.

Davidson, Joe P. L. "Ugly Progress: W. E. B. Du Bois's Sociology of the Future." *Sociological Review* 69, no. 2 (2021): 382–95.

Dery, Mark. *Escape Velocity: Cyberculture at the End of the Century*. New York: Grove Press, 1997.

Diop, Cheikh Anta. *The African Origin of Civilization: Myth or Reality*. Edited and translated by Mercer Cook. Chicago: Chicago Review Press, 2012.

Douglass, Frederick. *Narrative of the Life of Frederick Douglass: An American Slave, Written by Himself*. Cambridge: Harvard University Press, 2009.

Dove, Nah. "The Emergence of Black Supplementary Schools: Resistance to Racism in the United Kingdom." *Urban Education* 27, no. 4 (1993): 430–47.

Dow, George Francis. *Slave Ships and Slaving*. Mineola, NY: Dover, 2002.

Du Bois, W. E. B. "The African Roots of War." *The Atlantic*, May 1915.

Du Bois, W. E. B. *The Autobiography of W. E. B. Du Bois: A Soliloquy on Viewing My Life from the Last Decade of Its First Century*. New York: International Publishers, 1968.

Du Bois, W. E. Burghardt. *Black Folk Then and Now: An Essay in the History and Sociology of the Negro Race*. New York: Henry Holt & Company, 1939.

Du Bois, W. E. B. *Black Reconstruction in America, 1860–1880*. New York: Harcourt and Brace, 1935.

Du Bois, W. E. B. *Dark Princess*. Repr. ed. Jackson: University of Mississippi Press, (1928) 1995.

Du Bois, W. E. B. *Darkwater: The Givens Collection*. New York: Washington Square Press, 2004.

Du Bois, W. E. B. *Darkwater: Voices from Within the Veil*. Rahway, NJ: Harcourt, Brace and Howe, 1920.

Du Bois, W. E. B. *Dusk of Dawn: An Essay Toward an Autobiography of a Race Concept*. New York: Schocken, 1940.

Du Bois, W. E. B. "The Economic Future of the Negro." *Publications of the American Economic Association* 7, no. 1 (1906): 219–42.

Du Bois, W. E. B. "The Negro and Communism." In *Capitalism vs. Collectivism: The Colonial Era to 1945*, edited by M. Pohlmann. New York: Routledge, 2013.

Du Bois, W. E. B. "A Negro Student at Harvard at the End of the 19th Century." *Massachusetts Review* 1 (Spring 1960): 455.

Du Bois, W. E. B. *The Ordeal of Mansart*. New York: Oxford University Press, (1957) 2014.

Du Bois, W. E. B. *The Philadelphia Negro: A Social Study and History of Pennsylvania's Black American Population, Their Education, Environment and Work*. New York: Pantianos, 1899.

Du Bois, W. E. B. *The Problem of the Color Line at the Turn of the Twentieth Century: The Essential Early Essays*. Edited by Nahum Dimitri Chandler. New York: Fordham University Press, 2020. Originally published in *The Crisis* 32 (October 1926): 290–97.

Du Bois, W. E. B. *The Souls of Black Folk*. New York: Oxford University Press, 2008.

Du Bois, W. E. B. "The Talented Tenth Memorial Address." In *The Future of the Race*, edited by Henry Louis Gates Jr. and Cornel West. New York: Knopf, 1996.

Du Bois, W. E. B. "To the Nations of the World." Quoted in Alexander Walters, *My Life and Work*, 257–60. New York: Fleming H. Revell, 1917.

Du Bois, W. E. B. "The Twelfth Census and the Negro Problems." *The Southern Workman* 29, no. 5 (May 1900): 305–9.

Du Bois, W. E. B. "What of the Color-Line? Travels in the Reich, 1933–1945." In *Travels in the Reich, 1933–1945: Foreign Authors Report from Germany*, ed. Oliver Lubrich. Chicago: University of Chicago Press, 2012.

Elia, Adriano. "W. E. B. Du Bois's Proto-Afrofuturist Short Fiction: 'The Comet.'" *Il Tolomeo* 18 (2016): 173–86. https://edizionicafoscari.unive.it/media/pdf/article/il-tolomeo/2016/18/art-10.14277-2499-5975-Tol-18-16-12.pdf.

Ellison, Ralph. *Invisible Man*. New York: Penguin, 2016.

Forman, James. *Self-Determination and the African American People*. Seattle: Open Hand Publishing, 1981.

Franklin, John Hope. *The Color Line: Legacy of the Twenty-First Century*. Columbia: University of Missouri Press, 1993.

Gaines, Joseph H. "An Indelible Imprint of Literacy: The Olmec and African Presence in Pre-Columbian America." *International Journal of Learning* 14, no. 4 (2007).

Gibson, Richard. *African Liberation Movements: Contemporary Struggles against White Minority Rule*. Oxford: Oxford University Press, 1972.

Gordon, Lewis R. "Du Bois's Humanistic Philosophy of Human Sciences." *Annals of the American Academy of Political and Social Science* 568, no. 1 (March 2000): 265–80.

Grossman, Jonathan. "Black Studies in the Department of Labor, 1897–1907." *Monthly Labor Review* (June 1974): 12. https://www.dol.gov/general/aboutdol/history/blackstudiestext.

Guglieimo, Jennifer, and Salvatore Salerno. *Are Italians White? How Race Is Made in America*. New York: Routledge, 2004.

Handler, Richard. "Boasian Anthropology and the Critique of American Culture." *American Quarterly* 42, no. 2 (1990): 252–73.

Hood, R. W., Jr. "Study of Mysticism." In *Where God and Science Meet: How Brain and Evolutionary Studies Alter Our Understanding of Religion.* Praeger, 2006.

Hopkinson, Nalo. *Brown Girl in the Ring.* Aspect, 2001.

Hume, David. "Part I, Essay XXI: Of National Characters." In *The Philosophical Works of David Hume, including all the Essays, and Exhibiting the More Important Alterations and Corrections in the Successive Editions Published by the Author: Essays, Moral, Political, and Literary,* vol. 3, 217–36, 228–29. Edinburgh: Adam and Charles Black; Boston: Little, Brown and Company, 1854.

Ijere, Martin O. "W.E.B. Du Bois and Marcus Garvey as Pan-Africanists: A Study in Contrast." *Présence africaine* 1 (1974): 188–206.

Itzigsohn, José, and Karida L. Brown. "The Sociology of WEB Du Bois." In *The Sociology of W. E. B. Du Bois: Racialized Modernity and the Global Color Line.* New York: New York University Press, 2020.

Jaima, Amir. "Historical Fiction as Sociological Interpretation and Philosophy." *Transaction* 53, no. 4 (2017).

James, Joy. "The Profeminist Politics of W.E.B Du Bois: With Respects to Anna Julia Cooper and Ida B. Wells Barnett." In *WEB Du Bois on Race and Culture,* edited by Bernard W. Bell, Emily R. Grosholz, and James B. Stewart, 141–60. New York: Routledge, 2014.

Jefferson, Thomas. *Notes on Virginia.* 1834.

Karenga, Maulana. *Introduction to Black Studies.* Los Angeles: University of Sankore Press, 1993.

Katz, Jack. "On Becoming an Ethnographer." *Journal of Contemporary Ethnography* 48, no. 1 (2019): 16–50.

Keene, Jennifer D. "W. E. B. Du Bois and the Wounded World: Seeking Meaning in the First World War for African Americans." *Peace and Change* 26, no. 2 (2001): 135–52.

Kendi, Ibram X. *How to Be an Anti-Racist.* New York. One World, 2019.

Kidd, Dustin, and Christina Jackson. "Art as Propaganda: Bringing Du Bois into the Sociology of Art." *Sociology Compass* 4, no. 8 (2010): 555–63.

King, Mel. *Chain of Change: Struggles for Black Community Development.* Boston: South End Press, 1981.

Kodi, M. W. "The 1921 Pan-African Congress at Brussels: A Background to Belgian Pressures." *Transafrican Journal of History* 13 (1984): 48–73.

Kunjufu, Jawanza. *Countering the Conspiracy to Destroy Black Boys.* Chicago: African American Images, 1985.

Langfield, Michele. "The Welsh Patagonian Connection: A Neglected Chapter in Australian Immigration History." *International Migration* 36, no. 1 (1998): 67–91.

Lavender, Isiah, III, ed. *Black and Brown Planets: The Politics of Race in Science Fiction.* Jackson: University Press of Mississippi, 2014.

Lewis, David Levering. *W.E.B. Du Bois: Biography of a Race, 1868–1919*. New York: Henry Holt, 1993.

Logan, John R., and Mark Schneider. "Racial Segregation and Racial Change in American Suburbs, 1970–1980." *American Journal of Sociology* 89, no. 4 (1984): 874–88.

Lowrie, Donald. *My Life in Prison*. Createspace Independent Publishing Platform, 1912.

Marable, Manning. "A Conversation with John Hope Franklin." *Souls* (Summer 1999): 73–87.

Marable, Manning. *W.E.B. Du Bois: Black Radical Democrat*. Woodbridge, CT: Twayne, 1986.

Meer, Nasar. "W. E. B. Du Bois, Double Consciousness and the 'Spirit' of Recognition." *Sociological Review* 67, no. 1 (2019): 47–62.

Miller, Kelly. "The Education of the Negro." *U.S. Dept. of Interior Annual Report, FY Ending 1901; Report of the Commissioner of Education, vol. 1*, chapter 16. Washington, DC: Government Printing Office, 1902.

Molobi, Victor. "Ancestral Veneration of the Core of African Spiritual Renewal among the AICs in South Africa." *Studia Historiae Ecclesiasticae* 31, no. 1 (2005): 111–26.

Moore, B. Sharise. "Alla Our Stuff." *Journal of Pan African Studies* 4, no. 2 (2010): 415–19.

Morehouse, Henry Lyman. "The Talented Tenth." *American Missionary* 50, no. 6 (June 1896).

Morris, Aldon D. *The Scholar Denied: W.E.B. Du Bois and the Birth of Modern Sociology*. Berkeley: University of California Press, 2017.

Mullen, Bill V. "W. E. B. Du Bois Was the Father of Pan African Socialism." *Jacobin*, May 2, 2022.

Muller, Christopher. "Freedom and Convict Leasing in the Postbellum South." *American Journal of Sociology* 124, no. 2 (2018): 367–405.

Murphy, Michael. "Climate Change and the Color Line." *Class, Race, and Corporate Power* 1, no. 1 (2013).

Newman, Omarosa Manigault. *Unhinged: An Insider's Account of the Trump White House*. New York: Simon and Schuster, 2018.

Nzongola-Ntalaja, Georges. *Patrice Lumumba*. Columbus: Ohio University Press, 2014.

Okorafor, Nnedi. "Organic Fantasy." *African Identities* 7, no. 2 (2009): 275–86.

Omi, Michael, and Howard Winant. *Racial Formation in the United States*. New York: Routledge, 2014.

Padmore, George. *Pan-Africanism or Communism*. New York: Doubleday, 1971.

Petrie, William Matthew Flinders. *Letter from Sir William Matthew Flinders Petrie to W.E.B. Du Bois*. New York: Crisis Publishing, 1912.

Pinn, Anthony B. "Reading Du Bois Through Religion and Religious Commitment." *Journal of Religion* 94, no. 3 (2014): 370–82.

Porter, Eric. *The Problem of the Future World: W. E. B. Du Bois and the Race Concept at Midcentury*. Durham: Duke University Press, 2010.

Rabaka, Reiland. *Du Bois Dialectics: Black Radical Politics and the Reconstruction of Critical Social Theory*. New York: Lexington Books, 2008.
Rabaka, Reiland. "W.E.B. Du Bois and/as Africana Critical Theory: Pan-Africanism, Critical Marxism, and Male-Feminism." In *Africa and the Academy: Essays on Theory and Practice*, edited by James L. Conyers, 67–112. Jefferson, NC: McFarland, 2003.
Rabaka, Reiland. *W. E. B. Du Bois and the Problems of the Twenty-First Century: An Essay on Africana Critical Theory*. New York: Lexington Books, 2007.
Rabaka, Reiland. "W. E. B. DuBois's 'The Comet' and Contributions to Critical Race Theory: An Essay on Black Radical Politics and Anti-Racist Social Ethics." *Ethnic Studies Review* 29, no. 1 (2006): 22–48.
Rambsy, Howard. "Beyond Keeping It Real: OutKast, the Funk Connection, and Afrofuturism." *American Studies* 52, no. 4 (2013): 205–16.
Raper, Arthur F. *The Tragedy of Lynching*. Chapel Hill: University of North Carolina Press, (1933) 2017.
Rath, Richard C. "Echo and Narcissus: The Afrocentric Pragmatism of W. E. B. Du Bois." *Journal of American History* 84, no. 2 (September 1997): 461–95.
Rediker, Marcus. *The Slave Ship: A Human History*. New York: Penguin, 2008.
Reed, Adolph L., Jr. *W. E. B. Du Bois and American Political Thought: Fabianism and the Color Line*. New York: Oxford University Press, 1997.
Reed, Ismael. *Yellow Back Radio Broke-Down*. Dallas: Dalkey Archive Press, 2022.
Reid-Merritt, Patricia. *A State-by-State History of Race and Racism in the United States*. New York: Praeger, 2017.
Reviere, Ruth. "Toward an Afrocentric Research Methodology," *Journal of Black Studies* 31, no. 6 (2001): 709–28.
Robinson, Cedric. *Black Marxism: The Making of the Black Radical Tradition*. Chapel Hill: University of North Carolina Press, 2000.
Ross, Charles K. *Outside the Lines: African Americans and the Integration of the National Football League*. New York: New York University Press, 2000.
Rudwick, Elliott M. "Du Bois Versus Garvey: Race Propagandists at War." *Journal of Negro Education* 28, no. 4 (Autumn 1959): 421–29.
Saman, Michael J. "Du Bois and Marx, Du Bois and Marxism." *Du Bois Review: Social Science Research on Race* 17, no. 1 (2020): 33–54.
Sawyer, Mark Q., and Tianna S. Paschel. "'We Didn't Cross the Color Line, the Color Line Crossed Us': Blackness and Immigration in the Dominican Republic, Puerto Rico, and the United States." *Du Bois Review: Social Science Research on Race* 4, no. 2 (2007): 303–15.
Schiele, Jerome H. "An Afrocentric Perspective on Social Welfare Philosophy and Policy." *Journal of Sociology & Social Welfare* 24, no. 2 (1997).
Schiele, Jerome. "Organizational Theory from an Afrocentric Perspective." *Journal of Black Studies* 21, no. 2 (1990): 145–61.
Serequeberhan, Tsenay. *The Hermeneutics of African Philosophy: Horizon and Discourse*. London: Routledge, 1994.

Sheridan, Richard B. *Sugar and Slavery: An Economic History of the British West Indies, 1623–1775*. Chicago: Canoe Press, 1994.

Siegel, Fred, Stephan Thernstrom, and Robert Woodson Sr. "The Kerner Commission Report." Washington, DC: Heritage Foundation, 1998. https://www.heritage.org/poverty-and-inequality/report/the-kerner-commission-report.

Smith, Aaron X., ed. *Afrocentricity in AfroFuturism: Towards Afrocentric Futurism*. Jackson: University Press of Mississippi, 2023.

Smith, Darryl A. "Droppin' Science Fiction: Signification and Singularity in the Metapocalypse of Du Bois, Baraka, and Bell." *Science Fiction Studies* 34, no. 102 (2007): 201–19.

Snape, Steven. *Ancient Egyptian Tombs: The Culture of Life and Death*. New York: Wiley-Blackwell, 2011.

Squires, Gregory D., ed. *Redlining to Reinvestment*. Philadelphia: Temple University Press, 2011.

Sundquist, Eric J., ed. *The Oxford W. E. B. Du Bois Reader*. New York: Oxford University Press, 1996.

Szwed, John F. *Space Is the Place: The Lives and Times of Sun Ra*. Durham: Duke University Press, 2020.

Thomas, Sheree Renée, ed. *Dark Matter: A Century of Speculative Fiction from the African Diaspora*. London: Hachette, 2014.

Tillotson, Michael. *Invisible Jim Crow: Contemporary Ideological Threats to the Internal Security of African Americans*. Trenton, NJ: Africa World Press, 2011.

Turner, Christina. "How Racism Pushed Tina Turner and Other Black Women Artists Out of America." *Canvas Arts*, PBS News, April 22, 2021, 1–3.

Van Dyk, Sandra. "Molefi Kete Asante's Theory of Afrocentricity: The Development of a Theory of Cultural Location." PhD diss., Temple University, 1998.

Van Sertima, Ivan. "Death Shall Not Find Us Thinking That We Die." *Présence Africaine*, n.s., nos. 149–50 (1989): 321–30.

Van Sertima, Ivan. *They Came Before Columbus*. New York: Random House, 1976.

Vansina, Jan. "A Comparison of African Kingdoms." *Africa* 32, no. 4 (1962): 324–35.

Walker, S. J. "Frederick Douglass and Woman Suffrage." *Black Scholar* 4, nos. 6–7 (1973): 24–31.

Washington, Booker T. "Atlanta Compromise Speech." 1895. In *Encyclopedia of Race and Racism*, by Patrick L. Mason, 280–82. New York: Macmillan, 2013.

Washington, Booker. T. "The Atlanta Exposition Address, 1895." In *The Booker T. Washington Papers*, edited by Louis R. Harlan, vol. 3, 583–87. Urbana: University of Illinois Press, 1974.

Weinberg, Meyer, ed. *W.E.B. Du Bois: A Reader*. New York: Harper & Row, 1970.

Weiss, Jeff, and Evan McGarvey. *2pac vs. Biggie: An Illustrated History of Rap's Greatest Battle*. New York: Voyageur Press, 2013.

Weissman, Stephen R. "What Really Happened in Congo: The CIA, the Murder of Lumumba, and the Rise of Mobutu." *Foreign Affairs* 93, no. 4 (July/August 2014): 14–24.

Williams, Chad L. *The Wounded World: W.E.B. Du Bois and the First World War*. New York: Macmillan, 2023.

Williams, Chancellor. *Destruction of Black Civilization: Great Issues of a Race from 4500 BC to 2000 AD*. Morrisville, NC: Lulu Press, 2020.

Williams, Robert. "The Early Social Science of WEB Du Bois." *Du Bois Review: Social Science Research on Race* 3, no. 2 (2006): 365–94.

Wilson, William Julius. *The Declining Significance of Race*. Chicago: University of Chicago Press, 2012.

Womack, Ytasha L. *Afrofuturism: The World of Black Sci-Fi and Fantasy Culture*. Chicago: Chicago Review Press, 2013.

Yaszek, Lisa. "Afrofuturism, Science Fiction, and the History of the Future." *Socialism and Democracy* 20, no. 3 (2006): 41–60.

Zhang, Juguo. *W.E.B. Du Bois: The Quest for the Abolition of the Color Line*. New York: Routledge, 2001.

Index

activism/activists, 11, 16, 19, 20–22, 24, 37, 49, 51–53, 87, 98
affirmative action, 84
Africa/African culture: African agency, 20, 27, 57, 58, 59, 89–90, 99–102, 105, 112–13; Afrocentric Futurism, 61; Afrocentricity, 59–60; classical Africa, 25–26; Du Boisian legacy, 104; Du Bois's conception of, 6; Pan African movement, 13; relocations, 80–82, 97–98; socialism and the masses, 47–56; and the South, 5–6
African Americans: Afrocentricity, 59; agency, 6, 63; black organizations, 104–5; color line, 22, 37, 57, 75–87, 92, 95, 101, 110, 114; Committee of Twelve, 35–37; cultural and socioeconomic shifts, 109–14; democratic revolution, 47; double consciousness, 18–19, 90; economic situation of, 29–30, 111; equality for, 11, 13; farmers or farm laborers, 36–37; future of African American history, 49–50; historical alienation, 22–24; in the military, 99–100; Niagara Movement, 11–12; race and policies, 20–22; racial hierarchies, 112–13; racial identity, 20; racist and xenophobic reactions, 107; relocations, 82, 97–98; resistance to racism, 22; social condition of, 9; social construction of race, 75–87; socialism and the masses, 47–56; sociological studies, 9–10; Talented Tenth, 29–35; white gaze, 66
African Diaspora, 55, 59, 60–61, 92, 95–96, 98–102
African people: Afrocentricity, 59–60; Afrocentric tradition, 108–9; democracy and revolution, 45–46; emancipation of, 51–52; equal opportunity, 26–27; intersectionality, 77; orientation to race, 16; Pan Africanism and applied strategy, 98–102; religion and spirituality, 23; socialism and the masses, 49; study of in Philadelphia, 9; Talented Tenth, 29–31, 32, 34
Afrocentric Futurism, 57, 58, 60, 61, 62. *See also* "The Comet" (Du Bois)
Afrocentricity, 27, 50, 58, 59–60, 62, 89–91, 103–14
Afrocentricity in AfroFuturism (Smith), 57
Afrocentricity: The Theory of Social Change (Asante), 62
Afrofuturism, 58, 60–61, 63. *See also* "The Comet" (Du Bois)
Afrofuturism 2.0 (Anderson and Jones), 60
Agbeyebiawo, Daniel, 4–5
ageism, 80
agency reduction formation, 6
alienation, 24–26, 39, 90
American Academy of Political and Social Science, 9

American Baptist Home Mission Society, 32
American government, 13–14, 52–53
Anderson, Reynaldo, 60
antiracism, 17, 19, 24
apartheid, 71, 79
Aptheker, Herbert, 43
Arcade Hotel, Raleigh, NC, 1–2
Are Italians White? How Race Is Made in America (Guglieimo and Salerno), 18
Armstrong, Amaryah, 63
Asante, Molefi Kete, 47, 59, 62, 89–91, 95, 106–7
Association for the Study of Negro Life and History, 49
Atlanta, GA, 9–10, 32–34
Atlanta Baptist Seminary, 32–34
Atlanta Exposition, 12, 21–22, 30
Atlanta University, 9–10, 11, 12–13, 32

Baker, Josephine, 82, 98
Balaji, Murali, 54–55
Baldwin, James, 82, 98
Bass, Charlotta Amanda, 52–53
Beaumont, Gustave de, 44
Beavers, Herman, 85
Bentley, C., 11
Berkshire Valley, MA, 4
Berlin Conference of 1884–1885, 49
Bernier, Francois, 16
Between the World and Me (Coates), 46
birth and birthright, 72
The Birth of a Nation (Griffith), 20
Black Folk, Then and Now (Du Bois), 10–11, 81
Black History Month, 49
black inferiority, 17, 79–80
The Black Jacobins (James), 55
black leadership, 97, 104–5
Black Marxism (Robinson), 2
blackness, 26, 66

black organizations, integration of, 104–5
black poverty and white privilege, 86, 110
black progress, 33, 78, 84
Black Reconstruction in America (Du Bois), 10–11, 48, 51, 55, 64
black subjugation, 80
Bradford, George G., 9
Brodkin, Karen, 18
Brown, John, 11
Brown v. *Board of Education,* 84
Brussels, 96
Buffalo, NY, 11–12
Bureau of Labor Statistics, 9–10
Burghardt, Jack, 3
Burghardt, Mary, 4
Burghardt, Othello, 3
Burghardt, Thomas, 3

California Eagle (newspaper), 53
capitalism, 20, 55–56, 68–69
Carmichael, Stokely, 98
Carnegie Hall Conference, 35
Casely-Hayford, J. E., 107
Castronovo, Russ, 78
civil rights/civil rights movement, 10, 11–12, 30, 35, 43, 46, 51–53, 83
Civil War, 16, 29, 48, 51, 55
class, 20, 33–34, 39–40, 53, 63, 77–78, 82–83. *See also* Talented Tenth
classical Africa, 25–26
Clement, Rufus Early, 11
Coates, Ta-Nehesi, 46
color lie, 79, 82
color line, 22, 37, 57, 75–87, 92, 95, 101, 110, 114
"The Color Line" (Douglass), 110
"The Comet" (Du Bois), 57–73; invisibility and hypervisibility, 66–67; the story, 63–66; vault interpretations, 67–73

Committee of Twelve, 35–37
Communist Manifesto, 40
Communist Party, 43, 52–53, 100–102
Communist University for Eastern Peoples, 54
Congo, 81
Contee, Clarence, 82
convict leasing system, 71, 78
The Correspondence of W.E.B. Du Bois (Aptheker), 43
Council on African Affairs, 13
The Crisis (magazine), 12–13, 16, 33, 50, 78, 91, 96, 100
"Criteria of Negro Art" (Du Bois), 111
critical race theory, 84
Crummell, Alexander, 35, 109
Cullen, Countee, 14, 26
cultural maintenance, 109

Dark Matter (Thomas), 63
Darkwater (Du Bois), 4, 51, 63
Darling-Hammond, Linda, 84
Davis, Jefferson, 7, 8
Debs, Eugene V., 49
The Declining Significance of Race (Wilson), 20
Delany, Martin, 35
democracy, 13, 16, 44–47, 50–52
Dery, Mark, 60
Diagne, Blaise, 95–96, 99
Diop, Cheikh Anta, 25
discrimination, 4–5
dislocation, 1, 94, 102
double consciousness, 18–19, 90, 95
Douglass, Fredrick, 75–76, 109–10
Dove, Nah, 47
Du Bois, Alexander and John, 3–4
Du Bois, Alfred, 4
Du Bois, Burghardt Gomer, 14
Du Bois, Jacques, 3
Du Bois, James, 3
Du Bois, Nina Gomer, 14

Du Bois, Shirley Graham, 14, 53
Du Bois, William Edward Burghardt: African cultural defenses, 105–6; at Atlanta University, 9–13; *Black Folk, Then and Now,* 10–11, 81; *Black Reconstruction in America,* 10–11, 48, 51, 55, 64; classical Africa, 25–26; "The Comet," 57–73; Committee of Twelve, 35–37; conceptions of Africa, 6; "Criteria of Negro Art," 111; cultural and socioeconomic shifts, 109–14; *Darkwater,* 4, 51, 63; democracy and revolution, 45–47; double consciousness, 18–19; *Dusk of Dawn,* 10–11; "The Economic Future of the Negro," 111; as editor of *The Crisis,* 12–13; equal opportunity, 26–28; First Pan African Congress, 91–92; at Fisk University, 1–6; "The Freedmen's Bureau," 37; in Ghana, 13–14, 97–98; at Harvard University, 6–8; in his time, 37–39; historical alienation, 24–26; legacy, 103–14; marriage of, 14; Marxist influences, 62, 101–2; and Morehouse, 31–35; "The Niagara Movement Address to the Nation," 101; "On Christianity," 23; *The Ordeal of Mansart,* 22; origin, search for, 3–4; Pan Africanism, 89–102; Pan African movement, 13; performative biography, 1–14; performativity, 115n7; Philadelphia Negro, study of the, 8–9; *The Philadelphia Negro,* 9, 17, 20, 32, 35, 111–12; Porter's assessment, 109–10, 113; race and policies, 20–22; race discourse, contributions to, 15–28; racial identity, 20; religion and spirituality, 23; "Renaissance

of Ethics," 33–34; resistance to racism, 22; social construction of race, 75–87; socialism and the masses, 47–56; socialist revolutions, 43–44; *The Souls of Black Folk,* 14, 16, 18–19, 25, 35, 37, 97, 105, 107, 111; "The Study of the Negro Problem," 9; Talented Tenth, 29–31, 39–41; Third Pan African Congress, 93; "To the Nations of the World," 37; on the Tuskegee Machine, 97; at University of Pennsylvania, 8–9; and Washington, 10–12, 43
Du Bois, Yolande, 14
Du Bois Shrine, 14
Dunbar, William, 16
Dusk of Dawn (Du Bois), 10–11
duty, 33–34

"The Economic Future of the Negro" (Du Bois), 111
economics, 29–30, 35, 109–14
"The Education of the Negro" (Miller), 34–35
Egyptology, 25–26
elitism, 39, 80
Ellison, Ralph, 66
Encyclopedia Africana, 13–14, 43, 82, 103
Encyclopedia of the Negro, 10
"An End to the Neglect of the Problems of the Negro Woman!" (Jones), 53
Engels, Friedrich, 39–41
enslavement, 45–46, 57, 69–70, 78, 109
equal opportunity, 26–28
Eurobliviousness, 79
Eurocentricity, 7, 59–60, 104, 105–6
"Every Man His Own Reviewer" column, 105

February Revolution, 40

Ferris, William, 35–36
Fifth Pan African Congress. *See* Manchester Pan African Congress
First Pan African Congress, 13, 91–93, 95–96, 99–101
First World War, 92
Fisk University, 1–2, 3, 5–6, 8, 16, 18, 24, 97, 116n17
Floyd, George, 87
Fort Erie, Ontario, 11
Franklin, Benjamin, 18
Franklin, John Hope, 1–2, 115n3
Freedman's Bureau, 51
"The Freedmen's Bureau" (Du Bois), 37
Freedomways (journal), 53–54

Garvey, Marcus, 91, 96, 97, 99, 104, 105
gender, 77–78
Gendrone, Payton, 22
geopolitics, 78, 80–81
Germany, 16, 45, 51, 56, 83, 95
Ghana, 12, 13–14, 43, 52, 81–82, 97–98
Gordon, Lewis, 85
Great Barrington, MA, 3, 4–5, 6, 14, 16, 19, 44, 116n13
Griffith, D. W., 20
Grimké, Archibald, 35, 36
Grimké, Francis James, 35
Grossman, Jonathan, 10
Guglieimo, Jennifer, 18
Guiding Hundredth, 29, 40–41

Hampton University, 8, 50
Harpers Ferry, WV, 11
Harvard University, 1, 5, 6–8, 16
Hayes, Rutherford B., 46
Hershaw, A. M., 11
higher education, 5, 33, 35–36, 39, 84
Hispaniola, 86

historically black colleges and universities, 8, 23
Holt, Hamilton, 105
Hope, John, 32
Horizon (magazine), 12
Hosmer, Frank, 5
Howard University, 8
How Jews Became White Folks and What That Says About Race in America (Brodkin), 18
Humboldt University. *See* University of Berlin
Hume, David, 37–38
Hunton, Alphaeus, 13

identity, 18, 20, 46
Independent (magazine), 105
India, 56
Indian Removal Act of 1830, 45
industrial education, 10, 30–31, 35–36, 49
Industrial Revolution, 47
intermarriages, 3
International Workingmen's Association, 40
intersectionality, 76–78
intraracial segregation, 77
invisibility, 66
Invisible Jim Crow (Tillotson), 6
Invisible Man (Ellison), 66
Irish, 17–18, 27
Italians, 17–18

Jackson, Ada B., 53
Jackson, Andrew, 45
Jackson, Esther Cooper, 52–53
Jaima, Amir, 46
James, C. L. R., 55
James, William, 26, 33–34
Jefferson, Thomas, 38–39, 45
Jewish people, 17–18, 81, 83
Jim Crow, 78
Johnson, Lyndon Baines, 83–84
Jones, Charles E., 60

Jones, Claudia, 52–53
journalism, 78. *See also The Crisis* (magazine)
Journal of Negro History, 49
Jubilee Singers, 6, 116n17

Karenga, Maulana, 25, 78
Keene, Jennifer D., 50
Kendi, Ibram X., 19, 20
Kerensky, Alexander, 40
Kerner Report, 84
King, Martin Luther Jr., 26, 56, 95, 116n22

labor, 47–51
Langley, J. Ayodele, 96
leadership, 33, 39, 40, 97, 104–5
Lenin, Vladimir I., 39–41, 43
Lennep, Edward van, 5
liberal arts training, 32, 50
liberation, 40, 52, 76–77, 91, 93, 96, 100, 102, 106
The Life and Works of W.E.B. Du Bois (Agbeyebiawo), 4–5
Lincoln, Abraham, 12, 75
Lindsay, S. M., 32
location theory, 59
London, England. *See* First Pan African Congress
Lowrie, Donald, 70
lynching, 78

Madison, James, 45
Malcolm X, 83, 95, 116n22
Manchester Pan African Congress, 13, 34, 52, 55, 104
Mansart, Manuel, 22
Mao Zedong, 44
Marable, Manning, 1, 115n2
Marx, Karl, 39–41
Masses: of black people, 11, 22, 33, 47, 116n22; Committee of Twelve, 35–37; Pan African movement, 94; socialism,

narrative of, 43–44; socialism and the, 47–56; Talented Tenth, 30–31, 33–34, 39, 40; *See also* capitalism
mass incarceration, 71
mass revolutions, 44, 47
McFarlane, Arthur, 14
McKenzie, Fayette, 1
Miller, Kelly, 34–35, 36
The Miseducation of the Negro (Woodson), 50
"Molefi Kete Asante's Theory of Afrocentricity" (Van Dyk), 62
Montgomery Bus Boycott, 56
Morehouse, Henry Lyman, 30–34
Morehouse College, 32
Morrison, Toni, 66
mortality rates, 20, 79
Mullen, Bill, 52

NAACP (National Association for the Advancement of Colored People), 11–12, 13, 16, 20–22, 30, 36, 45–46, 100–101, 104–5, 111. See also *The Crisis* (magazine); Spingarn, Joel
National Advisory Commission on Civil Disorders, 84
National Endowment for the Humanities, 113
National Equal Rights League, 104
National Negro Committee, 12
Native Americans, 16–17, 45–46
Nazi Holocaust, 81
"Negro Problem," 24, 46
Negro spirituals, 5–6
Negro World (magazine), 96
Negro World Unity Congress, 55
New Deal, 36
New Negro, 49–50, 99
New York City, 11–12
Niagara Movement, 11–12, 36
"The Niagara Movement Address to the Nation" (Du Bois), 101

Nkrumah, Kwame, 13–14, 26, 43, 52, 56, 81–82, 103, 106
Nommo, 58, 73
nonracialism, 55
Notes on the State of Virginia (Jefferson), 38–39
Nyerere, Julius, 47

Oakes, James, 75
October Revolution of 1917, 40, 43, 51
Office of Strategic Services, 105
Omi, Michael, 20
"On Christianity" (Du Bois), 23
The Ordeal of Mansart (Du Bois), 22

Padmore, George, 52, 55
Painter, C. C., 5
Pan African Conference of 1900, 13, 37, 49, 89
Pan Africanism, 89–102; Afrocentric methodology, 89–91; applied strategy, 98–102; black leadership, 97; Du Boisian legacy, 104; Du Bois on, 93–95; First Pan African Congress, 13, 91–93, 95–96, 99–101; Manchester Pan African Congress, 13, 34, 52, 55; race and, 95–97; relocations, 97–98; Second Pan African Congress, 92, 96; Third Pan African Congress, 92, 93
Pan African socialism, 55
Paris Peace Conference, 92, 101
patriarchy, 34
Peace Information Center, 43
People's Republic of China, 44
Petrie, William Matthew Flinders, 25–26
Philadelphia, PA, 17, 39, 83
Philadelphia Negro, study of the, 8–9
The Philadelphia Negro (Du Bois), 9, 17, 20, 32, 35, 111–12
Phylon (journal), 11, 116n23

Phylon Institute, 100
Pinn, Anthony B., 23
Plekhanov, Alexander, 39–41
policy structures and systems, 20–22
Porter, Eric, 109–10, 113
poverty, 29
prison and imprisonment, 70–71
The Professor and the Pupil (Balaji), 54–55
Progressive Nations, 56
propaganda, 78–79, 83, 90, 99. See also *The Crisis* (magazine)
protests, 12, 51, 53, 75, 87

Rabaka, Reiland, 24, 39, 40, 51
Race, Rhetoric and Identity (Asante), 90
race and racism, 2–3, 15–28; biological notions of, 79–80; changing nature of, 17–18; and class, 20, 33–34, 39–40, 53, 63, 77–78, 82–83, 92; Committee of Twelve, 35–37; cultural and socioeconomic shifts, 109–14; democracy and revolution, 46–47; discrimination, 79–80, 84; double consciousness, 18–19; equal opportunity, 26–28; historical alienation, 24–26; incarceration, 71; orientation to race, 16–17; Pan Africanism, 95–97; policy structures and systems, 20–22; and Porter, 109–10, 113; racial agency, 98; racial domination, 18; racial hierarchies, 112–13; racial identity, 18, 20, 46; racialized demarcation, 85–86; racial oppression, 76, 80–81, 85, 90, 98; racial politics, 83–84; resistance to racism, 22; social construction of race, 75–87; term *race*, 16; and Weber, 107–8; white racial domination, 22, 56, 113; World War I, 50–51

racial formation theory, 20
Rath, Richard Cullen, 105–7
"Reading Du Bois Through Religion and Religious Commitment" (Pinn), 23
Reconstruction, 29
Reid-Merritt, Patricia, 15
religion and spirituality, 23, 64–66
relocations, 80–82, 97–98
"Renaissance of Ethics" (Du Bois), 33–34
Reviere, Ruth, 27
revolution, 44–47
Revolutionary War, 3
Robeson, Paul, 13, 26, 53–55
Robinson, Cedric, 2
Romanoff, Nicholas II, 40
Roosevelt, Franklin, 36
Russia, 39–41, 43, 51, 56
Russian Revolution of 1917, 57
Russian Social Democratic Labor Party, Bolshevik, 40

Salerno, Salvatore, 18
Samkange, Stanlake, 47
Sankofa, 58, 73
science fiction, 57, 60–61. See also "The Comet" (Du Bois)
Scottsboro Boys, 53
Second Pan African Congress, 92, 96
segregation, 36, 79
self-determination, 98, 102
Slater Fund scholarship, 7–8
Smith, Aaron X., 57, 58, 60, 79
Smith, C. S., 94
social condition of African Americans, 9
socialism, 34, 43, 47–56
socialist revolutions, 39, 43
Social Security, 36
sociology, 7, 8–9, 17, 39, 43, 103
The Souls of Black Folk (Du Bois), 14, 16, 18–19, 25, 35, 37, 97, 105, 107, 111

soundtracks and films, 60
South, 4, 6, 22, 24, 35, 36, 48, 51
South Africa, 13, 79, 82–83
Soviet Union, 43, 47–48, 54, 57
Spingarn, Joel, 96, 99
Spingarn Medal, 99, 111
Springfield Republican (newspaper), 5
Stamped from the Beginning and *How to Be an Antiracist* (Kendi), 19
A State-by-State History of Race and Racism in the United States (Reid-Merritt), 15
"The Study of the Negro Problem" (Du Bois), 9
Sunders, Eric J., 106

Talented Tenth, 26, 29–35, 39–41, 77, 80, 95, 113–14
"The Talented Tenth" (Morehouse), 30–31
"Talented Tenth Memorial Address" (Du Bois), 30
Taylor, Michelle, 27
technology, 60, 112
Third Pan African Congress, 92, 93
Tillotson, Michael, 6
Tocqueville, Alexis de, 44–45
tomb/pyramid, 72–73
"To the Nations of the World" (Du Bois), 37
"Toward An Afrocentric Research Methodology" (Reviere), 27
Trotter, William Monroe, 11, 35–36, 104–5
Trump, Donald, 98
Tuskegee Institute, 8, 10, 30, 32–34
Tuskegee Machine, 10–12, 20–21, 26, 33, 49–50, 97, 104
Tutu, Desmond, 47

Ubuntu, 47

United Negro Improvement Association and African Communities League (UNIA-ACL), 91
universal suffrage, 36
University of Berlin, 6–8, 16, 24
University of Massachusetts at Amherst, 113
University of Pennsylvania, 8–9, 17
uplift, 29–31, 32, 34, 35, 76, 84–86
urban sociology, 9, 17, 39

value of black life, 68–69
Van Dyk, Sandra, 62
victorious consciousness, 95, 102, 104
voter disenfranchisement, 78, 101

Washington, Booker T., 10–12; Atlanta Exposition speech, 21; Committee of Twelve, 35–36; cultural and socioeconomic shifts, 114; distinctions with Du Bois, 43; future of African American history, 49–50; leadership capabilities and institutional impacts, 96–97; race and policies, 20–21; racial hierarchies, 112; Talented Tenth, 30, 32–34; *See also* Tuskegee Machine
"W. E. B. Du Bois and the Wounded World" (Keene), 50
Weber, Max, 107–8
Whites: democracy and revolution, 45–46; dominance of the NAACP, 105; equal opportunity, 26; race and policies, 21; racial discourse, 15–17; racial identity, 20; resistance to racism, 22; social construction of race, 79–80; socialism and the masses, 48–56; Talented Tenth, 33–34; white gaze, 66; whiteness studies, 18; white privilege, 59, 86, 110; white

superiority, 17, 38–39, 48, 54;
    white supremacy, 15, 17, 22, 24, 39, 59, 61, 84, 111, 113
Wilberforce College, 8
Williams, Arnette Franklin, 14
Williams, Du Bois, 14
Williams, H. Sylvester, 13, 37, 49, 89
Wills, Matthew, 18
Wilson, William Julius, 20
Winant, Howard, 20
women, 52–53

Woodson, Carter G., 49–51, 103, 111
working class, 39–40
world events, 39–41, 81
World's Fair, Paris, 10
World War I, 49–51
Wright, Carroll D., 9

Xenia, OH, 8

Yaszek, Lisa, 62
Yergan, Max, 13

www.ingramcontent.com/pod-product-compliance
Ingram Content Group UK Ltd.
Pitfield, Milton Keynes, MK11 3LW, UK
UKHW042016140426
5217IPUK00015B/1213